MW00466907

ENDORSEMENTS

"W. Robert Godfrey is a gifted teacher. As a recognized historian, he helpfully sets the historical and ecclesiastical context for the writing of the Canons of Dort. As a trusted theologian, he clearly explains the exegetical and theological basis for each of the canons. As an experienced pastor, he carefully shows the practical nature of the doctrines of grace preserved in the Canons. In an age of constant change and theological amnesia, *Saving the Reformation* is an important contribution, an accessible treatment of one of the great documents of the Reformation."

—REV. JOEL E. KIM
President and assistant professor of New Testament
Westminster Seminary California, Escondido, Calif.

"*Saving the Reformation* is characteristic of Dr. Godfrey's engaging, clear, pastoral teaching that has benefited so many over the years. Guiding us through the history and biblical truth confessed in the Canons of Dort, he brings us to the reality of the sovereign goodness and all-sufficient grace of God in Christ for us: we are hell deserving sinners, saved, sanctified, and surrounded by God's all-powerful love. This is worth reading about."

—DR. WILLIAM VANDOODEWAARD
Professor of church history
Puritan Reformed Theological Seminary, Grand Rapids, Mich.

"*Saving the Reformation* confirms Dr. Godfrey's reputation as a premier student of the Synod of Dort and the Dutch Reformation. In a clear, accessible, and compelling way, Godfrey provides his readers with an account of the historical context and occasion for the convening of the Synod of Dort in 1618, as well as a helpful exposition of the teaching of the canons. He also provides a fresh translation of the Latin version of the Canons of Dort, and several useful appendices on their order and arrangement. These features combine to make this book an excellent resource for church members and scholars alike."

—Dr. Cornelis P. Venema
President and professor of doctrinal studies
Mid-America Reformed Seminary, Dyer, Ind.

SAVING *The* REFORMATION

SAVING *The* REFORMATION

THE PASTORAL THEOLOGY

OF THE

CANONS OF DORT

W. ROBERT GODFREY

 LIGONIER MINISTRIES

Saving the Reformation: The Pastoral Theology of the Canons of Dort
© 2019 by W. Robert Godfrey

Published by Ligonier Ministries
421 Ligonier Court, Sanford, FL 32771
Ligonier.org

Printed in York, Pennsylvania
Maple Press
0000523
First edition, fourth printing

ISBN 978-1-64289-030-3 (Hardcover)
ISBN 978-1-64289-031-0 (ePub)
ISBN 978-1-64289-032-7 (Kindle)

All rights reserved. No part of this publication may be reproduced, stored in
a retrieval system, or transmitted in any form or by any means—electronic,
mechanical, photocopy, recording, or otherwise—without the prior written
permission of the publisher, Ligonier Ministries. The only exception is brief
quotations in published reviews.

Cover design: Ligonier Creative
Interior design and typeset: Katherine Lloyd, The DESK

Unless otherwise indicated, Scripture quotations are the author's translation
from the Canons of the Synod of Dort and other documents.

Scripture quotations are from the ESV® Bible (The Holy Bible, English Standard
Version®), copyright © 2001 by Crossway, a publishing ministry of Good News
Publishers. Used by permission. All rights reserved.

Scripture quotations marked KJV are from the King James Version. Public
domain.

The Library of Congress has cataloged the Reformation Trust edition as follows:

Names: Godfrey, W. Robert, author. | Synod of Dort (1618-1619 : Dordrecht,
 Netherlands). Canones Synodi Dordrechtanae. English.
Title: Saving the Reformation : the pastoral theology of the Canons of Dort /
 W. Robert Godfrey.
Description: Orlando, FL : Reformation Trust Publishing, a division of Ligonier
 Ministries, [2019]
Identifiers: LCCN 2018031346| ISBN 9781642890303 (hardcover) | ISBN
 9781642890327 (kindle) | ISBN 9781642890310 (epub)
Subjects: LCSH: Synod of Dort (1618-1619 : Dordrecht, Netherlands) | Pastoral
 theology--History of doctrines--17th century. | Reformation--Netherlands
 --Sources. | Nederlandse Hervormde Kerk--Doctrines--History--Sources.
 | Pastoral theology--Netherlands--History--17th century--Sources. | Netherlands
 --Church history--17th century--Sources.
Classification: LCC BX9478 .G63 2019 | DDC 238/.42--dc23
LC record available at https://lccn.loc.gov/2018031346

For my family,

Mary Ellen
William
Mari and Mark
Robert and Catherine
Katrina, Kellan, Anne, William, and Emmaline

CONTENTS

PART I
HISTORICAL AND THEOLOGICAL BACKGROUND

PART II
THE CANONS OF THE SYNOD OF DORT—
A PASTORAL TRANSLATION

PART III
AN EXPOSITION OF THE CANONS OF DORT

APPENDICES

FOREWORD

Reformed confessional theology is a statement of faith set within a story of faith. As statements of believed truths, confessions express the mind of God's people embracing God's Word. If we neglect the church's historic statements of faith, we end up with mindless and spineless Christianity—more fit to drift like a jellyfish than to swim against the stream of this world. Confession of faith is an essential act of courageous Christianity, as we see from the living history of the people who wrote these declarations. They made their confession out of personal faith in Christ and fervent love for God—sealed with their tears and sometimes their blood, as was the case with Guido de Bres, the martyred author of the Belgic Confession. Reformed confessional theology was written not to pick a fight but to protect the church in the battles she already faces and to nurture people in the truth, as we see in that pastoral masterpiece the Heidelberg Catechism.

This book is an exposition of the Canons of Dort, the third document, with the Belgic Confession and Heidelberg Catechism, in the Dutch Reformed triumvirate known as the Three Forms of Unity. Of course, *canon* does not refer to artillery but to a rule to direct the church. The word derives from the Greek term *kanōn*, which literally refers to a rod or rule such as one used by builders and hence came to signify a standard for belief or conduct. After Paul's exposition of justification by faith alone and sanctification by the Spirit, the Apostle said, "As many as walk according to this rule [*kanōn*], peace be on them" (Gal. 6:16, KJV). The Canons of Dort furnish those who build up Christ's church with important tools for constructing right beliefs (orthodoxy) leading to right action (orthopraxy), both by the grace of God.

Unlike the Belgic Confession and Heidelberg Catechism, the Canons of Dort do not present a complete summation of the teaching of the Bible and the faith of the Reformed churches. Instead, here we find the Reformed doctrine of salvation focused to a point of intense and brilliant clarity. The Synod of Dort (1618–19) wrote the canons as a specific response to the Arminian challenge against salvation by God's grace alone—specifically, the objections to Reformed doctrine expressed in the five points of their Remonstrance. The synod was an international assembly of Reformed scholars who gathered to remedy the spreading infection of this false teaching that undermines the gospel.

Though an increasing number of Christians in the United States affirm the five points of Calvinism, few today have read the Canons of Dort, of which the five points are mere bullet-point summaries. The Synod of Dort produced one of the most mature and biblically balanced statements of the doctrine of salvation ever written. For example, the treatment of sovereign predestination begins with man's sin and the good news of salvation to all who believe in Jesus Christ. The treatment of particular redemption opens with the necessity of satisfying God's justice by the punishment of sin, which means that the salvation of sinners requires a substitute to die in their place. Thus, these distinctive Reformed doctrines are grounded in the gospel. It is important for all Christians to attain the biblical balance and gospel grounding that the Canons of Dort present, but it is particularly crucial for preachers and teachers of God's Word to do so.

Approaching a historic document can be somewhat intimidating, like hiking trails through the mountains. For the task, it helps to have an experienced trail guide, and few are more qualified to lead us through the canons than my friend W. Robert Godfrey. Having taught church history at Westminster Seminary, first in Philadelphia beginning in the 1970s and then in California since 1981, he brings to the task a wealth of wisdom as a historian and a theologian of the Reformed church. I have known Bob for decades and have always found his writings to be insightful and thought provoking. This book is no exception; in fact, Dutch Reformed church history and theology are two of his greatest strengths.

We experienced that firsthand at Puritan Reformed Theological Seminary when he taught a Dutch Reformation church history class that emphasized the Canons of Dort and their value for the church today.

Dr. Godfrey's treatment of the canons will be very helpful to students of the canons as well as to those who teach in church or seminary classes. He tells us the history behind the Synod of Dort so we can understand the conflict that gave birth to this statement. He gives a fresh translation of the canons for the modern reader. He walks us through each article of faith or refutation of error in the canons, offering brief comments to illuminate each section's meaning in its historical and theological context.

Godfrey also includes historical and analytical appendices, of which the first, third, and fifth are particularly valuable. In the first appendix, he argues that Jacobus Arminius was not a moderate Reformed theologian who was offended by extreme supralapsarianism and fell victim to a new, intolerant form of Reformed orthodoxy. Rather, Arminius sought to replace mainstream Reformed teaching with an altogether different theology—while claiming to be faithful to the Reformed confessions. The third appendix is a detailed outline of the canons, which teachers will find illuminating for organizing their presentations of its doctrines. The fifth appendix consists of a translation of the synod's statement on the Sabbath, which offers much-needed insight into Continental sabbatarian theology and its agreement with that of the British Puritans.

The Canons of Dort have meant a great deal to me for half a century now, ever since I was first converted. When I was a teenager, I struggled with the doctrine of predestination for months until I realized that the canons are scripturally accurate in their biblical, pastoral, sensitive, and warm presentation of this doctrine. Through reading the Canons of Dort, I learned as a teenager that the great question to be answered is not, How could God reject anyone and send His own creatures to hell? but rather, How could God elect anyone and bring His fallen, hell-worthy creatures into heaven to be with Him forever? The canons helped me be more amazed by "amazing grace" than I had ever been before. Later on, when doing a doctoral dissertation on assurance of faith for Westminster Theological Seminary, I came to appreciate and treasure the beauty and balance of the canons' treatment of this doctrine in head V. I saw as never before how the Canons of Dort paved the way for the Westminster Confession of Faith's magisterial treatment of assurance in its renowned chapter 18—a chapter that has codified the Reformed view of this doctrine ever since. More recently, the canons' Reformed stress on preaching, and its encouragement to pastors to boldly proclaim the lofty doctrines that it unpacks from a biblical, doctrinal, experiential, and practical vantage point, have moved me to write on this subject.[1]

In sum, though the Canons of Dort are a document worthy of historical and theological analysis, their value does not end with the intellectual or academic. The canons declare the redeeming love of God in Jesus Christ for fallen, corrupt, helpless sinners—the greatest love story of all. "We love him, because he first loved us" (1 John 4:19, KJV), and so the canons are a call to love the Lord our God with all our heart, soul, and strength, and our neighbor as ourselves.

The Canons of Dort cannot be rightly received or understood without prayer to God and faith in His Word. The synod was convened with prayer, and the canons call for prayer. The canons conclude with a prayer that God's Son, seated at the right hand of God, would empower and sanctify His servants so that they may glorify God and edify men. The Synod of Dort closed not with an academic debate but with a worship service, where the delegates heard a sermon on Isaiah 12:2–3: "Behold, God is my salvation; I will trust, and not be afraid: for the LORD JEHOVAH is my strength and my song; he also is become my salvation. Therefore with joy shall ye draw water out of the wells of salvation" (KJV).

Therefore, study the Canons of Dort with an open Bible, an open heart thirsting for Christ, and an open mouth proclaiming the praises of God.

—Dr. Joel R. Beeke
President, Puritan Reformed Theological Seminary
Pastor, Heritage Reformed Congregation of Grand Rapids, Mich.

INTRODUCTION

Most meetings of church assemblies are neither interesting nor significant. But throughout the history of the church there have been notable exceptions. The great Council of Nicaea (325) powerfully defended the eternal divinity of Jesus. The Council of Trent (1545–63) sealed the Roman Catholic Church in its rejection of the Reformation. The Synod of Dort (1618–19), the greatest of the Reformed church assemblies, preserved the great heritage of the Reformation for the Calvinistic churches. This synod is both interesting and significant, and its decisions are a theological and spiritual treasure for Christians. On the occasion of the four-hundredth anniversary of the synod, it is good to remember and be renewed in an appreciation of its accomplishments. But studying the canons is much more than a historical exercise. It will be spiritually profitable for Christians and churches today.

The Synod of Dort was in the first place theological in its concerns. It met to answer the Arminian doctrines and articulate the biblical alternative. One scholar said that the Arminian challenge was "the greatest crisis in dogma since the age of the first reformers."[1] As vital and central as that theological work was, the synod was significant for other reasons as well. Ecclesiastically, the synod expressed a clear vision of the church, its ministry, and its life. Politically, the synod met in cooperation with the state and in the context of wars to resolve tensions that might have threatened the very survival of the Dutch Republic. Ultimately, however, and most importantly, the synod was concerned with the deepest issues of the Christian religion.

The synod expressed the most profound religious truths: the absolute sovereignty of God, the effectiveness of the work of Christ and of the Holy Spirit, and the comfort Christians find in the gospel. This book will

1

explore great matters—theological, ecclesiastical, and political—but we must be careful never to lose sight of the underlying religious concern, which was always of greatest consequence. This book will concentrate on the fundamentally religious convictions of the synod and the canons.

In a profound sense, this synod saved the Reformation for the Reformed churches. While Lutherans would reject several elements of the canons, Calvinists saw clearly that a proper understanding of election was necessary to protect the Reformation's "grace alone." The proper understanding of Christ's atoning work was necessary to protect the Reformation's "Christ alone." A proper understanding of the regenerating and preserving work of the Holy Spirit and of the Christian's comfort in these doctrines was necessary to protect the Reformation's "grace alone" and "faith alone." Implicit in the canons' conclusions is their commitment to the Reformation's "Scripture alone" as the only source of religious truth.

As the Reformation was a revival of a biblical Augustinianism, so the Synod of Dort stands in the great Christian heritage that rejects Pelagianism and semi-Pelagianism. It stands in the tradition of Jesus against the Pharisees, Paul against the Judaizers, Athanasius against Arius, Augustine against Pelagius, and Luther against Erasmus. Dort against the Arminians continues that great commitment. The canons became the official teaching and sincere conviction of many churches and millions of Christians through the last four centuries.

The synod also met on the eve of a profound shift in Western thought. Increasingly after the synod, culminating with the Enlightenment, Western thought adopted a positive view of human nature and human abilities. The biblical view of fallen human nature and of a sovereign, personal God who acted in Christ, which was articulated by the Calvinists at Dort, increasingly seemed old-fashioned and wrong to modern thinkers. Yet Dort remained an invaluable witness to the truth of the Bible and of the Reformation. It also is a great resource to contemporary Christians for instruction and direction in understanding God's truth and Christian faith and living.

This book is intended to help churches and Christians appreciate and study the synod and its canons. The central part of the book is part

II, a new translation of the Canons of Dort. The canons were written for the church in a form designed to make them understandable for church members. This translation seeks to fulfill that aim. The translation does not simplify the vocabulary. Its main difference from earlier translations is to break the long Latin sentences of the original into shorter English sentences. A little of the precision of the Latin is lost in this process, but the result is a faithful translation that is much easier to read and understand for contemporary readers of English.

Part I of the book presents the historical and theological background to the synod. This material significantly helps with the understanding of the teaching of the canons in their original setting. Part I goes on to review the character and work of the synod itself. This section shows not only the situation for the writing of the canons, but also the broader work of the synod for the life and ministry of the church. Part III follows on the translation by presenting an analysis and exposition of the canons to help the reader understand the teaching of the canons. The aim is to see the general form of the canons as a whole and the meaning of each of the articles in itself and in relation to the other articles.

For those interested in more detail in these matters, this book contains several appendices. The first and longest is on the life and teaching of Jacobus Arminius. It challenges the dominant interpretation of Arminius' biography and as a result suggests an understanding of his role in the controversy in the Netherlands that is different from the one generally held today. The second appendix presents the general pattern of teaching in each of the heads of doctrine. The third appendix is a detailed outline of the teaching of the canons. The fourth appendix shows the relationship in each head of doctrine between the positive articles and the rejections of errors. Finally, the fifth appendix presents the statement of the Synod of Dort on the doctrine of the Sabbath.

Taken as a whole, this book seeks to help church members and pastors appreciate the important work of the Synod of Dort in the history of the church. But it aims even more at helping contemporary Christians to deepen their faith by seeing the greatness and goodness of God in His electing love and saving work in Christ.

—

PART I

HISTORICAL AND THEOLOGICAL BACKGROUND

—

Chapter 1

THE NEW CHURCH
AND THE NEW STATE

Interest in the Reformation appeared early in the Low Countries. The first Protestant martyrs—monks who adopted the views of Martin Luther—died there in the early 1520s. By the later 1520s, Anabaptism attracted a much larger following there than Lutheranism. These Anabaptists in the Netherlands were quite diverse in their convictions, ranging from pacifist Mennonites to the violent and revolutionary followers of John of Leiden. All of the Anabaptists were severely persecuted by the civil government.

Still later, in the 1540s, Calvinist preachers from Geneva and France began to enter the Low Countries from the south. Calvinism spread as a popular movement first in the French-speaking south and then more slowly in the Dutch-speaking north. The government strongly opposed this advance with vigorous persecution. The Reformed churches, however, grew steadily even while suffering "under the cross" as the persecuted.

These churches were like other Reformed churches throughout Europe in doctrine and worship. They organized themselves much like the Reformed churches of France. Local congregations were governed by ministers, elders, and deacons. The local churches assembled in regional meetings called classes. Delegates from each classis formed provincial synods (or in the case of the province of Holland with its large population, the particular synods of north Holland and south Holland). These regional synods at times met together as national synods.

The character of this church was from the beginning staunchly Calvinistic. Some ministers dissented, but they encountered strong disciplinary reaction from the church. The church adopted as its confessional standard the Belgic Confession (1561), written by the preacher Guido de Bres and modeled after the French Confession (1559), written largely by John Calvin. Beyond the material in the French Confession, de Bres expanded especially on the doctrine of the church and sought to distinguish clearly the Reformed teaching from both the Roman Catholic and the Anabaptist teaching. De Bres in his rejections of Anabaptism had the violent side of the movement particularly in mind. He died a martyr for his faith in 1567, making the Belgic Confession the only major Reformation confession sealed with the blood of its author. The other doctrinal standard adopted by the churches was the Heidelberg Catechism (1563), originally prepared for the Reformed churches of the Palatinate, an important part of the Holy Roman Empire. This catechism became a key teaching tool for spreading a thorough knowledge of the Reformed doctrines. The church required subscription to these standards by all ministers, elders, and deacons.[1]

The growth of the Reformed churches in the Low Countries took place at the same time that the state there was undergoing fundamental changes. The Low Countries had been composed of seventeen provinces that had passed to the sovereignty of the Holy Roman emperor Charles V. When he abdicated, in 1555, the Low Countries passed to his son, who had become King Philip II of Spain. By 1568, a revolt against Philip had begun, sparked by his insensitivity to historic liberties in the Low Countries and by his severe persecution of the Anabaptists and Calvinists. (This revolt in the Netherlands became known as the Eighty Years' War since it was not finally settled until 1648, when the Thirty Years' War in Germany also ended.) After decades of war in the Low Countries, the conflict reached a stalemate that in effect divided the land into two parts.

The southern part of about ten provinces remained under Spanish control and Roman Catholic in faith, and it ultimately became the country of Belgium. The northern part of about seven provinces organized itself on the basis of the Union of Utrecht (1579) into what became known as the United Provinces. These northern provinces, basically comprising what is today the Netherlands, were dominated by Protestants, although the Reformed church did not become the majority religion there until the later seventeenth century. After abjuring the rule of King Philip in the 1580s, the United Provinces tried to find a monarch, particularly hoping that Queen Elizabeth of England would rule over them. She was not willing, because she feared that they would ultimately be defeated by Spain. In time, the United Provinces became a republic and survived in that form until the Napoleonic era in the late eighteenth century. The United Provinces were formally governed by a legislative body called the States General. In this body, each of the seven provinces had one vote, and most important matters had to be decided unanimously.

The leading Protestant in the revolt against Spain was Prince William of Orange, who provided careful and heroic counsel to church and state until his assassination in 1584 by an agent of King Philip. After his death, executive leadership in the state passed to Jan van Oldenbarnevelt, an official from the province of Holland. William's son, Prince Maurits (sometimes rendered Maurice in English histories), became the military leader and a very successful strategist and warrior against Spain. He became the other dominant figure in the politics of the United Provinces in the late sixteenth and early seventeenth centuries.

Weary of war, the United Provinces arranged with Spain an armistice now known as the Twelve Years' Truce, which was signed in Antwerp on April 9, 1609. That year was significant also because on October 19 the Dutch Reformed minister and professor Jacobus Arminius died.

While the war with Spain raged, that external pressure had kept the strains in the state and church of the United Provinces somewhat in check. But with the truce, those strains came more to the fore. In the state, the merchants of Holland led by Oldenbarnevelt wanted a permanent peace for the sake of trade and commerce. But others, led by Maurits and supported by many Calvinists, wanted the war to continue. They wanted to keep the whole of the Low Countries united and to

9

liberate the southern provinces both from Spain and from the Roman Catholic religion.

Strain had also appeared in the church. The majority of the Calvinist ministers wanted the church to be more self-governing with less dependence on the state in matters of discipline and particularly in the calling of a national synod. These ministers knew that the church had had national synods before the formation of the United Provinces and thought that national synods should be used to address vital issues affecting the whole church. The Dutch Reformed churches according to their own reckoning had had five national synods before the Synod of Dort (1618–19): at Emden (1571), Dordrecht (1574 and 1578),[2] Middelburg (1581), and the Hague (1586). After the great Synod of Dort, no national synod of the Dutch Reformed churches was held for almost two hundred years.[3]

Arminius

A minority of ministers and many of the merchants in Holland wanted significant state control over the church, especially in matters of discipline. Such an approach to state control was called Erastian, after Thomas Erastus of Heidelberg, who had defended this view of church government. In addition to this difference over church polity, by 1609 it was also clear that a small group of ministers in the Reformed church dissented from the Calvinist orthodoxy of the majority. This theological difference would become very divisive and dangerous in the years after 1609.

For the background to this theological difference that would lead to the Synod of Dort, we must look to the life and work of one minister in particular, Jacobus (James) Arminius (1559–1609). He would, ironically, become the most famous theologian ever produced by the Dutch Reformed Church.

Arminius' biography is simple. He was born in the province of Holland in about 1559. His father had died in the war against Spain, leaving the family quite poor. Authorities supported his education, recognizing his academic talents. He was among the first students at the new University in Leiden, and from there he went for graduate study in Geneva and Basel. The leading professor in Geneva at that time was Calvin's successor, Theodore Beza. Arminius returned to Amsterdam, where he was ordained to the ministry and served as a pastor from 1588 to 1603. He was then appointed professor of theology at the University of Leiden, where he served until his death in 1609.

For most of his life, Arminius was not well known or widely influential. He caused some local controversy in Amsterdam among ministers for his sermons on Romans 7 and Romans 9. While these concerns seemed to be resolved, they were significant enough that some ministers criticized his appointment to teach theology at Leiden. In the latter years of his professorship, rumors circulated that he was undermining orthodoxy. The criticisms and rumors were hard to evaluate at the time because—as strange as it may seem—Arminius published none of his writings in his own lifetime.

The controversies that increasingly surrounded him came to a head in 1608. To express his views for the government investigation, he wrote his *Declaration of Sentiments*, presented to the government on October 30, 1608. This document, also not published in his lifetime, contained first a historical section reviewing his understanding of the past dissent from Calvinist orthodoxy in the Dutch churches. The second section was a theological section, in which he vehemently attacked one of the Calvinist understandings of election, called supralapsarianism:[4] "This doctrine completely subverts the foundation of religion in general, and of the Christian Religion in particular."[5]

Arminius then expressed his own view of predestination, which he very briefly summarized in terms of four decrees. Only the fourth of these decrees deals with predestination in relation to particular individuals; he stated that God decrees "to save and damn certain particular persons. This decree has its foundation in the foreknowledge of God, by which he knew from all eternity those individuals who would, through his preventing [i.e., prevenient] grace, believe, and through his subsequent grace would persevere."[6] This teaching was contrary to any Calvinist understanding of election and seemed very similar to the teaching of the

Spanish Jesuit Luis de Molina, first published in 1588. (For more details on Arminius and a reconsideration of his life, see appendix 1.)

Arminius' views as expressed in his *Declaration* would certainly have caused even greater controversy in the church, but his deteriorating health made further investigation difficult. He died on October 19, 1609. Some thought that his death might put an end to the troubles. But after the death of Arminius, it became clear that his teaching had had an impact and attracted a number of ministers. These ministers may have followed his teaching or may have simply felt liberated by his dissent to pursue their own forms of disagreement with Reformed orthodoxy. Whatever the actual direct influence of his thought, he became a symbol of the rejection of Calvinist orthodoxy, and his name became attached to various anti-Calvinist theologies.[7]

The Remonstrance of 1610

Those ministers influenced by Arminius at the time of his death recognized that their positions in the church were precarious. The vast majority of the ministers and elders of the church would have disciplined them for their views. To protect themselves, they prepared an appeal or petition to the civil government. They stated their theological positions and requested that the government ensure their toleration in the church. This petition—called a "remonstrance"—came to be known as the Remonstrance of 1610. Those who signed the petition and supported it came to be called the Remonstrants. In the United Provinces in the seventeenth century, the followers of Arminius were usually called Remonstrants rather than Arminians.

The Remonstrance of 1610 was a rather long document. The executive officer of the state, Jan van Oldenbarnevelt, saw immediately how explosive the document was and decided to keep it secret. As with most government secrets, it soon was widely known and evoked exactly the reaction that Oldenbarnevelt had feared. The orthodox Calvinists soon issued a written response that became known as the Counter-Remonstrance of 1611, and these Calvinists came to be called Counter-Remonstrants.

At the heart of the Remonstrance was a five-point summary of the doctrinal views that the Remonstrants wanted protected. So, in 1610, the five points of Arminianism were articulated. Although the Counter-Remonstrants initially responded in 1611 with seven points, ultimately the Synod of Dort would respond point by point to the Arminians, giving the world "the five points of Calvinism."

We should remember, however, that Calvinism has never summarized itself in five points. Calvinism is summarized in full confessional statements such as the Heidelberg Catechism, the Belgic Confession, and the Westminster Confession of Faith. To be very accurate, Calvinism does not have—and never has had—five points. Rather, it has five answers to the five errors of Arminianism.

The Canons of the Synod of Dort are not a full confession but are rather a clarification and defense of some points in the Belgic Confession and the Heidelberg Catechism. The Synod of Dort made this clear in the Form of Subscription that it prepared for ministers and others in the church. Ministers subscribed "the Confession and Catechism of the Dutch Reformed churches and also the Exposition [*declarationem*] of some articles of this doctrine made at the national synod of Dordrecht."[8]

The Remonstrance of 1610 is so important to the later controversies and to the synod that a new translation of the summary five points is provided here:

THE REMONSTRANCE OF 1610[9]

Article 1

God—by an eternal and unchangeable decree in Jesus Christ, His Son, before the foundation of the world—has determined, out of the fallen and sinful human race, to save in Christ, because of Christ, and through Christ those who, through the grace of the Holy Spirit, believe in this His Son Jesus and persevere in this belief and obedience even to the end, through this grace. On the other hand, God has determined to leave the unconverted and unbelieving in their sin and under wrath and to condemn them as separate from Christ. This is the word of the holy gospel in

John 3:36, "He who believes in the Son has eternal life, and he who is disobedient to the Son shall not see life, but the wrath of God remains on him." Other passages of the Scriptures teach the same.

Article 2

From this it follows that Jesus Christ, the Savior of the world, died for all men and for each man. He earned for them all, through the death of the cross, reconciliation and the forgiveness of sins. Still, Christ died in such a way that no one actually shares in this forgiveness of sins except those who believe. This is the word of the gospel of John 3:16, "God so loved the world that he gave his only Son, so that whoever believes in him, should not perish but have eternal life." And in the First Letter of John 2:2, "He is the reconciliation of our sins, and not only of ours, but of the sins of the whole world."

Article 3

Man does not have this saving faith from himself nor out of the power of his free will. Man in the state of apostasy and sin cannot, out of or from himself, think, will, or do any good that is truly good (as is particularly saving faith). But it is necessary that by God, in Christ, through His Holy Spirit, he be born again and renewed in understanding, affections, and will, and all powers so that he may rightly think, will, and do the truly good. This is the word of Christ, John 13:5, "Without me you can do nothing."

Article 4

This grace of God is the beginning, continuance, and completion of all good, so much so that even the regenerate man can neither think, will, or do the good nor resist any temptation to evil without prevenient or assisting, awakening, following, and cooperating grace. So, all the good deeds or works of which man can think must be ascribed to the grace of God in Christ. But as to the manner of the working of this grace, it is not irresistible. It is written of many that they have resisted the Holy Spirit, as in Acts 7 and many other places.

Article 5

Those who are united to Jesus Christ by a true faith and so come to share in his life-giving Spirit have abundant power to fight against Satan, sin, the world, and their own sin and to win the victory. But whether they of themselves through neglect can lose the beginning of their being in Christ, again take up with this present world, reject the Holy Spirit once given to them, lose their good conscience, and abandon grace, must first be sought out further from the Holy Scripture before we can ourselves teach it with the full confidence of our minds.

Conclusion

The Remonstrants who propose and teach these points consider that they are in conformity to the Word of God, are edifying, and in their content are sufficient for salvation, and that it is not necessary or edifying in these matters to climb higher or to descend lower.

Examining the Remonstrance of 1610

The Remonstrants or Arminians (forty-two ministers signed the petition) expressed their real theological convictions and concerns in this statement. They were also aware that they represented a small minority position in the church and that only the intervention of the civil government could protect them from the disciplinary actions of classes or synods. They expressed their views in their five points with an eye to presenting their views in the most sympathetic and attractive light.

Their five points were simple, straightforward, and cast in biblical terms. They were also clever, stating the issues in ways that played to their advantage. The central issue was predestination, but related issues were both strategically important and pastorally sensitive. The Arminians sincerely believed that their views were more biblical than those of the Calvinists, but they also wanted to attack the Calvinists at their weakest theological, pastoral, and rhetorical points.

In the first point of the Remonstrance, the Arminians recognized that the Bible taught predestination, and so they presented their view of predestination. In it, they express a thoroughly biblical truth: God saves those who believe and who persevere in faith and obedience. But they take that biblical truth and turn it into their doctrine of predestination. Unlike the Calvinists, who understand predestination as relating to individuals, the Arminians define predestination as relating to a class or condition of people. For Calvinists, God chooses individuals to salvation; for Arminians, He chooses qualifications for salvation that individuals must meet.

This point prominently stresses the work of Christ and the grace of the Holy Spirit—again showing the Remonstrants' efforts to appear biblical and Protestant—but it is not at all specific as to exactly what Christ and the Holy Spirit do. So, predestination is God's determination to save obedient believers and not to save disobedient unbelievers. The Remonstrants also quote a familiar biblical text to substantiate their position (John 3:36). The text does indeed teach about salvation. It does not, however, relate immediately or definitively to predestination.

Next, the Remonstrance turns to the death of Christ. Point 2 opens with a particularly clear statement: Christ died for all men and every man. Here is a sharp challenge theologically and rhetorically to the Calvinists. It was often hard for the Calvinists to express and defend their notion that the death of Christ was "limited." After its clear opening statement, the article then becomes exceedingly vague. Christ died for all, but not all are saved. Somehow, the effectiveness of the death of Christ is triggered by believing. The relationship between the work of Christ and the believing of an individual is completely undefined.

The great English Puritan John Owen provided the definitive analysis and refutation of this Arminian argument later in the seventeenth century in his work *The Death of Death in the Death of Christ*. The brief summary of Owen's case is this: If Christ died for all the sins of all men, did He die for the unbelief of the unbeliever? If unbelief is a sin, then Christ died for it, and the unbeliever is saved. If unbelief is not a sin, then God cannot condemn the unbeliever because of it. By its own inherent logic, the Arminian teaching on the atonement necessarily leads to universalism, however much Arminians try to deny that.

The issue of the extent of the atonement was for many the most emotional and controversial point of orthodox Calvinism. Yet the doctrine that Christ died for the elect was not unique to Calvinism but had been taught by a number of theologians in the Middle Ages. The greatest medieval textbook for theology, Peter Lombard's *Sentences*, declared that Christ had died sufficiently for all, but efficiently for the elect alone. Many Dutch Calvinists were particularly annoyed and offended by this emotional use of the work of Christ.

Point 3 aims to show that the Arminians have a Protestant view of the seriousness of sin. Again we have a clear statement, denying free will in fallen man and insisting that fallen man can on his own do nothing that is truly good. God must act to save this fallen man, who cannot save himself. As it stands, this point is perfectly acceptable to Calvinists. It is only as the thought begun in point 3 is continued in point 4 that Calvinists had trouble. (That is why the Canons of Dort in responding to the Remonstrants treat the third and fourth points together.)

If point 3 shows clearly the absolute necessity of grace to save fallen man, point 4 shows that that grace can be resisted and rejected by fallen man. Here again the effort is made to stress the centrality and pervasive activity of grace at all points of salvation. All the good in man must be attributed to grace alone. Still, that grace can be resisted. The will of fallen man can reject saving grace if he is determined to do so. Again, Scripture passages are cited to substantiate the position. For Calvinists, this sounds like a theology that tries to be as Augustinian as possible but in the end remains semi-Pelagian. In fact, it sounds very similar to the position taken by Erasmus in his criticism of Luther. Fallen man remains determinative as to whether grace is effective.

Point 5 continues the stress on the centrality of grace. God's grace

is powerfully sufficient to preserve the believer in the face of every difficulty and temptation. Nothing external to the believer can seriously
harm him. But the Arminians state that they need further study of the
Scriptures to decide if the believer can abandon Christ. In other words,
they believe that the sinner can reject grace at the beginning of grace's
contact with his life, but they are uncertain as to whether this grace can
be rejected later. Since this doctrine of perseverance had been a clear and
important teaching of Reformed Christianity since the days of Calvin,
Calvinists saw this uncertainty on the part of the Arminians as disingenuous, indeed dishonest. The Arminians had had a great deal of time to
study the matter and to reach a conclusion on it.

The brief conclusion to these five points insists on their orthodoxy,
piety, and sufficiency. The Calvinists would deny that these points present the teaching of the Scriptures on the matters they cover. Indeed, the
Calvinists would claim that the points of the Remonstrance reject the
clear teaching of the Bible. They would also insist that teachings that
are not true cannot be edifying. Finally, they would argue that the Bible
indeed has a much higher and deeper doctrine on these matters than the
Arminians realized. At the Synod of Dort, the Calvinists would lay out
the biblical truth on these matters, show their biblical fullness, and make
clear the truly edifying nature of genuine Reformed Christianity.

As problematic as the teachings of these points are, our study of the
Canons of Dort—especially the rejections of errors—will show how
much more radically Pelagian at least some of the Arminians had become
in less than a decade after 1610. Some of the Remonstrants, particularly
on points 3, 4, and 5, had gone much further theologically and become
much less cautious.

After the Remonstrance

In the years between the Remonstrance and the Synod of Dort, various
efforts were made to reconcile the Calvinists and Arminians, but the
differences were too great and too deep to be negotiated away. The civil
government did protect the Remonstrants from discipline by the church.
But the polarization of the two sides increased steadily, leading to the

edge of a split in the church. Some Calvinists refused to attend churches with Arminian ministers. Some Calvinists spoke of organizing secret classes, as they had done in the days of Roman Catholic persecution.

As long as the civil government remained united in its policy of toleration for the Remonstrants, the Calvinists' options were limited. But in 1617, Prince Maurits left his congregation, which had an Arminian minister, and started attending a church with a Calvinist pastor. Increasingly, he opposed the policies of Oldenbarnevelt. The polarization of Dutch society was complete. As the civil government, Oldenbarnevelt, and the peace party supported toleration for the Arminians, so Maurits, the army, and the war party came to support the Calvinists. The United Provinces were not far from civil war. But Maurits had the considerable advantage of an army to support him, whereas Oldenbarnevelt did not. Oldenbarnevelt was arrested for treason in 1618, which was a shameful act against a Dutch patriot and one of the low points for Dutch Calvinists. Years of frustration boiled over in excessive anger. The new government, led by Maurits, authorized the meeting of a national synod to address at last the Remonstrant theology.

Chapter 2

THE SYNOD

OF DORT

M any ministers in the Reformed church had been calling for a national synod to address the Arminian challenge for years. The new civil government authorized the calling of the national synod, and the decision was made for the synod to convene on November 13, 1618, in the city of Dordrecht.

Dordrecht is a port city in the province of Holland (the name of the city is often abbreviated in English as Dort or Dordt). This city was the site of the meeting of the first free gathering of the States General after the beginning of the revolt against Philip II of Spain. It was also the site of the meeting of two earlier synods, reckoned by the Calvinists as national synods, in 1574 and 1578. The associations of this city with great events in the history of the United Provinces underscore the importance of this synod. The hall in which the synod actually met no longer stands. But the building where some of the delegates were housed (the same building where the first free States General met) and the church where they often worshiped are still standing.

The Composition of the Synod

The Arminians objected sharply to the calling of the synod, insisting that it would be unfair, indeed a kangaroo court. They stated that a synod composed of their theological opponents could not fairly or objectively judge the theological issues in dispute. The Calvinist majority in the church responded that since they were simply upholding the standing doctrine of the church against the Arminian innovations, they were abundantly able to judge rightly.

To overcome any appearance of unfairness, the decision was made to invite international delegates as full members of the synod. Reformed ministers and professors from throughout Europe were invited. Where the civil government was Reformed, the invitation went to the government to decide on its delegates. Where the government was not Reformed, the invitation went to the Reformed church in that region. So, for example, the invitation went to King James VI and I to send delegates representing Great Britain. By contrast, the invitation went to the Reformed Church of France rather than to the Roman Catholic King Louis XIII.

These international invitations led to some embarrassing moments for the Dutch. When King James appointed an entirely English delegation to the synod, the Church of Scotland objected. James responded, somewhat ironically, by adding a Scot, Walter Balcanqual, to the delegation, but he was a member of the Church of England. James was theologically a Calvinist, but he much preferred dependent bishops to independent presbyters. The Church of Scotland was not happy.

The French and British delegations each notified the Dutch that they expected to have the most honored seats in the assembly hall. The French argued their right as they were coming from the greatest monarchy in Europe. The British argued that they were coming from the greatest Protestant monarchy in Europe. The Dutch were spared making a decision in this diplomatic difficulty when King Louis XIII refused to allow the French delegates to return to France if they attended. The Dutch left empty seats for the French (clearly visible in the well-known picture of the synod in session)—just below the British seats.

Another embarrassment awaited the Dutch. Apparently, someone neglected to invite the Genevans. An invitation was sent belatedly and accepted.

Other invitations went to the German-speaking Swiss (one

delegation was formed with representatives from Zurich, Bern, Basel, and Schaffhausen). Invitations also went to various German territories: the Palatinate, Hesse, Nassau, Bremen, and Emden. It was truly an international synod. Ultimately, the synod was organized around nineteen delegations or colleges—eight foreign and eleven domestic—as well as representatives of the civil government. Most of the domestic delegations were composed of four ministers and two elders each. The foreign delegations ranged in size from two to five delegates. The total number of delegates was eighty-two.

Many of the delegates were well known in their own day, but most have not remained famous through the years. The British delegates were particularly distinguished and influential, since the British had been the key ally of the Dutch in the war with Spain. The delegation was led by George Carleton, bishop of Llandaff. John Davenant was an important theologian at Cambridge University and a significant voice in the discussions on the second head of doctrine.

Other British, who were not delegates, attended all or parts of the synod. William Ames, an important Congregationalist Puritan in exile from England, was a secretary to the president of the synod. He was once asked if Arminianism was a heresy (meaning a false teaching so serious that its adherents could not be saved). He responded that Arminianism was not a heresy but a serious error tending to heresy.

Another important British observer was John Hales, chaplain to the English ambassador to the United Provinces, Dudley Carleton. Hales was sent to report to the ambassador, who in turn informed King James and George Abbot, archbishop of Canterbury. (Abbot, who was a Calvinist, took a great interest in the synod and later tried to have the Canons of Dort adopted as a doctrinal standard for all English clergy.) Hales wrote invaluable letters to Carleton recording many behind-the-scenes events.[1]

Other notables at the synod included Abraham Scultetus, who was a leading theologian from the Palatinate. Also important was Jean Diodati from Geneva. Professors of theology from Dutch universities formed a distinct group or "college" of delegates. The most famous of these was Franciscus Gomarus, who had taught with Arminius at Leiden.

Other delegates who were young at the time of the synod later became famous. The most notable of these delegates was Gisbertus Voetius. By the middle of the seventeenth century, he was the most celebrated and influential theologian in the Netherlands. He became a professor in Utrecht and was a staunch defender of Aristotelian philosophy, orthodox theology, and strict Sabbatarian piety. Another minister, Jacobus Triglandius, would later become a professor at Leiden and would write a long history of the Arminian controversy.

The Work of the Synod

The central work of the synod was to evaluate and respond to the teaching of the Arminians in the church. Much other work needed to be done, however, for the well-being of the church after more than thirty years during which no national synod had been held. This other work has been referred to as the Pro-Acta and Post-Acta of the synod.

The Pro-Acta were decisions made while the synod waited for the Arminians to answer the summons and arrive in Dordrecht. Three decisions were of particular importance for the life of the church. First, the synod called for the preparation of a new Dutch translation of the Bible. A translation committee was appointed and eventually produced the *Statenvertaling*, or state translation, which has had an influence and longevity in Dutch similar to that of the King James Version in English.

Second, the synod discussed how to promote effective catechism teaching for the young. One suggestion was that young people not be allowed to marry until they demonstrated an adequate knowledge of the catechism. Less draconian ideas were ultimately recommended to the churches.

Third, the synod addressed the question as to whether the children of heathen servants living in Dutch households in the Far East should be baptized. This question seems to be the first time a theological, missionary inquiry arose out of new European commercial interests outside of Europe. As Dutch traders began to live in the Far East, the issue of household baptism took on a new significance. The synod was not united in its response. A minority, led by the British delegation, believed that such children should be baptized. The majority taught that these children should be catechized and baptized only after they came to faith.

The Post-Acta were synodical decisions made after the canons were completed and the foreign delegates were dismissed with thanks on May 6, 1619. Several key actions were taken. The synod established an official text of the Belgic Confession, since slightly different versions had been circulating. It also adopted a form of subscription to the church's doctrine for all church officers as well as a church order and various liturgical forms. It also responded to an inquiry from the province of Zeeland about the proper understanding of Sunday as a Christian Sabbath. Zeeland had been influenced by English Puritan writing and wanted official synodical guidance on this subject. The synod replied that it did not have time for a full response but would issue a provisional statement. That statement was the only one made by a national synod on this issue for centuries. The Dutch Reformed Church in the course of the seventeenth century did become strictly Sabbatarian in its teaching and piety.[2]

The great French Reformed theologian and pastor Pierre Du Moulin, who had been delegated to the synod but was unable to attend, wrote a letter to the synod. The letter analyzed the Arminian theology and then made various proposals for Reformed and Protestant unity. One of his proposals was that the synod should write a new Reformed confession that would unite all the Reformed churches and demonstrate that unity to the world. Late in the meetings of the synod, it was recognized that there would not be time to undertake such a task. As a provisional response, however, the synod unanimously declared that the Belgic Confession is in conformity to the Word of God and acceptable as an expression of the Reformed teaching. The Belgic Confession, then, is the closest thing the Reformed have to a commonly accepted confession.[3]

Judging the Arminians

The Arminians arrived at the synod on December 6, 1618. Then the great work of the synod in evaluating and responding to the Arminian teaching began in earnest. A few particularly interesting and memorable moments occurred during those meetings of the synod. The first was the opening speech of Simon Episcopius, the leading Arminian at the synod. The speech lasted two hours, about which Hales commented that Episcopius finally came to the part for which they had all been eagerly waiting: the end.

Second, one of the debates on election among the orthodox delegates became quite heated. Gomarus was offended by a theological formulation presented by Martinius of Bremen. On the floor of the synod, Gomarus challenged Martinius to a duel. Cooler heads prevailed and peace was established between the two delegates without a duel.

Third, after several weeks of listening to the Arminians speaking at great length and in ways that were not responsive or helpful, Johannes Bogerman, the president of the synod, ran out of patience and ejected the Arminians from the sessions of the synod, instructing the Arminians to communicate with the synod only in writing. Hales called Bogerman's statement to them "a powdering speech." A number of delegates thought the president had exceeded his prerogatives, but the Arminians did not return.

After the dismissal of the Arminians in mid-January 1619, their views were judged from their writings. The decision was made to reduce the number of public sessions for a time and to have the various delegations or colleges meet separately and write their own responses to the Arminian theology following the five points articulated in the Remonstrance of 1610.

Each of the delegations produced their own *Judicia* or judgments on the Remonstrant teaching. Almost all of them were written in an academic, scholastic style. These judgments were then given to a committee that prepared the canons. This committee had nine members: the three leading officers of the synod (Johannes Bogerman, Jacobus Rolandus, and Hermannus Faukelius), three international delegates (George Carleton, Abraham Scultetus, and Jean Diodati), two Dutch professors (Johannes Polyander and Antonius Walaeus), and a Dutch minister (Jacobus Triglandius).

The canons were written in a form and with a character quite different from the form of most of the judgments (for a discussion of that form, see chapter 8 and appendix 2, on the general pattern of the canons.) The proposed canons were then presented to the synod with little opportunity for debate or amendment. This procedure annoyed some of the delegates, but in the end the canons were approved unanimously, not just by all the delegations but by all of the individual delegates. After many months and great labor, the canons were completed, and they have been a blessing to many churches inside and outside of the Netherlands.

The synod approved the canons on April 23, 1619, and two days later adopted a preface to the canons as a brief historical and theological introduction to the work of the synod and the canons. This preface has seldom been reprinted and is not regarded as an official part of the canons. Nevertheless, it is a useful introduction to them and is included here in a new translation.[4]

Preface

In the name of our Lord and Savior Jesus Christ, Amen.

Among the many comforts which our Lord and Savior Jesus Christ gave to His church militant in its troubled sojourn, one in particular is rightly celebrated. That one He left behind as He departed to His Father in the heavenly sanctuary, saying, "I am with you every day until the end of the age." The truth of this very delightful promise shines in the church of every time. She was attacked from the beginning not only in the open violence of enemies and the impiety of heretics, but also in the hidden cunning of seducers. Indeed, if ever the Lord had deprived her of the protection of the saving promise of His presence, long ago either the power of tyrants would have oppressed her or the fraud of deceivers would have seduced her to destruction. But the Good Shepherd has most constantly loved His flock for which He gave His life. He has always held back with His right hand at the right time the rage of persecutors, often openly and wonderfully. He has finished off and routed the crooked ways and fraudulent counsels of the seducers. Each time He showed His presence with His church. Clear proof of this truth stands in the histories of the pious emperors, kings, and princes, whom the Son of God so many times has raised up for the protection of His church. Inflamed with a holy zeal for His house, they restrained by their works the fury of the tyrants. They also took care of the church with the remedies of holy synods when contending with false teachers and those who in various ways counterfeit religion. In these synods, faithful servants of Christ joined together in prayer, counsel, and labor. They stood strong and immovable for the church and truth of God, opposed undaunted the ministers of Satan transformed into angels of light, suppressed the seeds of errors and discord, preserved the church in the harmony of pure religion, and transmitted sound worship to posterity undiminished.

With the same favor, our faithful Savior in this time has shown His gracious presence to the Dutch church, which was for many years very afflicted. This church was set free from the tyranny of the Roman Antichrist and the horrible papal idolatry by the powerful hand of God. It was preserved wondrously many times in the dangers of the long war. It has flourished in the harmony of true doctrine and discipline to the praise of God, the admirable growth of Republic, and the joy of the whole Reformed world.

Then Jacob Arminius and his followers, named Remonstrants, attacked this church with various errors, some old and some new, first privately and then openly. Scandalous dissensions and obstinately disordered schisms led to such division that this most flourishing church would have been consumed in the horrible fire of these dissensions and schisms unless the compassion of our Savior had intervened at the right time. Blessed forever be the Lord, who after He had hidden His face for a moment from us (who had provoked His wrath and indignation in many ways), has shown the whole world that He does not forget His covenant and does not scorn the sighing of His people. When it appeared that there was hardly any human hope of remedy, He inspired the minds of the Most Illustrious and Mighty States General of the Dutch federation, together with the counsel and direction of the Most Illustrious and Mighty Prince of Orange, to use those legitimate means which the Apostles themselves practiced. Those means, followed as examples by those who came after the Apostles, came down to us, sanctioned by long use in the Christian church and practiced before this with great fruit also in the Dutch church. These civil governors decided to face the raging evils before them, declaring by their authority that a synod be convened in Dordrecht from all their provinces. They also requested and procured for this Synod many most important theologians by the favor of the Most Serene and Powerful King of Great Britain, James, and of various Most Illustrious Princes, Counts, and Republics.

By the common judgment of so many theologians of the Reformed church, the teachings of Arminius and his followers would be judged accurately and by the Word of God alone, true doctrine established and false doctrine rejected, and—by the divine blessing—harmony, peace, and tranquility be restored to the Dutch churches. This is that blessing of God in which the Dutch churches exult. They humbly acknowledge the compassions of their faithful Savior and gratefully preach them.

Before the meeting of this venerable Synod, the authority of the highest magistrates called for and held gatherings of prayer and fasting in all the Dutch churches to avert the wrath of God and to implore His gracious help. The Synod then gathered in the name of the Lord at Dordrecht, inflamed by love of the divine majesty and of the well-being of the church. After calling on the name of God, it bound itself by a holy oath to have for its judgment only the standard of Holy Scripture, and in its proceedings to understand and to act in judgment with good and honest conscience, and to do this diligently. It bound itself with great patience to persuade the leading advocates of that teaching cited before them to present their conviction about the Five Heads of

Doctrine and to expound fully the reasons for that conviction. But when they repudiated the judgment of the synod and refused to respond to its questions, neither the warnings of the Synod nor the commands of the delegates of the Most Generous and Powerful States General could make progress with them. The Synod was forced to pursue another way by the order of their Lords and from the custom received from ancient synods. So the Synod examined their teachings on the five points from their writings, confessions, and declarations, some previously issued, others prepared for this Synod.

Through the singular grace of God, with the greatest diligence, faith, and conscience, this Synod achieved the absolute consensus of all and each member, to the glory of God. So, for the integrity of the truth of salvation, the tranquility of consciences, and the peace and well-being of the Dutch church, the Synod decided to promulgate the following judgment. By this judgment it both expounded the true conviction, which agreed to the Word of God about the previously mentioned Five Heads of Doctrine, and rejected the false conviction which differed from the Word of God.

This preface, written in the flowery language of the time, is an interesting historical document reflecting the synod's sense of its calling and work. It reflects the theological convictions of the synod as well as the spiritual confidence connected to those convictions. But this preface also shows that the synod is clearly strategic in its thinking about how it will communicate to the wider world.

The preface begins by remembering Christ's promise to be with His church and to preserve her from all sorts of enemies. Referring to this promise is a theological conviction about Christ's sovereign care of His church. It also reflects the piety of the church as it rests in the promises of God's Word. It is also strategically wise to begin with this expression of dependence on Christ's constant presence with His church. It also recalls how the church had been delivered from papal tyranny and idolatry, reminding the reader of what the Reformed church had accomplished in the Netherlands.

After resting in Christ's promise, the synod recalls how throughout the history of the church Christ has used pious magistrates to protect the church. Christ has also frequently used synods to protect her truth, her unity, and her worship. Christ has similarly promoted and protected the church in the Netherlands. Strategically, the synod connects itself with Christian magistrates—reaching back to Constantine, who called the Council of Nicaea in 325—and with the practice of the churches through the whole history of the church to meet in councils and synods to deal with problems.

The preface points to Arminius and his followers as those who have disturbed the church, undermining its teaching and unity. Here again we see a strategic cleverness in reminding the reader that it was the Arminians who had disturbed the peace and order of the church. After protracted struggles, the magistrates—both the States General and the prince of Orange (Maurits)—decided to follow the practice of the church through history and to call a synod to judge the issues in dispute. They were helped in this by many foreign magistrates and theologians, especially King James of Great Britain.

This synod committed itself to judge the Arminians by the Word of God alone in order to protect and unify the Dutch churches. When the Arminians refused to cooperate with the work of the synod, their views had to be judged from their writings. The synod unanimously agreed to both the statement of the true doctrine and the rejection of false teaching. The stress on the unanimity of the synod again pointed to the lack of any support for the Arminians in the European Reformed churches.

In this preface, the synod made clear what it believed it had accomplished. It acted for "the glory of God" and for "the integrity of the truth of salvation, the tranquility of consciences, and the peace and well-being of the Dutch church." The great goals and the real accomplishments of the Synod of Dort were to declare and defend the truth, to provide comfort for the souls of Christians, and to ensure the peace and blessing of the churches. The synod succeeded to a remarkable degree.

—

PART II

THE CANONS OF THE SYNOD OF DORT— A PASTORAL TRANSLATION

—

Chapter 3

FIRST HEAD OF DOCTRINE:

GOD'S PREDESTINATION

The Official Teaching
Of the Dutch Reformed Churches
On God's Predestination and Related Topics,
Adopted at the International Assembly of Churches
Meeting at Dordrecht, November 1618–May 1619[1]

Article 1

All people have sinned in Adam and so are subject to the curse and eternal death. God would not have been unfair to anyone if He had left everyone in sin and under the curse, and had willed to damn them all on account of sin. The Apostle teaches this: "The whole world is guilty under the condemnation of God"; "all have sinned and fallen short of the glory of God"; and "the wages of sin is death" (Rom. 3:19, 23; 6:23).

Article 2

Truly God shows His love in this, that He sent His only begotten Son into the world, so that each one who believes in Him, would not perish but have eternal life (1 John 4:9; John 3:16).

Article 3

God mercifully sends messengers of this most joyful news to those He will and when He will, so that people may be brought to faith. By this ministry, people are called to repentance and faith in Christ crucified. "How shall they believe in him of whom they have not heard? How will they hear without a preacher? How will they preach unless they are sent?" (Rom. 10:14–15).

Article 4

The anger of God remains on those who do not believe this gospel. Those who receive it and embrace Jesus the Savior with a true and living faith are freed by Him both from the anger of God and from destruction. They are given eternal life by Him.

Article 5

The cause of our guilt for this unbelief and for all other sins is not at all in God, but is in humans. However, faith in Jesus Christ and salvation through Him are the gracious gift of God. So it is written: "By grace you are saved through faith, and this not of yourselves, it is the gift of God" (Eph. 2:8). Also: "It is freely given to you to believe in Christ" (Phil. 1:29).

Article 6

The reality that some people are given faith by God in time, while others are not given faith, proceeds from God's eternal decree. "He knows all His works from eternity" (Acts 15:18; Eph. 1:11). According to this decree, He graciously softens the hearts of the elect, however hard, and inclines them to believe. He also leaves the nonelect according to His just judgment in their wickedness and hardness of heart. This decree most powerfully shows us God's profound, merciful, yet also just distinction among people equally lost. This decree of election and reprobation is revealed in the Word of God. And although the perverse, impure, and unstable twist it to their own destruction, it gives inexpressible comfort to holy and pious souls.

Article 7

Election is the immutable purpose of God, by which He chose to salvation in Christ, from the whole human race, a fixed multitude of particular persons. God's election is from before the foundation of the world in relation to people who fell from their original integrity into sin and destruction by their own fault. God chose His elect, according to the most free good pleasure of His will, out of mere grace. Those chosen were neither better nor more worthy than others, but were like others fallen into the common human misery. From eternity, God made Christ the Mediator and Head of all the elect and the foundation of salvation. God gave the elect to Christ to save them, and effectively to call them and draw them into communion with Him through His Word and Spirit. He decreed to give them true faith in Christ as well as to justify them, sanctify them, and finally, after powerfully preserving them in the communion of His Son, to glorify them. All this shows God's mercy for the praise of the riches of His glorious grace. So it is written: "God elected us in Christ with love, before the foundation of the world, so that we might be holy and blameless in His sight. He who predestined us, adopted us as sons, through Jesus Christ to Himself, according to the good pleasure of His will, to the praise of His glorious grace, by which He made us acceptable to Him in the beloved" (Eph. 1:4–6). And elsewhere: "Those whom He predestined, He also called; and those whom He called, He also justified; those whom He justified, He also glorified" (Rom. 8:30).

Article 8

This election is not of various kinds, but is one and the same for all those saved in the Old and New Testaments. For the Scripture teaches that God has one good pleasure, one purpose, and one counsel of His will, by which from eternity He elected us both to grace and to glory. He elected us both to salvation and to the way of salvation, which He prepared as the way in which we would walk.

Article 9

This very election was made not on the basis of foreseen faith, or of the obedience of faith, or of holiness, or of any other good quality and disposition, as the prerequisite cause or condition for electing anyone. Rather, this election is to faith, to the obedience of faith, to holiness, etc. And so election is the fountain of all saving good. From election flow faith, holiness, and all other saving gifts, even eternal life itself, as fruit and effect. As the Apostle wrote: "He chose us in love [not because we were, but] so that we might be holy and blameless in his sight" (Eph. 1:4).

Article 10

The cause of this gracious election is the good pleasure of God alone. The cause is not that God elected certain human qualities or actions out of all possibilities as the condition of salvation. Rather, He adopted as His own possession certain specific persons out of the common multitude of sinners. So it is written: "For the children, not yet born, and not having done anything good or evil . . . it was said [to Rebecca], the elder will serve the younger, as it is written: Jacob I loved, Esau I hated" (Rom. 9:11–13). And "all who were ordained for eternal life believed" (Acts 13:48).

Article 11

As God Himself is most wise, immutable, omniscient, and omnipotent, so the election made by Him cannot be interrupted, changed, recalled, or annulled. Just so, the elect cannot be lost or their number reduced.

Article 12

The elect become more certain of their eternal and unchangeable election to salvation in their own time, though in varying stages and different degrees. This certainty does not indeed come by curiously examining the secret and deep things of God. Rather, it comes by seeing in themselves, with spiritual joy and holy satisfaction, the fruit of infallible election taught in the Word of God. That fruit includes true faith in Christ, childlike fear of God, godly sorrow for sin, a hunger and thirst for righteousness, etc.

Article 13

As a result of this sense and certainty of election, the children of God daily find more reason to humble themselves before God, to adore the depth of His mercies, to purify themselves, and also eagerly to love Him who first loved them so greatly. So we see that this doctrine of election, and meditation on it, are far from making the children of God slack in observing the commandments of God or making them carnally secure. Rather, such slackness and carnal security are usually found according to the just judgment of God in those who do not want to walk in the ways of the elect. Such people either rashly presume on the grace of election or chat about it in an idle and shameless manner.

Article 14

This doctrine of divine election according to the most wise counsel of God was preached by the prophets, by Christ Himself, and by the Apostles, in the Old just as in the New Testament. It was notably preserved in the sacred Scriptures. So today it ought to be taught in the church of God, for which it was particularly intended, at the right time and place, with a spirit of discretion and in a manner that is religious and holy. Far from encouraging any curious examination of the ways of the Most High, it ought to be taught for the glory of the most holy divine name and for the lively comfort of His people.

Article 15

Additionally, what greatly shows the eternal and free grace of our election, and which the Holy Scripture commends to us, is the testimony that not all humans are elect. Rather, some are nonelect or are passed over in the eternal election of God. God in His most free, most righteous, blameless, and unchangeable good pleasure decreed to leave the nonelect in the common misery. They have plunged themselves into this misery by their own fault. God decreed not to give them saving faith and the grace of conversion. Instead, He left them under His righteous judgment to follow their own ways. He decreed at last to damn and eternally punish them not only because of their unbelief, but also for all their other sins, for the demonstration of His justice. And this is the decree of reprobation, which does not make God in any way the author of sin (which it is blasphemous to think). Rather, it shows Him to be a formidable, blameless, righteous judge and avenger.

Article 16

Some people do not yet effectively feel a living faith in Christ, a confident trust in the heart, peace of conscience, a desire for childlike obedience, or a glorying in God through Christ. But if such people nevertheless use the means through which God has promised to work these things in them, they ought not to be alarmed at the mention of reprobation or reckon themselves reprobate. Rather, they ought to persevere in the diligent use of the means and ought to desire ardently a time of fuller grace and to look for it with reverence and humility. The doctrine of reprobation should be much less terrifying for those who desire seriously to be converted to God, to please Him only, and to be delivered from the body of death, but cannot yet arrive at the life of piety and faith that they want. For the merciful God has promised that He will not quench the smoking flax or break the bruised reed. However, this doctrine is rightly terrifying to those who have forgotten God and the Savior Jesus Christ and have completely given themselves over to the cares of the world and the desires of the flesh, as long as they are not seriously converted to God.

Article 17

We are to judge the will of God from His Word. The Word testifies that the children of the faithful are holy, not by nature, but as a benefit of God's gracious covenant. These children together with their parents are included in this covenant. Therefore, pious parents ought not to doubt the election and salvation of their children whom God calls out of this life in infancy.

Article 18

To those who murmur against this grace of free election and the severity of just reprobation, we set against them this Apostolic word: "O man! Who are you to answer back to God?" (Rom. 9:20). And that word of our Savior: "Am I not allowed to do what I want with My own?" (Matt. 20:15). Truly, we adore this mystery piously when we exclaim with the Apostle: "O the depth of the riches both of the wisdom and the knowledge of God! How unsearchable are the judgments of God and how inscrutable are His ways! Who has known the mind of the Lord? And who has been His counselor? And who has first given to Him that it would be returned to him? For from Him, and through Him, and in Him are all things. To Him be glory forever. Amen" (Rom. 11:33–36).

THE REJECTION OF ERRORS

By which the Dutch Churches have been disturbed for some time. After expounding the orthodox doctrine of election and reprobation, the Synod rejects the following errors.

Rejection 1

The Synod rejects the error of those who teach:

"The whole and complete decree of election to salvation is the will of God to save those who would believe and would persevere in faith and the obedience of faith. Nothing else concerning this decree is revealed in the Word of God."

Those who teach this deceive the more simple people and clearly contradict the sacred Scripture. The Scripture testifies that God not only wills to save those who are going to believe. God has also elected from eternity a certain number of persons to whom, rather than to others, He will give in time faith in Christ and perseverance. As it is written, "I have made Your name known to the men whom You gave to me" (John 17:6), and, "As many as were ordained to eternal life believed" (Acts 18:48), and, "He chose them before the foundation of the world, that they might be holy" (Eph. 1:4).

Rejection 2

The Synod rejects the error of those who teach:

> "The election of God to eternal life is of several kinds. One is general and indefinite and another is particular and definite. Further, the particular and definite one either is incomplete, revocable, nondecisive, or conditional, or is complete, irrevocable, decisive, or absolute." Also, "one election is to faith, and another to salvation, so that election can be to justifying faith without being a decisive election to salvation."

This teaching is an invention of the human understanding devised outside the Scriptures. It corrupts the doctrine of election, and destroys the golden chain of salvation: "Those whom He predestined, He also called; and those whom He called, He also justified; those whom He justified, He also glorified" (Rom. 8:30).

Rejection 3

The Synod rejects the error of those who teach:

> "The good pleasure and purpose of God, which Scripture mentions in its doctrine of election, does not consist in

this, that God elected certain particular persons rather than others. But it consists in this, that God out of all possible conditions (among which are also works of the law) or out of the order of all things, elected the act of faith, in itself undistinguished, and the imperfect obedience of faith as the condition of salvation. He graciously reckoned this as perfect obedience and He wanted to consider it worth the reward of eternal life."

By this pernicious error the good pleasure of God and the merit of Christ are enervated. Also, men are distracted from the truth of gracious justification and the simplicity of the Scriptures to considering useless questions. By this, the statement of the Apostle is rendered false: "God called us with a holy calling; not because of works, but because of His own purpose and grace, which He gave to us in Christ Jesus before the times of the ages" (2 Tim. 1:9).

Rejection 4

The Synod rejects the error of those who teach:

"In the election to faith this condition is required, that men rightly use the light of nature and be pious, meek, humble, and disposed to eternal life, as if election to some extent depended on these things."

These things savor of Pelagius and in fact falsely undermine the Apostle who wrote: "We once lived in the passions of our flesh, carrying out the desires of the flesh and the mind, and were by nature children of wrath like the rest. But God who is rich in mercy, because of His great love with which He loved us, even when we were dead in offenses, He made us alive with Christ, by whose grace you are saved, and raised us up and seated us in the heavens in Christ Jesus, so that in the coming ages He might show the surpassing riches of his grace according to His kindness to us in Christ Jesus. By grace you have been saved through faith (and that not of yourselves, it is the gift of God), not of works lest anyone should boast" (Eph. 2:3–9).

Rejection 5

The Synod rejects the error of those who teach:

> "The election of particular persons to salvation is incomplete and nondecisive, made on the basis of foreseen faith, repentance, holiness, and piety, begun and continued for some time. It becomes complete and decisive on the basis of final perseverance of foreseen faith, repentance, holiness, and piety. This is the gracious and evangelical worthiness, on account of which he who is elect is more worthy than he who is not elect. Therefore faith, the obedience of faith, holiness, piety, and perseverance are not the fruit or effect of immutable election to glory. Rather, they are conditions or causes without which these persons are not completely elected, being prerequisites which are foreseen as fulfilled."

That teaching is repugnant to the whole Scripture, which repeatedly declares, in these texts and many others, to our ears and hearts: "Election is not from works, but from calling" (Rom. 9:11). "As many as were ordained to eternal life believed" (Acts 13:48). "He elected us in Him that we might be holy" (Eph. 1:4). "You did not chose Me, but I chose you" (John 15:16). "If by grace, then not by works" (Rom. 11:6). "In this is love, not that we loved God, but that He loved us, and sent His Son" (1 John 4:10).

Rejection 6

The Synod rejects the error of those who teach:

> "Not all election to salvation is immutable, but certain of the elect, without any decree of God preventing it, can perish and do perish eternally."

By this gross error they make God mutable and subvert the comfort of the pious in the constancy of their election. They also contradict the sacred Scriptures, which teach "the elect cannot be led astray" (Matt. 24:24). "Christ does not lose those given Him by the Father" (John 6:39). "Those whom God predestined, called, and justified, He also glorified" (Rom. 8:30).

Rejection 7

The Synod rejects the error of those who teach:

> "There is in this life no fruit, no sense, and no certainty of immutable election to glory except from a mutable and contingent condition."

Surely it is absurd to make certainty uncertain. It is contrary to the experience of the saints who rejoice with the Apostle in their sense of election. The saints celebrate this blessing of God. They "rejoice" with the disciples according to the Word of Christ "that their names are written in heaven" (Luke 10:20). Finally, they oppose their sense of election to the fiery attack of the devils, asking, "Who will bring any charge against God's elect?" (Rom. 8:33).

Rejection 8

The Synod rejects the error of those who teach:

> "God has not decreed, simply according to His just will, to leave anyone in the fall of Adam and in the common state of sin and condemnation or to pass over anyone in communicating the necessary grace for faith and conversion."

This Scripture stands against them: "He has mercy on whom He will; He hardens whom He will" (Rom. 9:18). And this: "It is given to you to know the mysteries of the kingdom of heaven; to them it is not given" (Matt. 13:11). Also "I glorify You, Father, Lord of heaven and earth, that You have hidden this from the wise and understanding, and revealed it to infants, because, Father, it was pleasing to You" (Matt. 11:25–26).

Rejection 9

The Synod rejects the error of those who teach:

> "The reason God sends His gospel to one people rather than to another is not merely and solely the good pleasure of God, but because one people is better and more worthy than another people to whom the gospel is not communicated."

Moses contradicts this saying to the people of Israel: "To Jehovah your God belong the heavens and the heavens of heavens, the earth and what is in it. Only to your forebears did Jehovah with love incline to love them and He chose their seed after them, indeed you, above all peoples, as it is today" (Deut. 10:14–15). And Christ: "Woe to you Chorazin, woe to you Bethsaida, because if the works which were done in you had been done in Tyre and Sidon, they would have repented long ago in sackcloth and ashes" (Matt. 11:21).

Chapter 4

SECOND HEAD OF DOCTRINE:

THE DEATH OF CHRIST
AND THE REDEMPTION OF HUMANS
THROUGH THAT DEATH

Article 1

God is not only supremely merciful, but also supremely just. His justice requires (as He has revealed in His Word) that our sins committed against His infinite majesty be punished. They must be punished both in body and soul, with eternal as well as temporal punishments. We cannot escape these punishments unless the justice of God be satisfied.

Article 2

We cannot satisfy for our sins or free ourselves from the anger of God. So God, out of His immense mercy, gave His only begotten Son as surety for our sins. This Son, so that He might satisfy for us, was made sin and curse on the cross for us and in our place.

Article 3

This death of the Son of God is the only and most perfect sacrifice and satisfaction for sins. It is of infinite value and worth, abundantly sufficient to expiate the sins of the whole world.

Article 4

Now this death is of such value and worth because of the person who experienced it. He is not only a true and perfectly holy human. But He is also the only begotten Son of God, of the same eternal and infinite essence with the Father and the Holy Spirit. It was necessary for such a person to be our Savior. His death is also of such value and worth because it was accompanied by the experience of the anger and curse of God, which we had merited for our sins.

Article 5

The promise of the gospel is that whoever believes in Christ crucified shall not perish, but shall have eternal life. This promise along with the command to repent and believe ought to be announced and proclaimed generally and indiscriminately to all peoples and humans to whom God according to His good pleasure sends the gospel.

Article 6

Many who are called by the gospel do not in fact repent or believe in Christ, but perish in unbelief. This loss is not because of any defect or insufficiency in the sacrifice of Christ offered on the cross. Rather, it is because of their own guilt.

Article 7

All those who truly believe are freed from destruction and saved from their sins through the death of Christ. They obtain this by the grace of God alone, which He owes to no one, but gave to them in Christ from eternity.

Article 8

It was the most free counsel and most gracious will and intention of God the Father that the living and saving efficacy of the most valuable death of His Son would extend to all the elect. To the elect alone He gives justifying faith and infallibly produces salvation through faith. God willed for Christ efficaciously to redeem through the blood of the cross (by which He confirmed the new covenant)—from every people, tribe, nation, and tongue—all those and only those who were elected to salvation from eternity and were given to Him by the Father. God willed that Christ give to the elect the faith that He acquired for them by His death, along with other saving gifts of the Holy Spirit. He also willed for Christ to cleanse them by His blood from all sin, both original and actual, committed before as well as after faith. He willed for Christ to preserve them faithfully even to the end, and finally to bring them, without spot or blemish, glorified into His presence.

Article 9

This plan, coming from God's eternal love toward the elect, has been powerfully fulfilled from the beginning of the world up to the present time. And it will be continually fulfilled in the future, despite the vain opposition of the gates of hell. So the elect in due time are gathered into one, and there will always be a church of believers. This church, founded in the blood of Jesus, constantly loves Him, perseveringly worships Him, and celebrates Him, now and in all eternity, as her Savior. He is the One who offered His own soul for her on the cross as a Bridegroom for His bride.

REJECTION OF ERRORS

After expositing the orthodox doctrine, the Synod rejects the following errors.

Rejection 1

The Synod rejects the error of those who teach:

> "God the Father destined His Son to the death of the cross without a certain and definite plan for saving anyone by name. Therefore the necessity, usefulness, and worth of what the death of Christ accomplished could have

remained perfect, complete, and whole in all its parts even if the accomplished redemption had not ever actually been applied to any individual."

This assertion is contemptuous of the wisdom of God the Father and the merit of Jesus Christ and is contrary to Scripture. Thus the Savior said: "I give My life for My sheep and I know them" (John 10:15, 27). And the prophet Isaiah wrote about the Savior: "When He will sacrifice Himself for sin, He will see His seed and prolong His days and the will of Jehovah will prosper in His hand" (Isa. 53:10). Finally, it overturns the article of faith [in the Apostles' Creed] in which we believe in the church.

Rejection 2

The Synod rejects the error of those who teach:

"The purpose of the death of Christ was not that He might actually establish a new covenant of grace. Rather, it was only that He might acquire for the Father the bare right of establishing again with men a covenant whether of grace or of works."

This denies the Scripture, which teaches that Christ "was made the Surety and Mediator of a better," that is, new "covenant" (Heb. 7:22). And, "A testament is of force where there has been a death" (Heb. 9:15, 17).

Rejection 3

The Synod rejects the error of those who teach:

"Christ through His satisfaction has not certainly merited for anyone the salvation and faith, by which this satisfaction of Christ is efficaciously applied for salvation. Rather, He has only acquired for the Father the power or the full will, for working anew with men and for prescribing new conditions as He might will. The fulfillment of these conditions so depends on the free will of man that it could be that either no one or every one might fulfill them."

These teachers think in an exceedingly low way about the death of Christ, and they do not at all recognize the preeminent fruit and benefit of His death. They recall the Pelagian error from hell.

Rejection 4

The Synod rejects the error of those who teach:

"That new covenant of grace, which God the Father, through the intervention of the death of Christ, made with men, does not consist in this: to the extent that faith accepts the merit of Christ, we are justified and saved before God. But rather the new covenant consists in this: God, having abrogated the demand of perfect legal obedience, counts faith itself and the imperfect obedience of faith for the perfect obedience of the law, and reckons it worthy of the gracious reward of eternal life."

These teachers contradict the Scripture, "They are justified freely by His grace, through the redemption made in Jesus Christ, whom God put forth as a propitiation in His blood through faith" (Rom. 3:24–25). They teach, like the impious Socinus, a new and strange justification before God, against the consensus of the whole church.

Rejection 5

The Synod rejects the error of those who teach:

"All men have been taken into the state of reconciliation and the grace of the covenant so that no one is subject to damnation or will be damned on account of original sin, but all are free from the guilt of this sin."

This conviction rejects the Scripture, which affirms, "We are by nature children of wrath" (Eph. 2:3).

Rejection 6

The Synod rejects the error of those who abuse the distinction between accomplishing and applying, so that they might instill in the careless and inexperienced this opinion:

> "God for His part wanted to confer on all men equally those benefits which were acquired by the death of Christ. That some participate in the remission of sins and eternal life, while others do not, depends on the proper use of their free will, applying themselves to the grace generally offered to all. It does not depend on a particular gift of mercy efficaciously operating in them by which they, rather than others, apply this grace to themselves."

For these teachers, while pretending to set forth this distinction in a sound sense, seek to give the people the pernicious poison of Pelagianism.

Rejection 7

The Synod rejects the error of those who teach:

> "Christ could not die, nor ought to have died, nor did die for those whom God loved most highly and elected to eternal life, since such people do not need the death of Christ."

They contradict the Apostle, who said, "Christ loved me and gave Himself for me" (Gal. 2:20). Also, "Who will bring any charge against God's elect? It is God who justifies. Who will condemn? It is Christ who died" (Rom. 8:33–34), namely, died for them. And the Savior asserted, "I give My life for my sheep" (John 10:15). And, "This is My command, that you love one another as I have loved you. Greater love has no one, than that he lay down his life for his friends" (John 15:12–13).

Chapter 5

———

THIRD AND FOURTH HEADS OF DOCTRINE:

THE CORRUPTION OF HUMANS, AND THE CONVERSION TO GOD WITH ITS WAY OF HAPPENING

Article 1

Man was created in the beginning in the image of God. He was adorned with complete holiness. In his mind he had the true and wholesome knowledge of his Creator and spiritual realities. In his will and heart he had righteousness, and in all his affections he had purity. But when he fell away from God by the instigation of the devil and by his own free will, he deprived himself of these excellent gifts. In contrast to the gifts given in creation, he caused in his mind blindness, horrible darkness, vanity, and perverseness of judgment, in his will and heart wickedness, rebellion, and hardness, and in all his affections impurity.

Article 2

The kind of man he became after the fall was the kind of children he fathered; namely, corruption produced corruption. By the righteous judgment of God, this corruption passed from Adam to all his posterity (Christ only excepted). This corruption passed not through imitation (as the Pelagians in the past said), but by the propagation of a depraved nature.

Article 3

So all men are conceived in sin. They are born children of wrath, incapable of any saving good, prone to evil, dead in sin, and servants of sin. Without the regenerating grace of the Holy Spirit, they neither can nor want to return to God, correct their depraved nature, or dispose themselves to such correction.

Article 4

Even after the fall, some light of nature remains in humans. This light preserves in man some knowledge of God, of natural matters, and of the difference between things honorable and foul. It also leads to some regard for virtue and outward discipline. But this light of nature is far from bringing a saving knowledge of God or enabling anyone to convert to God. Indeed, it cannot even be used correctly in matters natural and civil. Rather, it renders humans inexcusable before God because they completely pervert it in various ways and suppress it in unrighteousness.

Article 5

As it is with the light of nature, so it is with the Ten Commandments, which God gave through Moses to the Jews. This law particularly shows the greatness of sin and convinces humans more and more of their sin. But it does not impart the strength to escape misery, and so through the weakness of the flesh, the sinner remains under the curse. Through the law, man cannot obtain saving grace.

Article 6

What neither the light of nature nor the law could do, God accomplished by the power of the Holy Spirit. Through preaching or the ministry of reconciliation—which is the gospel of the Messiah—God is pleased to save humans who believe, both in the Old and in the New Testament.

Article 7

God revealed the mystery of His will to few in the Old Testament. In the New Testament He shows it to many without any distinction among peoples. The cause of this dispensation is not in the value of one nation above others or the better use of the light of nature. It results from the most free good pleasure and gracious love of God. Those to whom such grace is given, beyond and contrary to all merit, should acknowledge it with humility and a grateful heart. As to the rest, to whom this grace is not given, they ought to adore with the Apostle the severity and righteousness of the judgments of God and ought never to pry into it with curiosity.

Article 8

As many as are called through the gospel are seriously called. God seriously and most truly shows in His Word what is pleasing to Him, namely that those called would come to Him. He also seriously promises the rest of souls and eternal life to all who come to Him and believe.

Article 9

Many who are called through the ministry of the gospel do not come and are not converted. The fault for this is not in the gospel, nor in Christ offered in the gospel, nor in God who calls them through the gospel and who confers various gifts on them. Rather, the fault lies in those called. Some, secure in themselves, do not accept the Word of life. Others accept it but do not receive it into their hearts. After the joy of their temporary faith vanishes, they fall away. Still others choke out the seed of the Word by their difficult cares and worldly desires and produce no fruit. This our Savior teaches in the parable of the seed, Matthew 13.

Article 10

Some called by the ministry of the gospel do come and are converted. This cannot be ascribed to man as if by his free will he distinguishes himself from others provided with equal or sufficient grace for faith and conversion (as the proud heresy of Pelagius states). Rather, God, who elected them in eternity in Christ, effectively calls them in time, and gives to them faith and repentance. Rescuing them from the power of darkness, God transfers them into the kingdom of His Son. Those called and converted should then declare the power of Him who called them out of darkness into this marvelous light. They should glory not in themselves but in the Lord. So the Apostolic Scriptures testify throughout.

Article 11

So God executes His good pleasure in the elect and works true conversion in them. He does this not only when He causes the gospel to be preached outwardly to them, but also powerfully illumines their minds by the Holy Spirit. By this illumination they rightly understand and discern the things of the Spirit of God. By the efficacious work of this same Spirit, God penetrates the inmost parts of man, opens the closed heart, softens what is hardened, and circumcises what is uncircumcised. He infuses new qualities in the will and makes it alive out of death, good out of evil, willing out of unwilling, and obedient out of obstinate. God activates and strengthens the will so that like a good tree, it can bring forth the fruit of good actions.

Article 12

And this work of God is what is proclaimed so greatly in the Scriptures as regeneration, new creation, resurrection from the dead, and enlivening. God has worked this in us without our working. This is by no means accomplished only through externally spoken teaching or moral persuasion. God does not work in such a way that after the working of God, it remains in man's power to be regenerated or not to be regenerated, to be converted or not to be converted. Rather, this work is wholly supernatural, at once most powerful, secret, and ineffable. It is no less powerful, according to the Scripture (which is inspired by the Author of this work), than the work of creation or the work of raising the dead. All those in whose hearts God works in this amazing way are regenerated certainly, infallibly, and efficaciously so that they actually do believe. For this reason, man also himself is said rightly to believe and repent through this grace which he received.

Article 13

Believers cannot fully understand the way in which God works in this life. Yet for now they rest in this, that they know and experience that through this grace of God, they believe in their hearts and love their Savior.

Article 14

Faith is the gift of God. It is not a gift in the sense that it is offered by God for human choice. Rather, it is really conferred on, breathed into, and infused in man. It is not a gift in which God confers a power to believe, leaving it to the choice of man whether he will consent and perform the act of believing. Rather, God, who works both to will and to do, effects in man the will to believe and the believing itself. Indeed, He works all in all.

Article 15

God owes this grace to no one. For what might God owe to one who could give nothing to repay Him? Indeed, what might God owe to one who has nothing of his own except sin and falsehood? He, therefore, who receives that grace owes and gives eternal thanks to God alone. He who does not receive it either does not care at all about spiritual matters and is pleased with himself as he is, or he vainly boasts, secure that he has what he does not have. Further, following the example of the Apostles, we ought to judge and speak about those who outwardly profess faith and amend their lives in the most positive way. The secrets of their hearts are unknown to us. As for those not yet called, we should pray to God who calls things that are not as if they were. We ought in no way to be haughty toward those who do not believe as if we made ourselves to differ.

Article 16

Man by the fall did not cease to be man, endowed with understanding and will. And sin, which pervades the whole human race, did not destroy the nature of the human race, but depraved it and killed it spiritually. So also the divine grace of regeneration does not act in men as if they were tree trunks or logs, or take away the will and its properties, or force it violently and unwillingly. But this grace spiritually enlivens, heals, corrects, and at once sweetly and powerfully moves the will. Where before rebellion and resistance of the flesh fully dominated the will, now the ready and genuine obedience of the Spirit begins to rule there. In this the true, spiritual restoration and freedom of our will consists. For this reason, unless that admirable Maker of all good acts for us, there is no hope that man would be raised from the fall through free choice. That free choice in which he once stood rather plunged him into ruin.

Article 17

That omnipotent work of God, by which He produces and sustains our natural life, does not exclude but rather requires the use of means. Through these means, God wanted to exercise His power according to His infinite wisdom and goodness. So also this supernatural work of God, which was described before, by which He regenerates us, does not at all exclude or overturn the use of the gospel. The most wise God ordained the gospel as the seed of regeneration and the food of the soul. For this reason, the Apostles and those teachers who followed them have piously taught the people about this grace of God, to His glory and the deflation of all human pride. Still, by the holy admonitions of the gospel, all those teachers did not neglect to keep the people under the administration of the Word, sacraments, and discipline. So far be it from teachers or students to presume to test God by separating those things which God by His good pleasure has wished to be most strongly joined together. Grace is conferred through admonitions. And the more readily we do our duty, the more clearly this benefit of God is usually working in us and the more directly is His work advanced. To Him alone is owed all glory forever for the means He has given and for their saving fruit and efficacy. Amen.

REJECTION OF ERRORS

After expositing the orthodox doctrine, the Synod rejects the following errors.

Rejection 1

The Synod rejects the error of those who teach:

> "It cannot properly be said that original sin in itself is sufficient to condemn the whole human race or to deserve temporal or eternal punishments."

These teachers contradict the Apostle, who said: "Through one man sin entered the world, and through sin death, so that death passed to all men, in that all have sinned" (Rom. 5:12). And verse 16: "The guilt of one leads to condemnation." Also, "The wages of sin is death" (Rom. 6:23).

Rejection 2

The Synod rejects the error of those who teach:

> "Spiritual gifts, or good dispositions, and virtues, such as goodness, holiness, righteousness, could not have had a

place in the will of men when they were first created, and so cannot be separated from it in the fall."

This fights with the description of the image of God that the Apostle teaches in Ephesians 4:24, where it describes the image in terms of righteousness and holiness, which certainly have a place in the will.

Rejection 3

The Synod rejects the error of those who teach:

> "The spiritual gifts are not separated from the will of man in spiritual death since the will in itself has never been corrupted. It only was impeded through the darkness of the mind and the disordering of the affections. When these impediments are removed, the will makes natural use of its free faculty, that is, it can either will or choose the good put before it, or it can not will or not choose that good."

This is a novelty and an error that leads to elevating the powers of the free will, contrary to what was said by the prophet Jeremiah: "The heart is deceitful above all things and perverse" (Jer. 17:9); and by the Apostle: "Among whom [sinful men] we all also once lived in the desires of our flesh, following the will and understanding of the flesh" (Eph. 2:3).

Rejection 4

The Synod rejects the error of those who teach:

> "Unregenerate man is not properly or totally dead in sin or destitute of all powers for spiritual good. Rather, he can hunger and thirst after righteousness and life, and can offer the sacrifice of a contrite and broken spirit, which is acceptable to God."

Against this teaching stands the open testimonies of the Scripture: "You were dead in your trespasses and sins" (Eph. 2:1, 5).

And "The imagination of the thoughts of the heart of man is only evil all the time" (Gen. 6:5; 8:21).

Rejection 5

The Synod rejects the error of those who teach:

> "Corrupt, natural man could so rightly use common grace—which is to them the light of nature, or gifts remaining after the fall—so that by using this good he could gradually obtain more grace, indeed evangelical and saving grace and salvation itself. And for this reason, God for His part shows Himself ready to reveal Christ to all. God accomplishes for all both sufficiently and efficiently the means necessary for the revelation of Christ, faith, and repentance."

This is false, according to the experience of all times, about which Scripture also testifies. "He has shown His words to Jacob, His statutes and laws to Israel; He has not done this to any other nation; they do not know His laws" (Ps. 147:19–20). "In the past ages God let all nations walk in their own ways" (Acts 14:16). "They were prevented [Paul and others with him] by the Holy Spirit from speaking the Word of God in Asia," and "when they had come into Mysia, they tried to go into Bithynia, but the Spirit did not permit them" (Acts 16:6–7).

Rejection 6

The Synod rejects the error of those who teach:

> "In the true conversion of man, new qualities, dispositions, or gifts are not infused into his will by God. The faith by which we are first converted, and from which we are named the faithful, is not a quality or gift infused by God. It is only an act of man that can be said to be a gift in no other way than with respect to the power of attaining it."

These teachers contradict here the Holy Scriptures, which testify that God does infuse in our hearts new qualities of faith, of obedience, and of a sense of His love. "I will put My law in their minds and write it on their hearts" (Jer. 31:33). "I will pour out water upon the thirsty and streams upon the dry land; I will pour out My Spirit upon your seed" (Isa. 44:3). "The love of God is shed abroad in our hearts by the Holy Spirit who has been given to us" (Rom. 5:5). This is also repugnant to the continual practice of the church, which prays with the prophet, "Convert me, Lord, and I will be converted" (Jer. 31:18).

Rejection 7

The Synod rejects the error of those who teach:

> "The grace by which we are converted to God is nothing other than a gentle persuasion. Others explain this grace, the noblest manner of working in the conversion of man and the most appropriate to human nature, as working by persuasions. Nothing prevents this moral grace alone from rendering the natural man spiritual. Indeed, God does not produce the consent of the will in any other way than by moral means. In this consists the efficacy of divine working, by which the work of Satan is surpassed, namely, that God promises eternal goods while Satan promises only temporal goods."

This is entirely Pelagian and contrary to the whole Scripture. Scripture, against this error, recognizes another much more efficacious and divine manner of working by the Holy Spirit in the conversion of man. "I will give you My heart and I will give you a new spirit in place of the old. I will take away your heart of stone and I will give you a heart of flesh" (Ezek. 36:26).

Rejection 8

The Synod rejects the error of those who teach:

> "God in the regeneration of man does not use the powers of His omnipotence, by which He might powerfully and

infallibly turn man's will to faith and conversion. God has accomplished all the workings of grace which He uses for converting man. Nevertheless, man can resist and actually often does resist God when the Spirit intends man's regeneration and wills to regenerate him. Man can certainly impede his regeneration. Indeed, it remains in man's own power whether he will be regenerated or not."

This is nothing other than to remove all efficacy of the grace of God in our conversion. It subjects the action of the omnipotent God to the will of man, contrary to the Apostles, who teach: "We believe because of the efficacy of the strength of His might" (Eph. 1:19). And "God powerfully fulfills in us the gracious benevolence of His kindness and the work of faith" (2 Thess. 1:11). Also, "His divine power has given us all things which pertain to life and piety" (2 Peter 1:3).

Rejection 9

The Synod rejects the error of those who teach:

"Grace and free will are the partial causes concurring together for the beginning of conversion. Grace is not antecedent in the order of causality to the efficacy of the will." That is, "God does not efficaciously help the will of man to conversion before that the will of man moves and determines itself."

This teaching of the Pelagians was condemned long ago by the ancient church, in accordance with the Apostle: "It is not to him who wills or runs but to God who shows mercy" (Rom. 9:16). And "Who makes you different?" and "What do you have that you have not received?" (1 Cor. 4:7). Also "God Himself works in you to will and to do for His good pleasure" (Phil. 2:13).

63

Chapter 6

FIFTH HEAD OF DOCTRINE:

THE PERSEVERANCE OF THE SAINTS

Article 1

God, according to His purpose, calls people to communion with His Son our Lord Jesus Christ and regenerates them through His Holy Spirit. He liberates all of these people from the dominion and servitude of sin, but He does not liberate them completely from the flesh and the body of sin in this life.

Article 2

From this continuing sin, the daily sins of weakness arise and blemishes adhere to even the best works of the saints. These sins and blemishes provide a constant cause for the saints to humble themselves before God and to flee for refuge to Christ crucified. The saints seek to mortify the flesh more and more through the Spirit of prayer and through holy exercises of piety. They long for the goal of perfection, until, delivered from this body of death, they reign with the Lamb of God in heaven.

Article 3

Because of these remnants of indwelling sin and of the temptations of the world and Satan, the converted could not remain in this grace if they were left to their own powers. But God is faithful. He mercifully confirms them in the grace once given and powerfully preserves them in it even to the end.

Article 4

That power of God, which truly confirms and preserves the faithful in grace, is greater than that which could be overcome by the flesh. Still, the converted are not always so led and moved by God that they cannot in particular actions fall back from the leading of grace by their own fault. They can be seduced by the desires of the flesh and gratify them. For this reason, they ought always to watch and pray for themselves so that they might not be led into temptations. When they do not do this, they can be carried off by the flesh, the world, and Satan, even into serious and dreadful sins. Indeed, sometimes they actually are carried off by the just permission of God. This is shown by the sad falls into serious sin of David, Peter, and other saints as described in the Holy Scriptures.

Article 5

By such very great sins, the faithful certainly offend God, incur deadly guilt, grieve the Holy Spirit, interrupt the exercise of faith, and most gravely wound the conscience. Sometimes, for a time, they lose a sense of grace, until through serious repentance they return to life so that the fatherly countenance of God shines again upon them.

Article 6

God, who is rich in mercy, because of His immutable purpose of election, does not utterly take away the Holy Spirit from the converted even in their sad falls. Neither does He let them fall so far that they lose the grace of adoption or the state of justification. He does not let them commit the sin unto death or the sin against the Holy Spirit or be so utterly deserted by the Spirit as to rush into eternal destruction.

Article 7

In the first place, God conserves in the elect even in their falls His imperishable seed by which they were regenerated so that it might not be lost or cast away. Next, He renews them to repentance certainly and efficaciously through His Word and Spirit, so that they have heartfelt sorrow to God for their sins. Out of a contrite heart, through faith, they both seek and obtain forgiveness in the blood of the Mediator. They experience again the grace of a reconciled God, adore His mercies through faith, and then eagerly work out their salvation with fear and trembling.

Article 8

They obtain this not by their merits or powers but from the gracious mercy of God so that they do not fall away totally from faith and grace nor finally remain and be lost in their falls. Such loss not only could happen but certainly would happen if they were left to themselves. But with respect to God, it could not possibly happen, because His plan cannot be changed, His promise cannot fail, nor can the call according to His purpose be recalled. Neither could the merit, intercession, and protection of Christ be rendered void, nor could the sealing of the Holy Spirit be frustrated or destroyed.

Article 9

Concerning this protection of the elect for salvation and the preservation of true believers in faith, the believers themselves can be certain of it. Indeed, they are certain according to the measure of their faith. By that faith they certainly believe that they are and always will remain true and living members of the church and have the remission of sins and eternal life.

Article 10

This certainty is not derived from some particular revelation made beyond or outside the Word. But this certainty comes from faith in the promises of God, which God has revealed most abundantly in His Word for our comfort. It also comes from the testimony "of the Holy Spirit testifying with our spirit that we are the children and heirs of God" (Rom. 8:16). Next, it comes from a serious and holy desire for a good conscience and good works. And if in this life the elect of God were deprived of this solid comfort of obtaining the victory and of the unfailing guarantee of eternal glory, they would be of all men the most miserable.

Article 11

Further, Scripture testifies that believers in this life may be conflicted with various carnal doubts. They may in grave temptations not always experience the fullness of faith and certainty of perseverance. Truly, God, the Father of all comfort, will not let them be tempted beyond their ability, but with the temptation will provide the way of escape (1 Cor. 10:13). And through the Holy Spirit, He will awaken again in them the certainty of perseverance.

Article 12

This certainty of perseverance is far from making believers proud or carnally secure. On the contrary, it is the true root of humility, filial reverence, true piety, patience in all afflictions, ardent prayers, constancy in cross-bearing and in confessing the truth, and solid joy in God. The consideration of this benefit is a stimulus for serious and continual exercise of gratitude and good works, as is evident from the testimonies of Scripture and the examples of the saints.

Article 13

A revived confidence of persevering does not produce in those restored from a fall immorality or harm their piety. Rather, with much greater concern, they carefully keep the ways of the Lord which were prepared for them to walk in. In this way, they retain the certainty of perseverance, lest because of the abuse of His fatherly kindness, God would again turn away from them His favorable face and they would fall into more grievous torments of the soul. (The contemplation of His favor is sweeter to the pious than life; the loss of that favor is more bitter then death.)

Article 14

It has pleased God to begin His work of grace in us through the preaching of the gospel. So He preserves, continues, and completes this work through the hearing, reading, and meditating on its exhortations, threats, and promises and through the use of the sacraments.

Article 15

God has most abundantly revealed in His Word this doctrine concerning the perseverance of true believers and saints and its certainty. He revealed it for the glory of His name and the consolation of pious souls. He impresses it on the hearts of believers. The flesh does not understand this doctrine, Satan hates it, the world derides it, the ignorant and the hypocrites abuse it, and the spirits of error fight against it. But the bride of Christ has always loved it most tenderly as a treasure of incalculable value and she has constantly fought for it. God—against whom no plan can avail and no power can prevail—will take care that she will esteem it always.

REJECTION OF ERRORS

After expounding the orthodox doctrine, the Synod rejects the following errors.

Rejection 1

The Synod rejects the error of those who teach:

> "The perseverance of the truly faithful is not the effect of election or the gift of God acquired by the death of Christ.

Rather, it is a condition of the new covenant, which man must fulfill by his free will before his 'decisive' (as they called it) election or justification."

For the sacred Scripture testifies that perseverance follows from election, and that the power of the death, resurrection, and intercession of Christ is given to the elect. "The elect obtained it, the rest were hardened" (Rom. 11:7). Also, "He who did not spare His own Son, but gave Him up for us all, how will He not with Him give us all things? Who will bring any charge against the elect of God? It is God who justifies. Who is it who condemns? Christ is the One who died, who indeed was also raised, who also sits at the right hand of God, who also intercedes for us: who will separate us from the love of Christ?" (Rom. 8:32).

Rejection 2

The Synod rejects the error of those who teach:

"God indeed provides the faithful man with sufficient powers for perseverance, and is prepared to preserve them in him if he does his duty. God had done for everyone those things that are necessary for persevering in faith and that God wanted to use for preserving faith. But perseverance always depends on the choice of man's will whether he perseveres or does not persevere."

This conviction contains obvious Pelagianism, and while it wants to make men free, it actually makes them sacrilegious. It stands against the perpetual consensus of evangelical doctrine, which takes from man all matter for glorying, and ascribes the praise of this benefit to the grace of God alone. This conviction is contrary to the testimony of the Apostle: "God is the One who will confirm us blameless until the end in the day of our Lord Jesus Christ" (1 Cor. 1:8).

70

Rejection 3

The Synod rejects the error of those who teach:

"Those truly believing and regenerate can fall away finally and totally from being justified by faith, as well as from grace and salvation. More than that, they frequently actually do fall from them, and perish for eternity."

This opinion renders void the very grace of justification and regeneration and the perpetual care of Christ, against the express words of the Apostle Paul: "If Christ died for us, when we were still sinners, how much more will He through it save from wrath those justified in His blood?" (Rom. 5:8–9). Also against the Apostle John: "He who is born of God does not commit sin because His seed remains in him, and he cannot sin because he is born of God" (1 John 3:9). And also against the words of Jesus Christ: "I give eternal life to My sheep, and they will not perish in eternity, and no one may rip any of them from My hand. My Father who gave them to Me is greater than all, and no one can rip them from the hand of My Father" (John 10:28–29).

Rejection 4

The Synod rejects the error of those who teach:

"The truly faithful and regenerate can sin the sin unto death, or the sin against the Holy Spirit."

After the Apostle John (in 1 John 5:16–17) mentioned those who had committed the sin unto death and had forbidden to pray for them, he immediately joins verse 18 to it: "We know that whoever is born of God does not sin [namely, that kind of sin unto death], but God keeps him who is born of God, and the evil one does not touch him."

71

Rejection 5

The Synod rejects the error of those who teach:

> "No certainty of future perseverance can be had in this life without special revelation."

By this doctrine the solid comfort of the truly faithful in this life is taken away and the doubting of the papists is reintroduced to the church. The sacred Scripture throughout requires this certainty, not by special and extraordinary revelation, but from the proper signs of the children of God and the most constant promises of God. Especially the Apostle Paul teaches, "Nothing created can separate us from the love of God which is in Christ Jesus our Lord" (Rom. 8:39). And John, "All who keep His commandments, remain in Him, and He in them; and by this we know that we remain in Him, by the Spirit whom He gave us" (1 John 3:24).

Rejection 6

The Synod rejects the error of those who teach:

> "The doctrine of perseverance and the certainty of salvation, from its nature and inherent quality, is an easy seat for the flesh, and harmful to piety, good morals, prayers, and other holy exercises. On the contrary, to doubt this doctrine is truly praiseworthy."

These teachers show that they do not know the efficacy of divine grace and the working of the indwelling Holy Spirit. They contradict the Apostle John, who affirms the opposite with these express words: "My beloved, we are now the children of God, but it does not yet appear what we will be. We know that when He shall appear, we will be like Him, for we will see Him as He is. And whoever has this hope in Him, purifies himself, as He is pure" (1 John 3:2–3). Furthermore, the examples of the saints of the Old as well as the New Testament refute it, who, notwithstanding their certainty of perseverance and salvation, nevertheless were assiduous in prayers and other exercises of piety.

Rejection 7

The Synod rejects the error of those who teach:

> "Temporary faith does not differ at all from justifying and saving faith except in its duration."

For Christ Himself in Matthew 13:20ff. and Luke 7:13ff. clearly shows the difference between three kinds of those temporarily faithful and those truly faithful. Jesus says that the former receive the seed in rocky ground, while the latter receive it in good ground or good hearts; the former are without root, the latter have a firm root; the former are devoid of fruit, the latter produce their fruit in diverse measure, but constantly and perseveringly.

Rejection 8

The Synod rejects the error of those who teach:

> "It is not absurd that a man who has lost his regeneration, may be reborn again, even many times."

Through this doctrine these teachers deny that the seed of God by which we are reborn is incorruptible, against the testimony of the Apostle Peter: "Reborn not of corruptible seed, but incorruptible" (1 Peter 1:23).

Rejection 9

The Synod rejects the error of those who teach:

> "Christ has nowhere prayed for the unfailing perseverance of believers in faith."

These teachers contradict Christ Himself, who said, "I have prayed for you, Peter, that your faith fail not" (Luke 22:32). The gospel of John testifies (John 17:20) that Christ prayed not only for the Apostles, but also for all who would believe through their word. Also verse 11, "Holy Father, keep them in Your name," and verse 15, "I do not pray that You would take them out of the world, but that You would keep them from evil."

Chapter 7

_____

CONCLUSION

This is the clear, simple, and candid declaration of the orthodox doctrine on the five articles in the Netherlands, and the rejection of the errors with which the Dutch churches have been troubled for some time. The Synod judges this declaration and rejection to be taken from the Word of God and agreeable to the confessions of the Reformed Churches. So it appears clearly that some most improperly have wanted to inculcate in the people, against all truth, justice, and love, the following false claims:

- The doctrine of the Reformed Churches on predestination and subjects related to it, by its own proper inclination and tendency, leads the souls of men away from all piety and religion. It is an easy seat for the flesh and the devil and the bow of Satan with which he lies in wait for all, wounds very many, and lethally pierces many with the darts of either despair or false security.

- It makes God the author of sin, unjust, a tyrant, and a hypocrite. Nor is this anything other than a new form of Stoicism, Manicheism, Libertinism, and Turkism.

- This renders men carnally secure, for indeed by it they are persuaded that the salvation of the elect will not be hurt however they live, and they are so secure that they can perpetrate the most atrocious wickedness. It also teaches that the reprobate will not benefit even if they truly did all the works of the saints.

- This teaches that God, by a bare and pure choice of the will, without respect or consideration at all to any sin, created and predestined the greatest part of the world to eternal damnation.
- In the same way that election is the foundation and cause of faith and good works, reprobation is the cause of infidelity and impiety.
- Many infants of the faithful are ripped innocent from the breasts of their mothers and tyrannically thrown into hell so that neither baptism nor the prayers of the church at their baptism help them.

And we are accused of teaching many other things of this sort which the Reformed Churches not only do not acknowledge, but also detest with all our heart.

For this reason, the Synod at Dordrecht implores in the name of the Lord all those who piously call on the name of our Savior Jesus Christ not to judge the faith of the Reformed Churches from the calumnies heaped upon it. The Synod also implores them not to judge on the basis of private statements by some teachers, either old or more recent, often also cited in bad faith, or corrupted and distorted into an alien sense. Rather, the Synod implores them to judge the faith of the Reformed Churches from the public confessions of the churches themselves, and from this declaration of the orthodox doctrine unanimously affirmed by all and every member of the Synod. It seriously admonishes those calumniators to recognize how gravely they come under the judgment of God—both as those who present false testimony against so many churches and against so many confessions of churches, and as those who disturb the consciences of the weak, and are busy to render suspect the society of the many who are truly faithful.

Finally, this Synod exhorts all colleagues in the gospel of Christ, that in the handling of this doctrine, both in the schools and in the churches, they consider it piously and religiously. They need to accommodate themselves in speaking and in writing to the glory of the divine name, the holiness of life, and the consolation of troubled souls. They need to think as well as speak with the Scripture according to the analogy of faith. Finally, they need to abstain from all those phrases that exceed the limits prescribed for us in the genuine sense of the Holy Scriptures, and that could furnish a right occasion for the shameless sophists to insult or even falsely accuse the doctrine of the Reformed Churches.

May the Son of God Jesus Christ, who is seated at the right hand of the Father to give gifts to men, sanctify us in the truth, lead those who are erring to the truth, close the mouths of those who falsely calumniate sound doctrine, and provide the faithful ministers of His Word with the Spirit of wisdom and discretion so that all their communications may result in the glory of God and the edification of their hearers.

—

PART III

AN EXPOSITION
OF THE CANONS
OF DORT

—

Chapter 8

———

THE FORM
OF THE CANONS

The Synod of Dort had to make many decisions about how to formulate its response to the Arminian theology. Since discussion in the churches had been about the five points of the Remonstrance ever since 1610, the first decision was to shape the determinations of the synod in five chapters or "heads" of doctrine.[1]

This rather obvious decision had a problem. The third article of the Remonstrance of 1610 by itself was orthodox. The Arminians seemed to teach faithfully the doctrine of total depravity. Only when moving on to the fourth article, where the Arminians teach the resistibility of grace, did it become clear that they did not consistently maintain what they had said in article 3. For Calvinists, only irresistible grace can overcome true total depravity. To make that clear, the synod combined its response to the third and fourth articles as the third and fourth heads of doctrine. As a result, the synod made its five-point answer to the Arminians in four sections. The articles of the synod's five heads of doctrine together are called the canons[2] of the synod.

A much bigger decision was whether to write the canons in a style that would communicate to academic theologians or to the people of the church. To write for the theological scholars would have been easier in a sense. In clear, technical language, the Calvinist position could have been briefly stated. But the synod decided that the canons should be written for the people. The Arminian teaching had troubled the churches and the people, and so the synod wanted its response to be accessible to the people for their good. This book's new translation of the canons tries to make the canons readable for the people in contemporary English. (I have translated the quotations from the Bible in the canons as they read in the Latin text, so sometimes they differ from our English translations.)

The synod further decided that each of the heads of doctrine should be complete in itself. The leaders of the synod wanted someone concerned about perseverance, for example, to be able to possess in the fifth head of doctrine the whole of the synod's teaching on perseverance. They did not want the reader to have to know what was said in the other heads of doctrine in order to understand perseverance. What that means is that there is some redundancy in the heads of doctrine. Each head of doctrine addresses, for example, the justice of God, Christian living, and the importance of the means of grace. (For details, see appendix 2, "General Pattern in Each Head of Doctrine.")

Another critical decision at the synod was to begin each head of doctrine with a statement of catholic Christian teaching. One of the charges brought by the Arminians against the Calvinists was that Reformed theology was sectarian and a departure from the catholic consensus of the church. Neither the Arminians nor Calvinists meant Roman Catholic when they insisted on being catholic. Indeed, Protestants generally believed that the Roman Catholic Church had become sectarian, rejecting catholic truth by insisting on being Roman. The Protestants taught that one could not be both catholic (universal) and Roman (localized in one place) at the same time. At Dort, the Calvinists sought to show their catholicity by beginning each head of doctrine with an article with which Roman Catholics, Lutherans, and Reformed would all agree.

A model for writing in a popular style with a catholic beginning was offered at the end of the judgment on the first head of doctrine written by the Palatinate delegation. Their formal judgment followed the scholastic approach of other delegations, but at the end they included something of an addendum, titled "On the way we ought teach." The synod seems to have accepted this model and used it for the whole of the canons.[3]

From that catholic beginning, each head of doctrine then develops the doctrine under consideration, showing step by step that sound theology, building on a catholic theology must reach the mature Reformed teaching. Then the canons give one article in which the Reformed doctrine is expressed in summary form. After that summary article, various implications of the doctrine are worked out.

In addition to the positive statement of truth in each head of doctrine, the synod added a section titled "Rejection of Errors." The idea of adding such a section was suggested in several of the judgments. The delegates from Great Britain in their judgment adopted the form of stating orthodox theses followed by an explication and confirmation of those theses. After this, they added after the first head of doctrine "Heterodox theses on election that we reject." The delegates from South Holland also added after their judgment on election a section on what "they reject."

This approach clearly commended itself to the synod. The rejections of errors allowed the synod clearly to state certain Arminian positions and to answer them specifically and pointedly. The synod there could warn the churches about these serious errors, and it often cited biblical texts to support the Calvinist teaching. Some of these errors had gone far beyond the teaching of Arminius himself in a more Pelagian direction. The Calvinists had always believed that Arminianism was an unstable form of theology that tended to move from bad to worse. The remarkable movement among some of the Arminians theologically in the ten years since the death of Arminius shows the validity of this concern.

The Canons of Dort do not present exhaustive biblical arguments for their teachings, but they provide a number of biblical quotations and references to buttress the doctrines presented. Interestingly, the biblical references are more frequent in the rejections of errors than in the positive articles.[4] The very frequent appeals to the Bible in the rejections of errors are intended to show the faithful that the Arminian doctrine stands clearly against the Scriptures. The strategy of the synod was clear:

detailed exegesis of these texts was not necessary since it was obvious that the Arminians had contradicted them.

The rejection of error sections of the canons have often been ignored or skimmed by students of the canons. For example, Philip Schaff in his important *Creeds of Christendom* (vol. 3) presents the Latin text of the whole canons including the rejections of errors, but only translates the positive articles into English. Sometimes this neglect of the rejections of errors reflects a modern prejudice against being too negative. Sometimes it reflects a conviction that what we really need to know is present in the positive articles. It is also true that the rejection of error sections at time repeats material found in the positive articles.

These sections, however, do have considerable value and are well worth studying. There is a sharp, clear focus on a particular error in each rejection. There is also a brief but compelling statement of the character and danger of the error, usually along with a helpful citation from the Bible to indicate the scriptural foundation of the Reformed teaching. Each of the rejections relates to one or more of the positive articles (see appendix 4 for the connections) but focuses much more narrowly on a specific issue.

In the exposition that follows, each positive article and each rejection of error from the new translation will be cited, followed by comments on its theological and historical significance. In these articles and rejections, we will see in various ways the concern of the synod to teach sound theology, to encourage pious Christian living, and to refute strategically the efforts of the Arminians to deceive the church. The prime purpose of this section is to help the reader see the continuing usefulness and value of the canons for the theological and spiritual life of Christians today.

Chapter 9

FIRST HEAD OF DOCTRINE:

GOD'S PREDESTINATION

E lection was the central issue in the debate and the first one discussed in various writings and conferences and so at the synod itself. The other heads of doctrine treated matters that were ancillary to the doctrine of predestination.

Article 1: Man Is Lost in Sin

All people have sinned in Adam and so are subject to the curse and eternal death. God would not have been unfair to anyone if He had left everyone in sin and under the curse, and had willed to damn them all on account of sin. The Apostle teaches this: "The whole world is guilty under the condemnation of God"; "all have sinned and fallen short of the glory of God"; and "the wages of sin is death" (Rom. 3:19, 23; 6:23).

In discussing the great topic of predestination, there are many places where one might begin theologically. One could begin in eternity, in the mind of God, to consider the plans or decrees of God. The canons instead begin in history with the human problem of sin. Whereas beginning in eternity may lead quickly to speculation and controversy, beginning with human need more easily shows the practical, pastoral significance of predestination.

Additionally, beginning with the fallen human condition allows for a catholic statement of doctrine. All people are fallen in Adam and because of his sin deserve eternal death. All Roman Catholics, Lutherans, and Reformed agreed to that in 1619.

The article goes on to say that God was under no obligation to save sinners. Since the issue of justice and fairness is often raised in discussions of predestination, such discussions are anticipated here by saying that the eternal death of all would be justice. Justice does not require mercy. Any mercy goes beyond justice.

In this article, several passages of Scripture are cited. The citations of the Bible throughout the canons are to provide some evidence for the doctrine being argued. The intention is not to offer complete or exhaustive proof but to provide some support so that believers can see that the teaching is derived from the Bible. The synod did not provide biblical citations for every article, perhaps because in some cases no single, brief quotation would be decisive. In this first head of doctrine, one-half of the articles have quotations from the Bible.

Article 2: God Redeems through His Son

Truly God shows His love in this, that He sent His only begotten Son into the world, so that each one who believes in Him, would not perish but have eternal life (1 John 4:9; John 3:16).

This article moves from human lostness to the love of God, the gift of the Son, and the promise that everyone who believes in Jesus will be saved and have eternal life. One of the misrepresentations of predestination is that many people want to believe, or even actually do believe, but they cannot be saved because they are not elect. Such a misrepresentation is utterly rejected. Before the meaning of predestination is examined, the canons declare unequivocally that every person who believes in Jesus will be saved.

Article 3: God Sends Preachers of Redemption

God mercifully sends messengers of this most joyful news to those He will and when He will, so that people may be brought to faith. By this ministry, people are called to repentance and faith in Christ cru-cified. "How shall they believe in him of whom they have not heard? How will they hear without a preacher? How will they preach unless they are sent?" (Rom. 10:14–15).

So that sinners may believe, God out of His mercy sends preachers of the gospel of Jesus. This ministry calls people to faith and repentance. Here again the generous provision of God is declared. He sends preachers to carry the message of salvation. It is a message for all who hear. Still, the article acknowledges, as is obvious, that preachers do not reach every individual but only those to whom God sends them. The implicit point here is that God has always restricted His grace in various ways. It is restricted to some in predestination, but it is also restricted to some in the providence of God, which sends preachers to some and not others.

Article 4: Fruit of Faith and Fruit of Unbelief

The anger of God remains on those who do not believe this gospel. Those who receive it and embrace Jesus the Savior with a true and living faith are freed by Him both from the anger of God and from destruction. They are given eternal life by Him.

For those who do not believe the gospel, the wrath of God remains upon them. By contrast, those who do truly believe are delivered from wrath and have eternal life. Here again, the sure promise to believers is reiterated. The fruit of unbelief is contrasted with the fruit of faith.

Article 5: The Gift of Faith and the Guilt of Unbelief

The cause of our guilt for this unbelief and for all other sins is not at all in God, but is in humans. However, faith in Jesus Christ and salvation through Him are the gracious gift of God. So it is written: "By grace you are saved through faith, and this not of yourselves, it is the gift of God" (Eph. 2:8). Also: "It is freely given to you to believe in Christ" (Phil. 1:29).

As unbelievers and believers are contrasted in article 4, here the sources of unbelief and faith are contrasted. This article stresses a point repeated several times in the canons: fallen sinners bear the responsibility for their sins, whether rebellion or unbelief. The sovereignty of God is "not at all" the cause of sin. The canons do not explore in any detail how that can be. Reformed theologians had discussed that point at length and offered a variety of theological explanations. The function of the canons is not to enter into that kind of detail or choose among Reformed alternatives. Rather, they give basic theological truth as a confession of faith. The article goes on to say that while sinners bear the responsibility for their unbelief, those sinners who come to faith and salvation receive those blessings exclusively as a gift of God's grace. Believers do not receive any credit or merit for their believing. God alone gives this gift of faith and ensures its full fruition in the elect.

Article 6: God Gives Faith according to His Plan

The reality that some people are given faith by God in time, while others are not given faith, proceeds from God's eternal decree. "He knows all His works from eternity" (Acts 15:18; Eph. 1:11). According to this decree, He graciously softens the hearts of the elect, however hard, and inclines them to believe. He also leaves the nonelect according to His just judgment in their wickedness and hardness of heart. This decree most powerfully shows us God's profound, merciful, yet also just distinction among people equally lost. This decree of election and reprobation is revealed in the Word of God. And although the perverse, impure, and unstable twist it to their own destruction, it gives inexpressible comfort to holy and pious souls.

In this article, for the first time, the distinctly Reformed approach to predestination begins to emerge. We must notice how carefully this article follows as a necessary consequence from the previous article. If God alone sovereignly gives the gift of faith, why does He give that gift to some and not to others? The answer is simple: God in His eternal decree or plan had decided to whom He would give the gift. This plan includes God's decision to act in softening the hearts of the elect sinners and leading them to faith. It also includes the decision of God to leave other sinners in their sin and unbelief.

The two sides of this decree manifest different aspects of God's character. He gives the gift of faith to some, manifesting His great mercy, while He leaves other sinners in their sin, manifesting His justice.

This language reflects the language of the Belgic Confession, article 16. This confession, written in 1561 by the martyred pastor Guido de Bres, had been the binding confession of the Dutch Reformed Church for almost the whole history of the church. The allusion to the confession here makes the point that the Canons of the Synod of Dort are not creating new doctrine for the church but only maintaining historic teaching. The innovators were the Arminians.

The article insists, however, that this teaching is not in the first place a tradition of the church, but that it is the teaching of the Bible. The Bible teaches that God's plan includes not only the positive side of election but also the negative side of reprobation.

The final point of this article speaks to the two ways in which this doctrine can be used. The doctrine can lead to destruction for those wicked and unreliable persons who twist and distort it. No explanation is offered here as to what the twisting or destruction was, but it does not take much imagination to understand a reference to the Arminians. The Arminians had twisted the Reformed doctrine, accusing the Reformed of making God the author of sin while themselves making man the final determinator of salvation. Such twisted teaching, misrepresenting God and man, would lead to destruction. By contrast, for pious believers the doctrine of predestination provides extraordinary comfort. The comfort also is not specified here, but surely it is found in the assurance that salvation is in the hands of a faithful God rather than in the hands of sinners. The theme of comfort is another repeated teaching throughout the canons.

Article 7: Election Defined

Election is the immutable purpose of God, by which He chose to salvation in Christ, from the whole human race, a fixed multitude of particular persons. God's election is from before the foundation of the world in relation to people who fell from their original integrity into sin and destruction by their own fault. God chose His elect, according to the most free good pleasure of His will, out of mere grace. Those chosen were neither better nor more worthy than others, but were like others fallen into the common human misery. From eternity, God made Christ the Mediator and Head of all the elect and the foundation of salvation. God gave the elect to Christ to save them, and effectively to call them and draw them into communion with Him through His Word and Spirit. He decreed to give them true faith in Christ as well as to justify them, sanctify them, and finally, after powerfully preserving them in the communion of His Son, to glorify them. All this shows God's mercy for the praise of the riches of His glorious grace. So it is written: "God elected us in Christ with love, before the foundation of the world, so that we might be holy and blameless in His sight. He who predestined us, adopted us as sons, through Jesus Christ to Himself, according to the good pleasure of His will, to the praise of His glorious grace, by which He made us acceptable to Him in the beloved" (Eph. 1:4–6). And elsewhere: "Those whom He predestined, He also called; and those whom He called, He also justified; those whom He justified, He also glorified" (Rom. 8:30).

This article provides the summary statement of the Reformed doctrine of predestination. It is stated with the greatest care, both to teach the church clearly and to leave no place for Arminian evasions. The opening sentence makes two key points: first, that God's purpose in election cannot be changed or altered in any way; second, that election refers to specific individuals, chosen out of the whole human race for salvation in Christ. Election was not of classes of people or of conditions for salvation, as the Arminians taught, but of particular persons.

This election by God, the article declares, occurred in eternity and relates to fallen humans. By approaching the matter this way, the article (and indeed, the canons as a whole) took no position on the difference among Reformed theologians known by the labels *infralapsarianism* and *supralapsarianism*. The infralapsarians focused on the electing decree of God exclusively in relation to fallen mankind, while the supralapsarians wanted to consider election as a divine distinction even before any consideration of the fall into sin. The Arminians had sought to set the infralapsarian Calvinists against the supralapsarian Calvinists both before the synod and at the synod. Historically, however, the infralapsarians and the supralapsarians had had no trouble cooperating with one another and tolerating each other's views. The decisions of the synod, strongly supported by both the infras and supras, manifest that.

God did not choose the elect because they were better than others; rather, the elect were just as lost as the others. God appointed Christ as the head of the elect since He as the eternal second person of the Trinity participated in God's eternal plan of salvation. Christ is also the foundation of salvation since He would accomplish and fulfill in history all that was required in the divine plan of salvation. The Arminians had wanted to declare Christ the foundation of election, thereby placing election to some extent in history as well as in eternity. The synod rejected the Arminian teaching and clarified Christ's role in election and salvation.

The work of Christ in history carried out the decree of election. His work involved not only accomplishing redemption in His life, death, and resurrection but also applying redemption to the elect individually through His Word and Spirit. Christ's Word and Spirit provide true faith to the elect and ensure that they will be justified, sanctified, and glorified. All of these truths are the teaching of the Scriptures.

Article 8: One Kind of Election

This election is not of various kinds, but is one and the same for all those saved in the Old and New Testaments. For the Scripture teaches that God has one good pleasure, one purpose, and one counsel of His will, by which from eternity He elected us both to grace and to glory. He elected us both to salvation and to the way of salvation, which He prepared as the way in which we would walk.

The Arminians had sought to compromise the Reformed teaching on election by suggesting that there were different decrees of election. This article insists that there was only one decree of election that included both the end of election—salvation and glory—and the means to salvation—the various gifts of grace. Election is a unified, complete plan of God.

Article 9: Election Not Based on Foreseen Qualifications

This very election was made not on the basis of foreseen faith, or of the obedience of faith, or of holiness, or of any other good quality and disposition, as the prerequisite cause or condition for electing anyone. Rather, this election is to faith, to the obedience of faith, to holiness, etc. And so election is the fountain of all saving good. From election flow faith, holiness, and all other saving gifts, even eternal life itself, as fruit and effect. As the Apostle wrote: "He chose us in love [not because we were, but] so that we might be holy and blameless in his sight" (Eph. 1:4).

This article now examines some of the conditions for election that the Arminians had taught. Arminians claimed that God elected to eternal life those whom He foresaw would believe or persevere in holiness. This teaching fundamentally misrepresents the doctrine of the Bible. Election does not flow from faith or holiness, but rather, faith and holiness flow from election. Election is God's plan to save, which He works out in the lives of the elect, giving to them the gifts that they need for salvation.

Article 10: Election of Persons, Not Conditions

The cause of this gracious election is the good pleasure of God alone. The cause is not that God elected certain human qualities or actions out of all possibilities as the condition of salvation. Rather, He adopted as His own possession certain specific persons out of the common multitude of sinners. So it is written: "For the children, not yet born, and not having done anything good or evil . . . it was said [to Rebecca], the elder will serve the younger, as it is written: Jacob I loved, Esau I hated" (Rom. 9:11–13). And *"all who were ordained for eternal life believed" (Acts 13:48).*

Election is grounded on what God finds in Himself, not on what He finds or anticipates in us. God's good pleasure, that is, the purpose that pleases Him, is the motive of His plan. This reality ensures that God receives all the glory for salvation and that we are appropriately humbled before Him.

Article 11: Election Is Unchangeable

As God Himself is most wise, immutable, omniscient, and omnipotent, so the election made by Him cannot be interrupted, changed, recalled, or annulled. Just so, the elect cannot be lost or their number reduced.

Election reflects the very character of God. As God is immutable, so His purpose in election is immutable. Nothing can interfere with God's implementing His decree of election. In particular, the specific number of the elect cannot be reduced. This conviction is foundational to the doctrine of God and to predestination as well as to the teaching on assurance found throughout the canons.

Article 12: Election and Assurance

The elect become more certain of their eternal and unchangeable election to salvation in their own time, though in varying stages and different degrees. This certainty does not indeed come by curiously examining the secret and deep things of God. Rather, it comes by seeing in themselves, with spiritual joy and holy satisfaction, the fruit of infallible election taught in the Word of God. That fruit includes true faith in Christ, childlike fear of God, godly sorrow for sin, a hunger and thirst for righteousness, etc.

One of the distinctive elements of the Reformed understanding of election is the teaching that the elect can know that they are elect. By contrast, the great medieval theologian Thomas Aquinas taught a thoroughly

Augustinian doctrine of predestination but denied that a Christian ordinarily could know that he is elect. Since Thomas recognized that Paul, for example, clearly had certainty of his salvation, he accounted for that by teaching that Paul and others had that certainty only by the special revelation from God.

This article teaches that ordinary means are available for Christians to know that they are elect. That knowledge does not always come to individual Christians at the same speed or with the same clarity. Some have a weaker and some a stronger sense of assurance. The means to this knowledge is not by climbing into heaven and examining God's Book of Life. No such access to the mind of God is ordinarily available. Rather, that knowledge and assurance comes to Christians from seeing the fruit of election manifested in themselves. Since only the elect will ever have true faith and repentance, as well as a real desire for holiness, where faith, repentance, and the beginnings of obedience are found, there surely is evidence of election. This evidence leads to assurance.

Article 13: Election and the Fruit of Assurance

As a result of this sense and certainty of election, the children of God daily find more reason to humble themselves before God, to adore the depth of His mercies, to purify themselves, and also eagerly to love Him who first loved them so greatly. So we see that this doctrine of election, and meditation on it, are far from making the children of God slack in observing the commandments of God or making them carnally secure. Rather, such slackness and carnal security are usually found according to the just judgment of God in those who do not want to walk in the ways of the elect. Such people either rashly presume on the grace of election or chat about it in an idle and shameless manner.

For Roman Catholic theologians, the Reformed doctrine of assurance was not only false but very dangerous spiritually. They reasoned that if one was certainly assured of salvation, it would lead to terrible arrogance and a lawless indifference to the pursuit of holiness. By contrast, the canons insist that a proper understanding of assurance leads to growing humility and gratefulness as well as great motivation to pursue holiness and love for God. The basic conviction here is that indifference to God and to the life of faith is found not in true Christians who have assurance of faith but in the unbelieving and unregenerate. Those who have received the gift of life will grow in their joy and love of the Lord and His will. Presumption in life or talk is not the fruit of faith or of sound doctrine. This article is very important for seeing the proper relationship of truth and life. The implications of theology for piety were always a concern for the synod.

Article 14: Election and Preaching

This doctrine of divine election according to the most wise counsel of God was preached by the prophets, by Christ Himself, and by the Apostles, in the Old just as in the New Testament. It was notably preserved in the sacred Scriptures. So today it ought to be taught in the church of God, for which it was particularly intended, at the right time and place, with a spirit of discretion and in a manner that is religious and holy. Far from encouraging any curious examination of the ways of the Most High, it ought to be taught for the glory of the most holy divine name and for the lively comfort of His people.

Some critics of Calvinism had suggested that even if predestination were true, it should not be spoken of in the public preaching of the church. This criticism is implied in point 1 and in the conclusion of the Remonstrance of 1610. This article responds by noting that throughout the Bible, predestination was taught and preached by the prophets, by Christ, and by the Apostles. Scripture has preserved the doctrine on its pages and has shown us how to teach it. So today it needs to be preached in the churches. This article recognizes that good judgment should be used by the preacher as to when and how much it should be preached. It should not be talked about all the time. It should be preached in a way that is reverent and careful. But it must be preached.

Predestination should never by approached or taught with a spirit of curiosity. Curiosity was regarded as a sin in the medieval church—very much in line with the saying "Curiosity killed the cat." Such curiosity was arrogantly speculative. Predestination is not revealed to encourage strange, abstract questions but to promote the adoration of the glories of God. It is also revealed for the comfort of God's people. It is not too much to say that if predestination is not a comfort to the people of God, it has not been rightly taught or understood. The comfort comes from recognizing that God has done for us—including His plan in eternity— what we could never have done for ourselves. The comfort also comes from knowing that God is a much better protector of our salvation than we could ever be.

Article 15: Reprobation Defined

Additionally, what greatly shows the eternal and free grace of our election, and which the Holy Scripture commends to us, is the testimony that not all humans are elect. Rather, some are nonelect or are passed over in the eternal election of God. God in His most free, most righteous, blameless, and unchangeable good pleasure decreed to leave the nonelect in the common misery. They have plunged themselves into this misery by their own fault. God decreed not to give them saving faith and the grace of conversion. Instead, He left them under His righteous judgment to follow their own ways. He decreed at last to damn and eternally punish them not only because of their unbelief, but also for all their other sins, for the demonstration of His justice. And this is the decree of reprobation, which does not make God in any way the author of sin (which it is blasphemous to think). Rather, it shows Him to be a formidable, blameless, righteous judge and avenger.

The Reformed have always taught that a stable doctrine of election requires not only the positive side of the teaching but also a clear teaching of the negative side. (This is sometimes called double predestination.) They insist that reprobation is not only theologically necessary but also clearly taught in the Scriptures. The article does not cite a passage of the Bible, but Romans 9 easily comes to mind.

Reprobation refers, then, to the nonelect or those who are passed over and not given the fruits of election. The critical point the article wants to make is that there is nothing unjust about God's leaving sinners in their sin. Sinners bear the responsibility for being sinners, and when God leaves them in their sin, He does nothing unjust. Further, at the last day, God will judge and condemn sinners because of all of their sins, not just for the sin of unbelief. This condemnation will be entirely just.

This article stresses that the final judgment will be in terms of all sins, first because that seems to be the clear teaching of Scripture (e.g., Matt. 25), but also to refute the Arminians. The Arminians had taught that Christ had paid for all sins except the sin of unbelief, so that no one would be condemned unless they had committed the sin of unbelief.

Some questions about the relation of divine sovereignty to the origins of sin are left unaddressed here by the synod. Different Reformed theologians had discussed these questions in a variety of ways. On one point only the article is adamant: God is not the author of sin. He is not responsible for evil or sin in the world. With all confessional Reformed theologians, the canons declare that such an idea is not only false but blasphemous. God is always good and just in all His dealings with mankind.

Article 16: Assurance and Reprobation

Some people do not yet effectively feel a living faith in Christ, a confident trust in the heart, peace of conscience, a desire for childlike obedience, or a glorying in God through Christ. But if such people nevertheless use the means through which God has promised to work these things in them, they ought not to be alarmed at the mention of reprobation or reckon themselves reprobate. Rather, they ought to persevere in the diligent use of the means and ought to desire ardently a time of fuller grace and to look for it with reverence and humility. The doctrine of reprobation should be much less terrifying for those who desire seriously to be converted to God, to please Him only, and to be delivered from the body of death, but cannot yet arrive at the life of piety and faith that they want. For the merciful God has promised that He will not quench the smoking flax or break the bruised reed. However, this doctrine is rightly terrifying to those who have forgotten God and the Savior Jesus Christ and have completely given themselves over to the cares of the world and the desires of the flesh, as long as they are not seriously converted to God.

This article returns to the subject of assurance, which had been raised in articles 12 and 13. This article wants to reassure those who do not yet feel that they experience in themselves the fruits of regeneration (such as faith, peace of conscience, and a desire for obedience). Those who do not yet feel spiritually what they would like to feel are counseled to continue to use diligently the means of grace through which God works to accomplish His purposes. Implicitly, this article calls such people to listen carefully to preaching and to pray for the blessing of the Lord. Such people certainly should not count themselves as reprobate.

The article then addresses those who have some feelings of desire for God and for living for Him but do not find in themselves those feelings as fully as they would like. They are assured that God will bless those beginnings of faith. Allusion is made to Isaiah 42:3: "A bruised reed he will not break, and a faintly burning wick he will not quench" (ESV). Jesus applies this prophecy to His own work on behalf of the needy (Matt. 12:20). This teaching is similar to the statement of William Perkins: "The desire for grace is an evidence of grace."

The doctrine of reprobation should not terrify the spiritually concerned but should terrify those who are completely indifferent spiritually. But while the doctrine should terrify such people, it does not prove that they are in fact reprobate in the eternal counsel of God. Rather, their terror might lead to awakening and even true conversion. No one living can know that he is reprobate (except by special revelation, as was the case with Judas Iscariot).

Article 17: Covenant and Reprobation/Election

We are to judge the will of God from His Word. The Word testifies that the children of the faithful are holy, not by nature, but as a benefit of God's gracious covenant. These children together with their

*parents are included in this covenant. Therefore, pious parents ought
not to doubt the election and salvation of their children whom God
calls out of this life in infancy.*

This article at first glance seems surprising and perhaps out of place.
The subject matter does not seem to follow logically from what had preceded it. In fact, however, it is quite important and logical. The Arminians
criticized the Calvinists not only for their theology but also for the pastoral consequences of that theology. In an age where many children died
in infancy, the spiritual state of those children was a pressing question
for families and ministers. This reality made this article theologically,
spiritually, and strategically critical.

The Arminians wanted to turn the Calvinistic doctrine of election
into a mysterious, unknowable, and threatening reality, suggesting that
parents could have no knowledge of whether their dead children had
gone to heaven or hell. They hoped to use this issue to lead people to
reject Calvinism generally. The Counter-Remonstrants in 1611 had
rejected this charge, and the synod returns to it again in the conclusion
of the canons.

The synod's response, while brief, is very important. It begins by
reminding us that we must not speculate about the will of God but must
know it from studying the Bible. In this case specifically, we must study
what the Bible says about the children of believers. Such children are
holy, according to 1 Corinthians 7:14. This holiness is not the natural
state of all children but is the covenant blessing of God given to the
children of the faithful. That is clearly the context of Paul's discussion in
1 Corinthians 7. The reasoning of the article is simple: "holy" children,
who have not rejected the covenant when they die in infancy, must be
elect and saved. The God of the covenant of grace would not send holy
children to hell but would instead take them to heaven.

Although the canons do not refer to 2 Samuel 11–12, it is the clearest example in the Scripture of a child of the covenant dying in infancy.
The child, conceived of David's adultery with Bathsheba, died shortly
after his birth, despite David's fervid prayers and fasting. After the child's

death, David said: "Why should I fast? Can I bring him back again? I shall go to him, but he will not return to me" (12:23, ESV). David seemed comforted (v. 24), so his words cannot mean that his son was dead and one day he would be dead too. Rather, he anticipated a personal reunion with his son in heaven.

How could David know that his son is in heaven? There is no evidence that he had a special revelation, so he must have known this from the character of the covenant of grace. He knew that his child was holy, and having died in the holiness of the covenant of grace, the child must be in heaven.

For the Calvinists at the Synod of Dort, election did not threaten or undermine the covenant of grace. Christians individually could know their election by the reality of the covenant of grace at work in their lives. Real faith, repentance, love of God, etc., showed that they were elect. That covenant knowledge then could also apply to their children dying in infancy. Election was always a comforting doctrine, not the doctrinal threat and spiritual uncertainty alleged by the Arminians.[1]

Article 18: The Glory of God in Election

To those who murmur against this grace of free election and the severity of just reprobation, we set against them this Apostolic word: "O man! Who are you to answer back to God?" (Rom. 9:20). And that word of our Savior: "Am I not allowed to do what I want with My own?" (Matt. 20:15). Truly, we adore this mystery piously when we exclaim with the Apostle: "O the depth of the riches both of the wisdom and the knowledge of God! How unsearchable are the judgments of God and how inscrutable are His ways! Who has known the mind of the Lord? And who has been His counselor? And who has first given to Him that it would be returned to him? For from Him, and through Him, and in Him are all things. To Him be glory forever. Amen" (Rom. 11:33–36).

This last article implicitly answers the complaints of the Arminians and others in the history of the church against the supposed unfairness of election. The response is an appeal to the sovereignty and wisdom of God. The world, especially fallen sinners, belongs to God, and He is free to do as He will with it. But this sovereignty is not arbitrary or capricious. What God does, He does in accord with His wisdom and for His glory. Therefore, we can always trust Him and glorify Him. This response is the proper fruit of knowing God's electing purpose, as Paul teaches very clearly and pointedly in Romans 11.

REJECTION OF ERRORS

Rejection 1: Election and One Decree

The Synod rejects the error of those who teach:

"The whole and complete decree of election to salvation is the will of God to save those who would believe and would persevere in faith and the obedience of faith. Nothing else concerning this decree is revealed in the Word of God."

Those who teach this deceive the more simple people and clearly contradict the sacred Scripture. The Scripture testifies that God not only wills to save those who are going to believe. God has also elected from eternity a certain number of persons to whom, rather than to others, He will give in time faith in Christ and perseverance. As it is written, "I have made Your name known to the men whom You gave to me" (John 17:6), and, "As many as were ordained to eternal life believed" (Acts 18:48), and, "He chose them before the foundation of the world, that they might be holy" (Eph. 1:4).

The error rejected here is a teaching that oversimplifies the whole discussion of election. This teaching states that God's sole decree of election is the appointment of three conditions for salvation. Anyone who meets those conditions is elect and saved. The first condition is faith, the second is persevering in faith, and the third is Christian obedience that flows from faith. This error insists that the Scriptures teach nothing else about election except this.

This teaching is shockingly contrary to basic Reformation theology. While the Bible certainly calls people to faith, perseverance, and obedience and also promises these as gifts to the elect, they are not the bases of election or salvation. To confuse these gifts of God with conditions for election is indeed to try to confuse simple people in the church. The error here is basically the one stated in the first point of the Remonstrance of 1610.

One of the great elements of sound theology is to make proper distinctions. Both in the history of theology and today, great harm is done to the church by muddling and mingling matters that ought to be distinguished. We see that today in many discussions of the relation of faith and works in theology. The Arminian error rejected here is a classic example of such confusion.

One of the great accomplishments of Protestant scholastic theology is the clarity of thought and truth achieved by proper distinctions. Consider this statement of Francis Turretin about the function of faith in the covenant of works and in the covenant of grace:

> Nor can it be objected here that faith was required also in the first covenant and works are not excluded in the second (as was said before). They stand in a far different relation. For in the first covenant, faith was required as a work and a part of the inherent righteousness to which life was promised. But in the second, it is demanded—not as a work on account of which life is given, but as a mere instrument apprehending the righteousness of Christ (on account of which alone salvation is granted to us). In the one, faith was a theological virtue from the strength of nature, terminating on God, the Creator; in the other, faith is an evangelical condition after the manner of supernatural grace, terminating on God, the Redeemer. As to works, they were required in the first as an antecedent condition by way of a cause for acquiring life; but in the second, they are only the subsequent condition as the fruit and effect of the life already acquired. In the first, they ought to precede the act of justification; in the second, they follow it.[2]

Many modern books on faith, works, and justification would not have been necessary if the church had remembered this paragraph by Turretin.

The synod here gives a succinct but pointed refutation of the error stressing God's gifts to His elect. It then adds scriptural quotations that show God has decreed and given particular graces to elect individuals, specifically, the gifts of revelation, faith, and holiness. The true character of God's great electing plan is laid out carefully and fully in article I.7.

Rejection 2: Election and Many Decrees

The Synod rejects the error of those who teach:

> *"The election of God to eternal life is of several kinds. One is general and indefinite and another is particular and definite. Further, the particular and definite one either is incomplete, revocable, nondecisive, or conditional, or is complete, irrevocable, decisive, or absolute." Also, "one election is to faith, and another to salvation, so that election can be to justifying faith without being a decisive election to salvation."*

> *This teaching is an invention of the human understanding devised outside the Scriptures. It corrupts the doctrine of election, and destroys the golden chain of salvation: "Those whom He predestined, He also called; and those whom He called, He also justified; those whom He justified, He also glorified" (Rom. 8:30).*

This second error addressed by the synod stands in contradiction to the first and no doubt is intended to show that the Arminians differed significantly among themselves. Indeed, the synod does not label the errors as Remonstrant or Arminian. It does not say that all Arminians hold these views. It simply says that the teachings it rejects are errors deviating from the Word of God.

If the first error oversimplified election, the second error creates unnecessary complications and confusion by making distinctions that are not proper or helpful. This error says that one can speak of general and particular election and that under the topic of particular election one can distinguish between incomplete and revocable election on the one hand and complete and irrevocable election on the other. Further, this error teaches that one may be elected to justifying faith but not be elected to salvation.

All of these distinctions amount to this: one may be elect in many ways and receive many gifts from God and still be lost eternally. These distinctions are labeled "human inventions" and demonstrate the tendency of Arminian theology to press human logic in theology to insist that man rather than God is ultimately determinative in salvation. Against this, the synod cites Romans 8 and its "golden chain," showing the unbreakable connection between the purposes and gifts of God for the salvation of the elect. This one purpose of God for both the grace and glory of the elect is clearly stated in article I.8.

Rejection 3: Election and Faith

The Synod rejects the error of those who teach:

> *"The good pleasure and purpose of God, which Scripture mentions in its doctrine of election, does not consist in this, that God elected certain particular persons rather than others. But it consists in this, that God out of all possible conditions (among which are also works of the law) or out of the order of all things, elected the act of faith, in itself undistinguished, and the imperfect obedience of faith as the condition of salvation. He graciously reckoned this as perfect obedience and He wanted to consider it worth the reward of eternal life."*

By this pernicious error the good pleasure of God and the merit of Christ are enervated. Also, men are distracted from the truth of gracious justification and the simplicity of the Scriptures to considering useless questions. By this, the statement of the Apostle is rendered false: "God called us with a holy calling; not because of works, but because of His own purpose and grace, which He gave to us in Christ Jesus before the times of the ages" (2 Tim. 1:9).

This error returns to the claim that election is not a matter of particular persons but of conditions to be met. The focus here is particularly on faith as a condition of election. Here the Reformation doctrine of faith is completely misunderstood or indeed denied. The error here treats faith as one good work among many. Instead of requiring perfect obedience to the law, now God graciously in the new covenant accepts faith and its imperfect obedience as the condition of salvation.

As the Scripture cited by the synod shows, however, faith is not a work, but a looking away from oneself and all one's good works to Christ alone. Faith rests in Christ and in the perfection of His work for us. The Arminians have not only abused the true doctrine of faith, they have corrupted in a very serious way other doctrines as well. They have rejected the teaching of the Bible that election rests on the good pleasure of God alone. Rather than flowing out of the will and pleasure of God, election now rests on factors in the elect. The Arminians' teaching also undermines the meaning of the death of Christ as a meritorious, substitutionary atonement. It also turns justification into a reward earned rather than a gift given. Finally, it distracts Christians from the clear teaching of the Bible—recovered in the Reformation—about Christ, grace, and faith. This Arminian teaching is indeed pernicious. This rejection is a very helpful expansion on what is taught in article I.10.

Rejection 4: Election and Preparation

The Synod rejects the error of those who teach:

> "*In the election to faith this condition is required, that men rightly use the light of nature and be pious, meek, humble, and disposed to eternal life, as if election to some extent depended on these things.*"

These things savor of Pelagius and in fact falsely undermine the Apostle who wrote: "We once lived in the passions of our flesh, carrying out the desires of the flesh and the mind, and were by nature children of wrath like the rest. But God who is rich in mercy, because of His great love with which He loved us, even when we were dead in offenses, He made us alive with Christ, by whose grace you are saved, and raised us up and seated us in the heavens in Christ Jesus, so that in the coming ages He might show the surpassing riches of his grace according to His kindness to us in Christ Jesus. By grace you have been saved through faith (and that not of yourselves, it is the gift of God), not of works lest anyone should boast" (Eph. 2:3–9).

The error here is that sinners can, and indeed must, prepare themselves for grace in order to receive grace. Sinners can, with the truth available to them in nature, pursue a life that has elements of piety and humility and actually desire eternal life. Such preparation certainly seems to deny the total depravity of the fallen. Election depends on such preparation to come to fruition.

The synod rightly observes that such teaching smells Pelagian, in the sense that it declares that nature does not need grace to move toward God. Against such teaching, a rather long quotation from the Apostle Paul is presented, which shows that whatever good we may have is a gift of grace. Again, this rejection is an expansion on article I.9, as is rejection I.5.

Rejection 5: Election and Foreseen Qualities

The Synod rejects the error of those who teach:

> "The election of particular persons to salvation is incomplete and nondecisive, made on the basis of foreseen faith, repentance, holiness, and piety, begun and continued for some time. It becomes complete and decisive on the basis of final perseverance of foreseen faith, repentance, holiness, and piety. This is the gracious and evangelical worthiness, on account of which he who is elect is more worthy than he who is not elect. Therefore faith, the obedience of faith, holiness, piety, and perseverance are not the fruit or effect of immutable election to glory. Rather, they are conditions or causes without which these persons are not completely elected, being prerequisites which are foreseen as fulfilled."

That teaching is repugnant to the whole Scripture, which repeatedly declares, in these texts and many others, to our ears and hearts: "Election is not from works, but from calling" (Rom. 9:11). "As many as were ordained to eternal life believed" (Acts 13:48). "He elected us in Him that we might be holy" (Eph. 1:4). "You did not chose Me, but I chose you" (John 15:16). "If by grace, then not by works" (Rom. 11:6). "In this is love, not that we loved God, but that He loved us, and sent His Son" (1 John 4:10).

The error rejected here is in one sense a very common one and in another sense is a very subtle one. Many Arminians have argued through the centuries that God elects to life those whom He has foreseen will respond well to the grace He offers them. This teaching seems attractive because the Bible itself speaks of the foreknowledge of God, sometimes in the very context of verses that Calvinists love to quote about predestination (for example, Rom. 8). Calvinists have insisted that biblical foreknowledge is God's knowledge of what He will do in the future, not foreknowledge of what sinners will do.

The foreknowledge of the Arminians includes final perseverance among all the other conditions required for salvation: faith, repentance, piety, and holiness. Only in light of that foreseen final perseverance can anyone be seen as certainly elect and saved. The really wicked part of this teaching is that it makes Christians better and worthier than non-Christians. Christians are those who made proper use of the grace offered and so are superior to those who have not made use of that grace. Such teaching destroys one of the most basic Christian virtues, namely, humility. "What do you have that you did not receive?" (1 Cor. 4:7, ESV). Calvinists may not always be as humble as they ought to be, but they recognize theologically that they are not better in themselves apart from grace than others. Humility and gratitude are foundational to Christian living.

The subtle side of the teaching of foreknowledge is found in the teaching of Luis de Molina, the Spanish Jesuit theologian. He developed the doctrine of middle knowledge, which holds that God foreknew every possible action that might be taken by the human free will of every individual. In the light of that knowledge, God so ordered human history that human free will always did what God wanted it to do. Arminius was influenced by this teaching (see appendix 1, the section "Unchanging Theology?" on page 191). The synod rejects this subtle teaching on foreknowledge both in its teaching on total depravity and in its recognition of the true biblical doctrine of election. Molinism has had a revival recently in some evangelical circles where there is a desire to maintain both human free will and divine sovereignty. It is always attractive to have your cake and eat it too. The problem is that Molinism does not work theologically and is not biblical.

Rejection of Error 6: Election and Perseverance

The Synod rejects the error of those who teach:

> *"Not all election to salvation is immutable, but certain of the elect, without any decree of God preventing it, can perish and do perish eternally."*

By this gross error they make God mutable and subvert the comfort of the pious in the constancy of their election. They also contradict the sacred Scriptures, which teach "the elect cannot be led astray" (Matt. 24:24). "Christ does not lose those given Him by the Father" (John 6:39). "Those whom God predestined, called, and justified, He also glorified" (Rom. 8:30).

The error here is the teaching that some kind of election can fail in its purpose to save the elect. Such election is changeable and does not lead the "elect" to persevere in faith. Such teaching has two serious errors. The first is that it corrupts the doctrine of God. God in His being is immutable. To teach that He changes is to make him capricious, arbitrary, and unpredictable—the very opposite of the God revealed to us in the Bible. While the Arminians may not have intended this result of their teaching, the synod rightly sees that it is the necessary consequence of it.

The doctrine of God is an important one in our day again as a number of theologians in the evangelical world have been challenging the classic Christian doctrine of God. They believe that the doctrine of God has been too much influenced by static Greek philosophical concepts and does not adequately express the dynamic picture of God presented in the Bible. Such teaching may seem attractive and biblical at first glance, but will not stand the test of careful and profound examination. The classic Christian doctrine of God has been constructed over centuries of thorough reflection and study of the Bible. The great Christian textbooks on theology make that clear. The current revisionists are at least as dangerous as the seventeenth-century Arminians, and this brief rejection of error here in the canons should alert us to the danger. This doctrine of God is stated briefly in article I.11.

The second error rejected here is a changeable election that must undermine the comfort of the pious. For the synod, election is not a dangerous or threatening doctrine for Christians but rather is always an encouragement. It is a vital comfort to know that He who began a good work in us will bring it to completion (Phil. 1:6) and that God begins that work according to His unchangeable, eternal plan (Eph. 1:4).

Rejection 7: Election and Assurance

The Synod rejects the error of those who teach:

> *"There is in this life no fruit, no sense, and no certainty of immutable election to glory except from a mutable and contingent condition."*

Surely it is absurd to make certainty uncertain. It is contrary to the experience of the saints who rejoice with the Apostle in their sense of election. The saints celebrate this blessing of God. They "rejoice" with the disciples according to the Word of Christ "that their names are written in heaven" (Luke 10:20). Finally, they oppose their sense of election to the fiery attack of the devils, asking, "Who will bring any charge against God's elect?" (Rom. 8:33).

Perhaps the most distinctive Reformed doctrine is that the Christian can not only know that he is in a present state of salvation but can know that he is elect and will persevere in faith to the end. This teaching is rejected by the error addressed here. The error states that since our present state as Christians is changeable and not certain to continue, we cannot reason from this present state to our future state. However reasonable such logic initially appears, the synod rejects it as unsound and unbiblical. Christians must speak of certainty because the Scriptures so plainly do (e.g., 2 Tim. 1:12). But to describe that certainty as uncertain is nonsense.

In the Scriptures, this knowledge of certain salvation is the source of great joy and confidence in the life of the saints. Since true faith is a gift of God that is irrevocable, the saints can indeed know and rejoice that their names are written in heaven. This point is developed further in article I.12.

Rejection 8: Election and Passing Over (Preterition)

The Synod rejects the error of those who teach:

> *"God has not decreed, simply according to His just will, to leave anyone in the fall of Adam and in the common state of sin and condemnation or to pass over anyone in communicating the necessary grace for faith and conversion."*

This Scripture stands against them: "He has mercy on whom He will; He hardens whom He will" (Rom. 9:18). And this: "It is given to you to know the mysteries of the kingdom of heaven; to them it is not given" (Matt. 13:11). Also "I glorify You, Father, Lord of heaven and earth, that You have hidden this from the wise and understanding, and revealed it to infants, because, Father, it was pleasing to You" (Matt. 11:25–26).

Part of the doctrine of reprobation is the doctrine of "passing over" or, more technically, of preterition. The Arminians deny this teaching, insisting that God has not decreed to leave anyone in their sins and to pass over them, not giving them the grace necessary for salvation. This Arminian teaching seems logical and fair to many, and the Arminians often pressed it in their criticism of Calvinism.

Interestingly, the synod in rejecting this Arminian error does not present theological reasoning or arguments, but simply quotes the Bible. The Arminians' argument is not with Calvinists but with the Bible. The biblical citations make clear that God is not a passive bystander in reprobation but is active in "hardening" and in not giving. This biblical teaching is difficult for many who want to ignore it, but it is clearly revealed in the Bible. The reality and spiritual value of reprobation and preterition are discussed in articles I.6 and III–IV.15.

Rejection 9: Election and Worthiness

The Synod rejects the error of those who teach:

> *"The reason God sends His gospel to one people rather than to another is not merely and solely the good pleasure of God, but because one people is better and more worthy than another people to whom the gospel is not communicated."*

Moses contradicts this saying to the people of Israel: "To Jehovah your God belong the heavens and the heavens of heavens, the earth and what is in it. Only to your forebears did Jehovah with love incline to love them and He chose their seed after them, indeed you, above all peoples, as it is today" (Deut. 10:14–15). And Christ: "Woe to you Chorazin, woe to you Bethsaida, because if the works which were done in you had been done in Tyre and Sidon, they would have repented long ago in sackcloth and ashes" (Matt. 11:21).

Church history shows that the gospel is preached in different parts of the world at different times and with differing degrees of success. The sending of the gospel in this way is part of the mysterious providence of God. The error rejected here tries to lessen the mystery and teaches instead that the gospel is sent by God to those who are more worthy of receiving it.

We have seen the spiritual dangers of this idea of superiority and greater worthiness in our discussion of rejection of error I.5. Here again the synod responds simply by quoting Scripture. The Old Testament shows that God chose Israel not because of her superiority to other nations but only because of His love. The New Testament quotation actually says that God sent the gospel to Chorazin and Bethsaida despite the fact that Tyre and Sidon would have been more receptive. Clearly, it is not worth but God's good pleasure that is decisive. See also articles I.3 and I.5.

This particular rejection of error perhaps deserves special attention. The seventeenth century would see the rapid expansion of European commercial contacts with Africa, Asia, and the New World. Commercial success often led to colonization and sometimes slavery. Much of modern history is about the successes and tragic failures of colonialism. At the heart of European failures was their profound sense of their superiority to the peoples they colonized and enslaved. How different that history might have been had those Europeans really grasped the teaching here and understood that they were not more worthy than others in the eyes of God. Then they might have embraced the virtue of humility implied in this teaching. Very regrettably, many Calvinists were no better than most non-Calvinists in really living out this teaching.

Chapter 10

SECOND HEAD OF DOCTRINE:

THE DEATH OF CHRIST
AND THE REDEMPTION OF HUMANS
THROUGH THAT DEATH

The biggest surprise at the Synod of Dort for the orthodox delegates was the discovery that they were not as agreed among themselves on the extent of the atonement as they had assumed. In fact, for a time, the synod had a great deal of difficulty finding a way forward to a statement on the death of Christ that all could accept. As a result, the second head of doctrine is a very carefully articulated compromise, as we will see in our exposition of the articles.

Article 1: God's Justice Requires Satisfaction for Sin

God is not only supremely merciful, but also supremely just. His justice requires (as He has revealed in His Word) that our sins committed against His infinite majesty be punished. They must be punished both in body and soul, with eternal as well as temporal punishments. We cannot escape these punishments unless the justice of God be satisfied.

As did the first head of doctrine, this head of doctrine begins with a common Christian conviction. That God is merciful and just is certainly

113

a common Christian teaching, as well as the explicit teaching of the Belgic Confession on election (article 16). God's Word makes clear that justice requires that sin be punished. Sin must be punished because it offends God. Today, if people think about sin at all, they focus on the inherent evil of sin and the problems it brings to human relationships. Here, the article rightly focuses on how sin violates the infinite majesty and goodness of God. The Bible shows that this infinite offense will be punished in the body and soul of the sinner, both in this life and everlastingly in hell. Today, many ask if everlasting punishment for temporal sin is fair. This article provides the answer. Yes, it is fair because the sin is against the infinite justice of the infinite God. The harmony of God's mercy with His justice requires that His justice be satisfied for His mercy to be manifested.

Article 2: Jesus Satisfies for the Sin of His People

We cannot satisfy for our sins or free ourselves from the anger of God. So God, out of His immense mercy, gave His only begotten Son as surety for our sins. This Son, so that He might satisfy for us, was made sin and curse on the cross for us and in our place.

We finite creatures, who are ever adding to our sins, cannot satisfy or liberate ourselves from the demands of God's justice. God in mercy provides for us a substitute to do for us what we could never do for ourselves. On the cross, Jesus took our sin upon Himself and bore the curse of God's wrath that should have fallen on us.

This article refers to Christ's work for "us," but it is not clear at this point who is included in this "us." What is clear is that the work of Christ is specific and complete. It accomplishes its purpose for those for whom it was intended.

Article 3: The Infinite Value of the Death of Christ

This death of the Son of God is the only and most perfect sacrifice and satisfaction for sins. It is of infinite value and worth, abundantly sufficient to expiate the sins of the whole world.

This article does not proceed to answer the question of for whom the death of Christ was intended. Rather, it focuses on further consideration of the character of that death. Only the death of Christ can satisfy for sin, and that satisfaction is perfect. The inherent value of that death is infinite and so is sufficient to save the whole world and—as theologians sometimes said—a thousand worlds besides.

Mentioning the sufficiency of the death here is very significant in the compromise reached at Dort among the orthodox. Many medieval theologians had embraced the formula of Peter Lombard, who had written the basic medieval text on theology, *The Sentences*, that Christ's death was sufficient for the whole world but efficient for the elect alone. This distinction between sufficiency and efficiency implied a dual intention in the death of Christ: an intention for the whole world and an intention for the elect. Exactly how these intentions were to be understood and how they related to one another was the subject of considerable debate.

By the late sixteenth century within the developing Reformed orthodoxy, Theodore Beza of Geneva and his followers had taken the position that the whole idea of sufficiency should be rejected. They taught that the exclusive purpose and intention in the death of Christ were to save the elect. Talk of sufficiency implied some intention in that death for the whole world, which they said was not true and could easily be confusing. Therefore, it was best not to use that category at all.

Others at the synod, particularly John Davenant in the British delegation, thought that sufficiency was an important category and that Christ had indeed had an intention in His death for the whole world. Davenant believed that Christ established a conditional covenant with the whole world on the cross, the condition being true faith. He was concerned that such sufficiency would be the foundation of preaching the gospel to all people and telling them that Christ had died for them.

Still, the majority at the synod believed that the distinction between sufficiency and efficiency was a useful and traditional distinction but did not believe that sufficiency necessarily carried with it some intention on Christ's part for the whole world. Article II.3 clearly does use the category of sufficiency—representing a concession on the part of the Bezans.

This concession reminds us that the canons were a compromise and that Calvinist theologians could be flexible in uniting against serious error.

Article 4: Christ Satisfies as God and Man

Now this death is of such value and worth because of the person who experienced it. He is not only a true and perfectly holy human. But He is also the only begotten Son of God, of the same eternal and infinite essence with the Father and the Holy Spirit. It was necessary for such a person to be our Savior. His death is also of such value and worth because it was accompanied by the experience of the anger and curse of God, which we had merited for our sins.

This article presents the character of the Christ who could offer such a perfect sacrifice. He is both a perfectly holy human and the eternal, only begotten Son of God. He is true God and true man. Only such a Savior could bear human sin as a human and pay an infinite price as God. He truly bore the curse that was due to us.

While the word *sufficiency* is not used in this article, the article does seem to explain that the sufficiency of Christ's death was related to the intrinsic value of it. The person of Christ does make His death of infinite value. A further meaning of *sufficiency* in terms of an intention of Christ for the world is neither affirmed nor denied. Again, we can see that the canons do not feel the need to take a position on all theological differences and in fact leave a place for differences on all these implications of sufficiency within the bounds of orthodoxy.

Article 5: The Call to Believe Is to Be Preached to Everyone

The promise of the gospel is that whoever believes in Christ crucified shall not perish, but shall have eternal life. This promise along with the command to repent and believe ought to be announced and proclaimed generally and indiscriminately to all peoples and humans to whom God according to His good pleasure sends the gospel.

This article addresses the preaching of the gospel. This preaching must declare that all who believe in Jesus will have eternal life. The promise of life in Christ as well as the command to repent of sins and believe in Jesus is to be proclaimed to all. Here is an unequivocal call to preach Christ to all. The only limitation noted here is God's providential ordering of history. Throughout history, God has sent preachers to some places by opening doors and not sent them to others. But wherever God makes it possible, the gospel must be preached to all.

What is noteworthy here is that no explicit link is made between the command to preach the gospel to all and the death of Christ. Here again the canons state what all Calvinists at the synod agreed on—that the gospel must be preached to all—and left open the question of whether or how this command was tied to the death of Christ. We see the compromise again.

Article 6: The Cause of Unbelief Is in the Unbeliever, Not in Christ

Many who are called by the gospel do not in fact repent or believe in Christ, but perish in unbelief. This loss is not because of any defect or insufficiency in the sacrifice of Christ offered on the cross. Rather, it is because of their own guilt.

This article raises the question of responsibility for unbelief. The matter of responsibility recurs in various forms throughout the heads of doctrine. Here the issue is whether unbelief is the result of some deficiency in the death of Christ. The Arminians had regularly accused Calvinist theology of failing to make grace available to those who sincerely sought it. The Calvinists sought to answer these serious theological and pastoral challenges.

Here the Calvinists insist that unbelief is the result of the guilt of sinners who persevere in their sin and reject the command to believe. Implicit in what is said here is that no one who sincerely desires grace is denied it.

Article 7: Christ Is the Cause of Faith

All those who truly believe are freed from destruction and saved from their sins through the death of Christ. They obtain this by the grace of God alone, which He owes to no one, but gave to them in Christ from eternity.

All who believe will surely be saved. Again, implicitly, this is a rejection of the Arminian charge that some who believe were not elected and so would not be saved. Faith is a gift of God's grace, and that grace was purchased on the cross, as was planned from all eternity. All who have true faith have that faith only as result of God's grace.

Article 8: Christ Died for the Elect Alone

It was the most free counsel and most gracious will and intention of God the Father that the living and saving efficacy of the most valuable death of His Son would extend to all the elect. To the elect alone He gives justifying faith and infallibly produces salvation through faith. God willed for Christ efficaciously to redeem through the blood of the cross (by which He confirmed the new covenant)—from every people, tribe, nation, and tongue—all those and only those who were elected to salvation from eternity and were given to Him by the Father. God willed that Christ give to the elect the faith that He acquired for them by His death, along with other saving gifts of the Holy Spirit. He also willed for Christ to cleanse them by His blood from all sin, both original and actual, committed before as well as after faith. He willed for Christ to preserve them faithfully even to the end, and finally to bring them, without spot or blemish, glorified into His presence.

Here is the defining article of this head of doctrine. The earlier articles have set the stage for this one by answering clearly a variety of theological questions often raised to distract from a simple consideration of the question: For whom did Christ die efficaciously? The answer is simple:

Christ died for all the elect and only for the elect efficaciously—that is, certainly and completely—to ensure their salvation. He died to save the elect alone, and He fully accomplished that purpose.

Such an efficacious death is what the Father planned from eternity and what the Son accomplished on the cross. It was the will of the Father that the Son out of His saving work would by the Holy Spirit give to each one of the elect true, justifying faith and all other saving gifts. Christ's death covers all the sins of the elect, both those committed before faith and those committed after faith. The will of the Father is that the death of Christ would effect salvation for the elect from beginning to end. So Christ not only gives faith, but He also preserves the elect and glorifies them at last. The key pastoral point here is that Christ is the full and complete Savior both in the earning and in the giving of salvation. The sinner contributes nothing to salvation except his sin. All the grace that we have is purely and entirely a gift from God.

This article buttresses and clarifies the teaching of the Belgic Confession on the work of Christ: "For any to assert that Christ is not sufficient, but that something more is required besides Him, would be too gross a blasphemy; for hence it would follow that Christ was but half a Savior. . . . Jesus Christ, imputing to us all His merits, and so many holy works which He has done for us and in our stead, is our righteousness" (article 22). Christ is indeed the complete and effective Savior.

Article 9: Christ Will Always Have a Church

This plan, coming from God's eternal love toward the elect, has been powerfully fulfilled from the beginning of the world up to the present time. And it will be continually fulfilled in the future, despite the vain opposition of the gates of hell. So the elect in due time are gathered into one, and there will always be a church of believers. This church, founded in the blood of Jesus, constantly loves Him, perseveringly worships Him, and celebrates Him, now and in all eternity, as her Savior. He is the One who offered His own soul for her on the cross as a Bridegroom for His bride.

The wonderful and saving plan of God has been worked out in every generation in the history of the church. The elect are always gathered, but that work of God is opposed by the devil. Among the strategems of the devil surely has been an attack on the truth of God's saving plan, as he seeks to create unbelief. But God's grace always triumphs in the elect. The elect, who have received the grace of God, are renewed to the service of God. Far from leading to the neglect of a holy life, the grace of God leads the elect into the church, where they love, worship, and serve their Savior. This church will always be filled with the praises of God for His grace and mercy.

REJECTION OF ERRORS

Rejection 1: Atonement and Effectiveness

The Synod rejects the error of those who teach:

> *"God the Father destined His Son to the death of the cross without a certain and definite plan for saving anyone by name. Therefore the necessity, usefulness, and worth of what the death of Christ accomplished could have remained perfect, complete, and whole in all its parts even if the accomplished redemption had not ever actually been applied to any individual."*

This assertion is contemptuous of the wisdom of God the Father and the merit of Jesus Christ and is contrary to Scripture. Thus the Savior said: "I give My life for My sheep and I know them" (John 10:15, 27). And the prophet Isaiah wrote about the Savior: "When He will sacrifice Himself for sin, He will see His seed and prolong His days and the will of Jehovah will prosper in His hand" (Isa. 53:10). Finally, it overturns the article of faith [in the Apostles' Creed] in which we believe in the church.

The Arminians have always made much of their commitment to a general or unlimited atonement. They say enthusiastically that Christ died for all the sins of all individuals. They insist that these individuals, for whom Christ died, must decide whether His death will be embraced by them and so save them.

This rejection looks at a necessary implication of such teaching and how foolish and impossible it is. If the atonement is not particularly planned by the Father for any particular persons, then it is possible that no person will actually be saved. If the free choice or free will of man is determinative, then all might choose not to embrace Christ's death. Then Christ would never have a people whom He had actually saved.

The synod rightly judges such teaching to be absurd, demeaning to the wisdom of God in planning salvation and to the merit of Christ in achieving salvation. By contrast, the Scriptures teach that Christ did die for a specific people and that He succeeds in saving His own. The synod also appeals to the Apostles' Creed, specifically to the article "I believe a holy catholic Church." If Christ had not actually purchased a people on the cross, we could not believe with certainty that there would be a church. (Rejections II.1–5, 7 expand on elements of article II.8.)

Rejection 2: Atonement and Covenant

The Synod rejects the error of those who teach:

> *"The purpose of the death of Christ was not that He might actually establish a new covenant of grace. Rather, it was only that He might acquire for the Father the bare right of establishing again with men a covenant whether of grace or of works."*

This denies the Scripture, which teaches that Christ "was made the Surety and Mediator of a better," that is, new "covenant" (Heb. 7:22). And, "A testament is of force where there has been a death" (Heb. 9:15, 17).

This error focuses on the relationship of the atonement and the new covenant. Rather than seeing the death of Christ in very personal and saving terms, this error sees the death in abstract and very strange terms.

It says Christ died to empower the Father to make a covenant that can be of whatever character the Father wants. Christ's death fulfills the old covenant, apparently, but seemingly liberates the Father to do whatever He wants for the future.

The synod rejects such teaching, seeing that the Bible declares that Christ intentionally established the new covenant as a covenant of grace in the form in which we now know it. The Father and the Son, together with the Holy Spirit, in eternity planned the whole reality of salvation. This plan included the death of Christ and the establishment of the covenant of grace in that death. This covenant is personal, specific, and effective.

Rejection 3: Atonement and Free Will

The Synod rejects the error of those who teach:

> *"Christ through His satisfaction has not certainly merited for anyone the salvation and faith, by which this satisfaction of Christ is efficaciously applied for salvation. Rather, He has only acquired for the Father the power or the full will, for working anew with men and for prescribing new conditions as He might will. The fulfillment of these conditions so depends on the free will of man that it could be that either no one or every one might fulfill them."*

These teachers think in an exceedingly low way about the death of Christ, and they do not at all recognize the preeminent fruit and benefit of His death. They recall the Pelagian error from hell.

This error focuses on the affirmation of free will. What Christ accomplished on the cross was, as we saw in the last rejection, to empower the Father to set new conditions for salvation. These new conditions so depend on the exercise of the free will of man that either every individual or no individual might be saved.

The synod rejects this error for two reasons. The first reason is that this error seriously degrades the death of Christ by making it ineffectual in itself. The second reason is that by elevating the free will of man, the error revives the condemned heresy of Pelagius. Pelagius was the opponent of Augustine in the debate over the will of man, the grace of God, and predestination. Pelagius defended the freedom of the will against Augustine, who taught the bondage of the will after the fall. The church had since the sixth century decisively condemned Pelagianism as heresy.

Rejection 4: Atonement and Faith

The Synod rejects the error of those who teach:

> *"That new covenant of grace, which God the Father, through the intervention of the death of Christ, made with men, does not consist in this: to the extent that faith accepts the merit of Christ, we are justified and saved before God. But rather the new covenant consists in this: God, having abrogated the demand of perfect legal obedience, counts faith itself and the imperfect obedience of faith for the perfect obedience of the law, and reckons it worthy of the gracious reward of eternal life."*

These teachers contradict the Scripture, "They are justified freely by His grace, through the redemption made in Jesus Christ, whom God put forth as a propitiation in His blood through faith" (Rom. 3:24–25). They teach, like the impious Socinus, a new and strange justification before God, against the consensus of the whole church.

This error is a variant on one that we saw before in rejection I.3. Here, as there, the essential Reformation understanding of faith is abandoned and faith is made an imperfect good work that God accepts for justification.

Those who teach this error are accused of joining the impious and novel views of Socinus. Faustus Socinus is most famous for promoting in the latter sixteenth century a form of Unitarianism. He denied the eternal divinity of Jesus and the doctrine of the Trinity. But in the seventeenth century, he was also notorious for his doctrine of justification, which insisted that Christ did not pay for our justification on the cross but only manifested God's love for us there. Faith did not receive Christ's merit instrumentally for justification but was one condition among many for continuing in a state of justification. The synod utterly rejects this denigration of the merit of the death of Christ.

Rejection 5: Atonement and Original Sin

The Synod rejects the error of those who teach:

> *"All men have been taken into the state of reconciliation and the grace of the covenant so that no one is subject to damnation or will be damned on account of original sin, but all are free from the guilt of this sin."*

This conviction rejects the Scripture, which affirms, "We are by nature children of wrath" (Eph. 2:3).

The errors about the atonement addressed by the synod in this head of doctrine extend in many different directions from the plans of God for the atonement (errors 1, 2) to the effects of the atonement on man (errors 3, 4). Generally, these errors make the atonement in itself ineffectual, as it must wait on human response to be effectual. In error 5, a rather different false teaching is answered. The error is that the death of Christ is so effective that it removes all the guilt of all individuals that resulted from original sin.

Original sin is another Christian doctrine that can strike people as unfair. Why should I be guilty of and suffer the consequences for Adam's sin? That question makes particular sense to those living in a very individualistic culture such as ours. But the Bible is more communal in its thinking, and so salvation as well as guilt is conceived of in corporate terms. If it is not true that in Adam all die, then how can it be true that in Christ all will be made alive (1 Cor. 15:22; cf. Rom. 5)?

The error rejected here wants to eliminate original sin as a continuing problem for justification after the death of Christ. Individuals are guilty of and responsible for only the sins that they individually commit. This error subtly undermines the whole effect and significance of original sin in understanding the human predicament. Here again we see a Pelagian tendency, for it was Pelagius who rejected the biblical and Augustinian teaching of original sin.

The synod rejects this error quite simply and briefly. It cites just part of one Bible verse: Ephesians 2:3. Paul, writing to the Ephesians after the death of Christ on the cross, declares that we are children of wrath. The death of Christ has clearly not removed the guilt of original sin from all.

Rejection 6: Atonement Accomplished and Applied

The Synod rejects the error of those who abuse the distinction between accomplishing and applying, so that they might instill in the careless and inexperienced this opinion:

> *"God for His part wanted to confer on all men equally those benefits which were acquired by the death of Christ. That some participate in the remission of sins and eternal life, while others do not, depends on the proper use of their free will, applying themselves to the grace generally offered to all. It does not depend on a particular gift of mercy efficaciously operating in them by which they, rather than others, apply this grace to themselves."*

For these teachers, while pretending to set forth this distinction in a sound sense, seek to give the people the pernicious poison of Pelagianism.

As we have seen, proper distinctions are essential to sound theology. One of those distinctions is between what Christ accomplished on the cross and what Christ applied to the life and experience of sinners. In a broad sense, we can say that the second head of doctrine is about the accomplishment of redemption and the third and fourth heads of doctrine, as well as the fifth head, are about the application of redemption.

This orthodox and useful distinction between accomplishment and application, however, can be perverted and misused in a way to confuse those who are not well instructed in theology. It is the abuse of this distinction that is addressed in this rejection. The error here is the Arminian claim that the death of Christ accomplished salvation for all, but that the benefits of that death are applied only to those who use their free will to receive it.

This use of the distinction tends to Pelagianism because it rests actual salvation on free will. In orthodox theology, God is sovereign both in the accomplishment and in the application of redemption. This distinction is used properly in articles II.8, 9.

Rejection 7: Atonement and the Love of God

The Synod rejects the error of those who teach:

> *"Christ could not die, nor ought to have died, nor did die for those whom God loved most highly and elected to eternal life, since such people do not need the death of Christ."*

They contradict the Apostle, who said, "Christ loved me and gave Himself for me" (Gal. 2:20). Also, "Who will bring any charge against God's elect? It is God who justifies. Who will condemn? It is Christ who died" (Rom. 8:33–34), namely, died for them. And the Savior asserted, "I give My life for my sheep" (John 10:15). And, "This is My command, that you love one another as I have loved you. Greater love has no one, than that he lay down his life for his friends" (John 15:12–13).

The error addressed here is closely related again to the Socinian error considered in rejection 4 above. Socinus argued that if God loved and freely forgave sinners, then no payment for sin would be or could be required. Love is enough. Orthodox theologians devoted long and sophisticated arguments to answer the Socinians on this point. The summary of this orthodox argument is this: While the forgiveness of sin is free to the sinner, the justice of God must be satisfied and is satisfied in the work of Christ on the cross.

Again, the synod does not enter into a theological argument on this matter but rather cites several texts of the Bible to refute it. These texts all show that the death of Christ is the source of salvation and flows from the love of God.

Chapter 11

THIRD AND FOURTH HEADS OF DOCTRINE:

THE CORRUPTION OF HUMANS, AND THE CONVERSION TO GOD WITH ITS WAY OF HAPPENING

The synod responded to the third and fourth points of the Remonstrance together because only the Arminian teaching on the resistibility of grace clearly shows that their apparently sound teaching on total depravity was not truly meant. The synod titled this section of the canons the third and fourth heads of doctrine, developing the topics of total depravity and irresistible grace together without a break or separation.

Article 1: Man's Created Goodness and Fallen Wickedness

Man was created in the beginning in the image of God. He was adorned with complete holiness. In his mind he had the true and wholesome knowledge of his Creator and spiritual realities. In his will and heart he had righteousness, and in all his affections he had purity. But when he fell away from God by the instigation of the devil and by his own free will, he deprived himself of these excellent gifts. In contrast to the gifts given in creation, he caused in his mind blindness, horrible darkness, vanity, and perverseness of judgment, in his will and heart wickedness, rebellion, and hardness, and in all his affections impurity.

The common Christian conviction at the beginning of this head of doctrine is that man was created by God in the garden of Eden good and in the image of God. Man's holiness was complete in his mind, will, and affections. This threefold theological anthropology was familiar and traditional. The mind as created had true knowledge of God, as the will was righteous and holy, and the affections or emotions were pure.

The goodness of man as created was lost because of the temptations of the devil and by the exercise of Adam's free will. Man was created with free will and freely exercised his will to rebel against God. So Calvinists do indeed believe in human free will—in Adam. In his rebellion, Adam lost the great gifts with which he had been created.

His mind lost his knowledge of God, so that his mind was blind, not seeing the truth. His mind became vain, self-centered, and self-impressed. It became perverse, deliberately accepting the lie. The point here is not that the fallen mind cannot know anything, but that, left to itself, it cannot truly know anything reliable about God.

His will lost its holiness. It became wicked in rebellion against God. It was also hardened against God and His ways. Implicitly, this fallen will is no longer free, but it is now chained to its rebellion. Again, the point is not that the will never chooses anything good from a human point of view but that the will always chooses against God.

Man's affections became impure. The emotions no longer rejoiced in the good but rather rejoiced in the evil. Again, it is not that the emotions never respond to the good or beautiful but that they do not rejoice constantly in God.

Article 2: Original Sin

The kind of man he became after the fall was the kind of children he fathered; namely, corruption produced corruption. By the righteous judgment of God, this corruption passed from Adam to all his pos-terity (Christ only excepted). This corruption passed not through imitation (as the Pelagians in the past said), but by the propagation of a depraved nature.

Fallen man can only propagate fallen progeny. Here is the doctrine of original sin. The sin originally committed by Adam is passed on to all his descendants. This passing on of Adam's sin to his children was according to the righteous judgment of God. So all humans are born guilty and corrupt in Adam.

In the early fifth century AD, a British theologian named Pelagius challenged the doctrine of original sin being taught by Augustine, the bishop of Hippo in North Africa. Pelagius taught that humans were sinners because they learned to copy the lives of other sinners. Although the bad examples around them led most people into becoming sinners, they had the free will to reject sin if they wanted to do so—and some actually had. They were not compelled by anything in their natures to sin. By contrast, Augustine taught that all humans are born guilty and corrupted by Adam's sin, none have free will, and all live in rebellion against God unless liberated by His grace.

In the history of the Western church, Augustine's theology had decisively triumphed over that of Pelagius. For more than a thousand years before the synod, to call someone a Pelagian was to call him a heretic and to condemn his theology. The synod, in raising the name of Pelagius here, is explicitly identifying with the long-standing Augustinian heritage of the church but is also implicitly identifying the Arminians with the Pelagians. The synod explicitly connects the Arminians to the Pelagians a number of times in the rejections of errors as both a theological reality and a valuable strategy.

Article 3: Total Depravity Defined

So all men are conceived in sin. They are born children of wrath, incapable of any saving good, prone to evil, dead in sin, and servants of sin. Without the regenerating grace of the Holy Spirit, they neither can nor want to return to God, correct their depraved nature, or dispose themselves to such correction.

This article elaborates on the meaning and consequences of original sin, defining total depravity. All humans are born dead in sin, incapable of any saving good, and live out their lives in sin and for sin. They are therefore under the wrath of God. They cannot help themselves. They are so lost that they are unable to turn to God, and perhaps even worse, they do not want at all to turn to God or be changed. The only hope for these utterly lost people is for God to take the initiative and act. God must regenerate the lost by His grace for them to be saved.

Article 4: Nature Cannot Regenerate Sinners

Even after the fall, some light of nature remains in humans. This light preserves in man some knowledge of God, of natural matters, and of the difference between things honorable and foul. It also leads to some regard for virtue and outward discipline. But this light of nature is far from bringing a saving knowledge of God or enabling anyone to convert to God. Indeed, it cannot even be used correctly in matters natural and civil. Rather, it renders humans inexcusable before God because they completely pervert it in various ways and suppress it in unrighteousness.

While the canons clearly and unequivocally teach total depravity, the synod here declares that human separation from God does not mean that man cannot know anything at all. The light of nature still shines. This light of nature shines in the general revelation of God in creation and in the remnants of the image of God remaining in fallen man. So, man is not as bad as he could possibly be. Total depravity in relation to God does not mean absolute depravity in every possible way. Fallen man can know some things, even the existence of God. He can learn things about this world and even make some correct moral distinctions in life. He recognizes that some order must be maintained in human relationships to avoid chaos and horror.

This light of nature, however, cannot provide a saving knowledge of God or spark a desire to turn to that God. Indeed, this light of nature is not even sufficient to provide reliable knowledge and action in human matters. Yet, this light shines brightly enough that man is left inexcusable before the judgment of God. As the Apostle Paul teaches in Romans 1, fallen humans reject and suppress the light of a knowledge of God that shines around them. They will not be able to plead ignorance on the last day.

Article 5: The Law Cannot Regenerate Sinners

As it is with the light of nature, so it is with the Ten Commandments, which God gave through Moses to the Jews. This law particularly shows the greatness of sin and convinces humans more and more of their sin. But it does not impart the strength to escape misery, and so through the weakness of the flesh, the sinner remains under the curse. Through the law, man cannot obtain saving grace.

The light of nature has been given to all men. Beyond that light, God has given His law as special revelation to some. At Mount Sinai, God gave Israel His law, summarized in the Ten Commandments, through Moses. This law has great profit for the people of God. This article stresses that the law shows us how great our sin is. The law teaches clearly who we are as sinners. The better we know the law, the more fully we learn our sinfulness.

While the law tells us the truth about ourselves, it does not give us the strength to live differently. The flesh remains powerless, and so the sinner remains lost and hopeless in himself. The law does not and cannot bring grace to the sinner.

Article 6: Regeneration by the Holy Spirit through Preaching

What neither the light of nature nor the law could do, God accomplished by the power of the Holy Spirit. Through preaching or the ministry of reconciliation—which is the gospel of the Messiah—God is pleased to save humans who believe, both in the Old and in the New Testament.

This article is both a statement of catholic conviction and the beginning of a section on how God works regeneration. The only hope and source of regeneration is God's working in the sinner by the power of the Holy Spirit. It takes divine power to change sinners. This article does not detail what the power of the Holy Spirit does, but it focuses on just two elements at this point. Perhaps surprisingly, the article stresses the importance of preaching the gospel of Christ in regeneration. The Spirit uses preaching and the ministry to accomplish His purpose of regeneration. This teaching is very much in harmony with Heidelberg Catechism 65: "Since, then, we are made partakers of Christ and all his benefits by faith only, whence comes this faith? From the Holy Spirit, who works it in our hearts by the preaching of the holy Gospel, and confirms it by the use of the holy sacraments." Regeneration is not to be regarded as so mysterious and so individualistic that the ministry of the church is irrelevant. Quite the opposite. The church and its ministry are central to regeneration.

The other element highlighted here is faith. God regenerates to faith. Faith is at the heart of the life of the redeemed. This salvation for those who believe is essentially the same in the Old Testament and the New Testament. In all times, salvation is by the powerful work of the Holy Spirit in regenerating sinners to faith. Faith alone, the great slogan of the early Reformation, is still being stressed here.

Article 7: Sovereign Regeneration

God revealed the mystery of His will to few in the Old Testament. In the New Testament He shows it to many without any distinction among peoples. The cause of this dispensation is not in the value of one nation above others or the better use of the light of nature. It results from the most free good pleasure and gracious love of God. Those to whom such grace is given, beyond and contrary to all merit, should acknowledge it with humility and a grateful heart. As to the rest, to whom this grace is not given, they ought to adore with the

*Apostle the severity and righteousness of the judgments of God and
ought never to pry into it with curiosity.*

Contrary to the universalistic concerns of the Arminians, this article
shows that God has always focused His saving work on some and not
others. In Old Testament times, one small people were the almost exclusive concern of God's redemptive revelation and work. In the time of the
gospel, that work was extended to many peoples and many parts of the
world, but it has still not reached all. The limited focus of God's work is
not the result of the superiority or moral value of some people above others. Rather, it is solely the result of the choice and good pleasure of God.

In the history of the church—from the time of Paul, through the
time of Augustine, into the Reformation and beyond—many have
rejected the vision of the sovereign will and purpose of God presented in
this article. They feel that it undermines the goodness and love of God.

Two responses are relevant here. First, Calvinists eagerly uphold the
goodness and love of God as revealed in the Scriptures. Goodness and
love are not abstractions to be defined as we will. They must be understood as presented in the Bible. That is why this article refers as it does
to the revelation of the character of God in His saving actions in the Old
Testament and the New Testament.

Second, all must face the serious ethical problem posed in affirm-
ing that the decisive factor in whether a person is redeemed rests in the
person. If the redeemed have made themselves to be the redeemed, then
indeed those redeemed must be in some way superior to those who have
not chosen salvation. (See implications of this doctrine for European history, discussed in the exposition of rejection I.9.) A proper understanding
of God's regenerating work in sinners must create in them humility and
amazement that they are the objects of such love. It must also produce
profound gratitude for such a gift.

As the redeemed come to understand the severity of God's judgment
on those whom He does not regenerate, they will increasingly worship
Him for His righteousness—as they have worshiped Him for His mercy.
God's true character is revealed in both His mercy and His judgment.

But the redeemed must also avoid "curiosity." In medieval theology, curiosity was dangerous speculation into theological matters about which God had not revealed the truth. Curiosity usually sought information that was not spiritually profitable and a desire to know the mind of God beyond what humans could comprehend. Some Reformed theologians have also become curious in trying to understand the ways of God beyond what is revealed to us. The redeemed must learn to replace curiosity with contentment. They can be helped to do that by reading passages in the Bible such as Job 38–39.

Article 8: Sincere Call to Believe

As many as are called through the gospel are seriously called. God seriously and most truly shows in His Word what is pleasing to Him, namely that those called would come to Him. He also seriously promises the rest of souls and eternal life to all who come to Him and believe.

This article again addresses certain caricatures of Calvinism: first, that God does not sincerely and truly call all sinners to Himself in the preaching of the gospel, and second, that He might not accept all who come and believe. The article vehemently rejects both. When the gospel is preached, all who hear it are sincerely and truly called to repent and believe. And everyone who does repent and believe will certainly be saved.

We can see this article as closely related to article 6 above. The mysterious and sovereign work of the Holy Spirit in regenerating the elect does not undermine or render irrelevant the ministry of the Word. Rather, the Spirit works in and through such ministry to call the elect. Preaching remains central and essential.

Article 9: Why Some Do Not Believe

Many who are called through the ministry of the gospel do not come and are not converted. The fault for this is not in the gospel, nor in Christ offered in the gospel, nor in God who calls them through the

*gospel and who confers various gifts on them. Rather, the fault lies
in those called. Some, secure in themselves, do not accept the Word of
life. Others accept it but do not receive it into their hearts. After the
joy of their temporary faith vanishes, they fall away. Still others choke
out the seed of the Word by their difficult cares and worldly desires
and produce no fruit. This our Savior teaches in the parable of the
seed, Matthew 13.*

The article begins with observing that in fact not all who hear the
Word are converted. Why does that happen? The fault is not in God
or in the sincerity of the call to believe. The fault is in the sinners who
refuse to come. In the spirit of Matthew 13:1–23 (the parable of the
sower), the article mentions various reasons why sinners reject the Word.
Some are so secure in the life they are living—whether in false religion or
worldliness—that they see no need to repent or change. Others respond
with "temporary faith." This was a traditional Reformed category. Since
the Bible uses the word *faith* in a variety of ways, not all of which refer
to true, saving faith, Reformed theology distinguished and defined those
uses. One way in which faith was used was labeled "historical faith,"
which meant simply knowing the facts of religion. Such faith even the
devils can have. Another is "temporary faith," which is an impermanent
enthusiasm, but it possesses no real root and has no genuine trust in
Christ. It may seem similar to real faith for a time, but it is entirely different in reality. Still others seem to have a kind of temporary faith, but they
become distracted by the problems of daily life and are led away from the
Word by the attractions of the world. Where the Word is not fruitful, the
fault is in the heart of the hearers, not in God or in His Word.

Article 10: Faith as a Gift of God

*Some called by the ministry of the gospel do come and are converted.
This cannot be ascribed to man as if by his free will he distinguishes
himself from others provided with equal or sufficient grace for faith
and conversion (as the proud heresy of Pelagius states). Rather, God,
who elected them in eternity in Christ, effectively calls them in time,*

and gives to them faith and repentance. Rescuing them from the power of darkness, God transfers them into the kingdom of His Son. Those called and converted should then declare the power of Him who called them out of darkness into this marvelous light. They should glory not in themselves but in the Lord. So the Apostolic Scriptures testify throughout.

Some who hear the gospel accept it and are truly converted. This response must not be credited to the free will and good sense of the hearer. Those lost in sin do not have free will or good sense. Their response must be seen as a gift of God. In a beautiful summary statement, this article reminds us that God gives this gift of faith. First, the article notes that from eternity God had decreed in Christ to give this gift to the elect. Second, in time, He works effectively by His Word and Spirit to call the elect to hear the truth. Third, He gives to the elect who hear the Word the gift of faith and repentance so that they trust the promises of Christ and turn from sin. Fourth, by this gift the elect are rescued from the power of the evil one and transferred into the new life of the kingdom of the Son.

The responsibility of the elect who have received such a marvelous gift is to give all the glory to God. The article alludes to 1 Peter 2:9: "But you are a chosen race, a royal priesthood, a holy nation, a people for his own possession, that you may proclaim the excellencies of him who called you out of darkness into his marvelous light" (ESV). As Peter makes clear, those who receive such extraordinary gifts from God must acknowledge that all they have comes from God. They must not talk about how much they have done and contributed to their own salvation, because in fact they have contributed nothing. This is indeed the testimony of Scripture in many places.

Article 11: God's Work of Regeneration in the Elect Defined

So God executes His good pleasure in the elect and works true conversion in them. He does this not only when He causes the gospel to be preached outwardly to them, but also powerfully illumines their

minds by the Holy Spirit. By this illumination they rightly under-
stand and discern the things of the Spirit of God. By the efficacious
work of this same Spirit, God penetrates the inmost parts of man,
opens the closed heart, softens what is hardened, and circumcises
what is uncircumcised. He infuses new qualities in the will and
makes it alive out of death, good out of evil, willing out of unwilling,
and obedient out of obstinate. God activates and strengthens the will
so that like a good tree, it can bring forth the fruit of good actions.

This article is the one that defines the distinctive Reformed doctrine of God's regenerating and converting work in the elect. It reminds us that God works outwardly for the elect in giving them the preaching of the gospel. God also works inwardly to illumine the minds of those who were previously blind in sin. This illuminating work of the Holy Spirit causes the minds of the elect to understand and discern the truths that they did not see or accept before.

The Spirit also works inwardly to renew the will that had previously been corrupt and self-centered. The renewal of will is presented in several expressions. The inmost person is said to be penetrated, and the heart is said to be opened, softened, and circumcised. The elect are given life, goodness, willingness, and obedience. These expressions come from various places in the Scriptures and explain in various ways the effects of regeneration on the will in the elect. All of this is the result of the efficacious work of the Spirit in and on the will. This renewed will certainly brings forth good fruit in the life of the Christian. This article is really a celebration of the new life that God produces in the elect.

One statement in this article has evoked some discussion among theologians: "He infuses new qualities in the will." Does this imply that the regenerate possess ontological properties that the unregenerate do not possess? Does this mean the regenerate do not share a full common humanity with the unregenerate? While these questions may be interesting, they are really irrelevant to the teaching and purpose of the article. The "new qualities" here are moral and spiritual, not ontological. We can see that clearly by comparing this article with rejection 6 in this head of doctrine. The Arminian error rejected there is this: "In the true conversion of man, new qualities, dispositions, or gifts are not infused into his will by God. The faith by which we are first converted, and from which we are named the faithful, is not a quality or gift infused by God." The orthodox assertion is this: "God does infuse in our hearts new qualities of faith, of obedience, and of a sense of His love." We see that here, as throughout the canons, "will" and "heart" are used as synonyms and that what is infused is faith and obedience. Ontology is clearly not the issue here. Spiritual rebirth is what is meant by these new qualities.

Article 12: Regeneration by God Alone

And this work of God is what is proclaimed so greatly in the Scriptures as regeneration, new creation, resurrection from the dead, and enlivening. God has worked this in us without our working. This is by no means accomplished only through externally spoken teaching or moral persuasion. God does not work in such a way that after the working of God, it remains in man's power to be regenerated or not to be regenerated, to be converted or not to be converted. Rather, this work is wholly supernatural, at once most powerful, secret, and ineffable. It is no less powerful, according to the Scripture (which is inspired by the Author of this work), than the work of creation or the work of raising the dead. All those in whose hearts God works in this amazing way are regenerated certainly, infallibly, and efficaciously so that they actually do believe. For this reason, man also himself is said rightly to believe and repent through this grace which he received.

In this exposition of the canons, I have used the word *regeneration* rather freely, as is the practice in Reformed theology. But in this article, the term *regeneration* is used for the first time in this discussion of irresistible grace. That word has come to be used often in Reformed theology to speak of the sovereign, ineffable work of God in renewing our hearts so that we will believe. This usage represents a change from the way in which the word was used by the Reformed in the sixteenth century. Then, regeneration was used as a synonym for sanctification. (We can see that use in Belgic Confession, article 24, which begins: "We believe that this true faith, being wrought in man by the hearing of the Word of God and the operation of the Holy Spirit, regenerates him and makes him a new man, causing him to live a new life.") But Dort is using *regeneration* in a more limited and technical way, not to refer to the whole course of the new life implanted by the Holy Spirit, but to refer to that operation of the Holy Spirit in bringing new life at the beginning of Christian experience.

Regeneration refers here to that working of God alone, without our working at all. This working of God is not only external through the preaching of the gospel. It is also not a working in the heart that only goes so far as to allow the one worked on either to believe or not to believe. It is not the working of a new ability that may be exercised or not.

Rather, regeneration is a powerful work of God that cannot be seen or fully understood in its operation. The Bible reminds us how supremely powerful this work really is—a truth that we are inclined to forget or undervalue. The power to regenerate the heart of a sinner is as exclusively God's as was His work to create out of nothing at the beginning or to raise the dead back to life. This work is amazing and should be the source of great and humble praise. This regenerating work in the hearts of God's elect certainly produces faith in those hearts. The Christian does indeed believe and repent as an exercise of his mind and will, but he does that only as the result of regenerating grace at work in his heart.

Article 13: What We Do Not Know and What We Do Know

Believers cannot fully understand the way in which God works in this life. Yet for now they rest in this, that they know and experience that through this grace of God, they believe in their hearts and love their Savior.

God works in many ways in history and in our individual lives that we do not fully understand. We may not understand His purpose or His means or all His effects. That is also true of aspects of our regeneration, and it should render us properly humble before the divine majesty. Yet Christians can and do know that they believe in and love Christ. This faith shows them that grace has worked in them even if they do not understand all those workings of grace. This article encourages us to be content with the reality of faith that we experience rather than to become curiously introspective about the mysterious operations of regenerating grace.

Article 14: How Faith Is a Gift

Faith is the gift of God. It is not a gift in the sense that it is offered by God for human choice. Rather, it is really conferred on, breathed into, and infused in man. It is not a gift in which God confers a power to believe, leaving it to the choice of man whether he will consent and perform the act of believing. Rather, God, who works both to will and to do, effects in man the will to believe and the believing itself. Indeed, He works all in all.

This article continues to specify the effective character of God's gift in regeneration. He gives the power to believe and the believing itself. Nothing is left for man to determine. In some ways, this article repeats points that have been made earlier. In this sense, the canons are like preaching, reiterating the truth from different angles. Here the focus is particularly on believing. The canons preserve the Reformation stress on the centrality of faith. If justification is by faith alone, then the source and character of faith must be a central concern—as it is.

Article 15: Reactions to This Grace

God owes this grace to no one. For what might God owe to one who could give nothing to repay Him? Indeed, what might God owe to one who has nothing of his own except sin and falsehood? He, therefore, who receives that grace owes and gives eternal thanks to God alone. He who does not receive it either does not care at all about spiritual matters and is pleased with himself as he is, or he vainly boasts, secure that he has what he does not have. Further, following the example of the Apostles, we ought to judge and speak about those who outwardly profess faith and amend their lives in the most positive way. The secrets of their hearts are unknown to us. As for those not yet called, we should pray to God who calls things that are not as if they were. We ought in no way to be haughty toward those who do not believe as if we made ourselves to differ.

In this article, the synod stresses that God was and is under no obligation to give His grace to any sinner. The sinner in rebellion against God can have no claim on Him or on His mercy. The one, then, who experiences the grace of God must and will be filled with thanksgiving for such an extraordinary and undeserved gift.

By contrast, those who do not receive the grace of God are of two sorts. One sort consists of people who are completely indifferent to all things spiritual and completely self-satisfied in their state. The other sort consists of people who believe that they are Christians and safe even though they do not have true faith at all. Both kinds of unregenerate people are not aware of or concerned about their sin and selfishness.

The fact that some may think that they have faith when they do not might lead people to try to examine and judge the hearts of others seeking to determine if they have true faith. This article warns against such a practice. When Christians relate to other Christians, they must do so as the Apostles did. They must not try to examine the hearts of others but must evaluate people on the basis of what they say and how they live. If they profess the Christian faith and live a life in conformity with Christian standards, they must be received as Christians.

This article also addresses the question as to how Christians should relate to non-Christians. It stresses the call to pray for unbelievers that the Lord would be pleased to give the gift of faith. God alone can know and change hearts. Also Christians must avoid all pride and sense of superiority over unbelievers, for we can claim no credit for the grace of faith that is ours.

Article 16: God Preserves Our Humanity

Man by the fall did not cease to be man, endowed with understanding and will. And sin, which pervades the whole human race, did not destroy the nature of the human race, but depraved it and killed it spiritually. So also the divine grace of regeneration does not act in men as if they were tree trunks or logs, or take away the will and its properties, or force it violently and unwillingly. But this grace spiritually enlivens, heals, corrects, and at once sweetly and powerfully moves the will. Where before rebellion and resistance of the flesh fully dominated the will, now the ready and genuine obedience of the Spirit begins to rule there. In this the true, spiritual restoration and freedom of our will consists. For this reason, unless that admirable Maker of all good acts for us, there is no hope that man would be raised from the fall through free choice. That free choice in which he once stood rather plunged him into ruin.

As the canons stress the powerful and effective action of God in regeneration, so this article makes clear that the objects of grace remain truly and fully human. The saving work of God in no way violates the personal character of the human worked on. As some put it, the Calvinist view of regeneration is no rape of the will. Neither the understanding nor the will of man is ignored or bypassed in the work of God. By grace, the human nature is renewed, enlivened, and sweetly moved. As grace renews the mind and will, the mind and will rejoice in the goodness of what they are receiving. This liberation from blindness and rebellion is freedom indeed.

By contrast, the freedom of the will proclaimed by the Arminians is an illusion and a deception. Their kind of freedom is what led Adam to the fall into sin. The freedom we need is renewal and preservation in grace. Sinners have no freedom to choose God. God must choose and act for them.

Article 17: The Means of Grace

That omnipotent work of God, by which He produces and sustains our natural life, does not exclude but rather requires the use of means.

142

Through these means, God wanted to exercise His power according to His infinite wisdom and goodness. So also this supernatural work of God, which was described before, by which He regenerates us, does not at all exclude or overturn the use of the gospel. The most wise God ordained the gospel as the seed of regeneration and the food of the soul. For this reason, the Apostles and those teachers who followed them have piously taught the people about this grace of God, to His glory and the deflation of all human pride. Still, by the holy admonitions of the gospel, all those teachers did not neglect to keep the people under the administration of the Word, sacraments, and discipline. So far be it from teachers or students to presume to test God by separating those things which God by His good pleasure has wished to be most strongly joined together. Grace is conferred through admonitions. And the more readily we do our duty, the more clearly this benefit of God is usually working in us and the more directly is His work advanced. To Him alone is owed all glory forever for the means He has given and for their saving fruit and efficacy. Amen.

This article first looks to nature and to God's work of creation in order to understand the means God uses to accomplish His purposes. God acts sovereignly to sustain our physical lives, but He does that through various natural means. God gives us our daily bread, but He does that through our sowing, harvesting, grinding, and baking. So also in spiritual and supernatural matters, God uses means to accomplish His ends.

In particular, God uses the means of preaching the gospel to achieve His purposes. As we have seen before, regeneration must not be separated from the Word. While God's work of regeneration in the soul is ineffable and mysterious, it is with and by the Word, just as God created by the Word and Spirit in Genesis 1.

(Again, we must remember that the canons are a statement of confessional conviction, not an exhaustive, systematic theology. They are looking at what theologians have often called the "ordinary" way in which God works. They are not necessarily saying that God cannot or does not work in extraordinary ways in the special cases of those who cannot hear the Word, such as infants who die in infancy or those who are severely mentally handicapped.)

This article states that the Word is the "seed of regeneration," a clear allusion to 1 Peter 1:23: "Since you have been born again, not of perishable seed but of imperishable, through the living and abiding word of God" (ESV). The idea of the Word as seed is also prominent in Matthew 13.

As we begin with the Word, so we continue with the Word, the sacraments, and discipline. These three elements of the life of the church are called the marks by which the church can be identified in the Belgic Confession, article 29. But they are more than that. They also sustain, encourage, and build up the life of the church as a whole and the life of individual Christians. The ministry of the church is used by the Spirit to preserve and grow the seed of new life planted in us. This unity of Word and Spirit is appointed by God and must most carefully be maintained by us. The more careful we are, the greater will be our blessing.

REJECTION OF ERRORS

Rejection 1: Sin and Original Sin

The Synod rejects the error of those who teach:

> *"It cannot properly be said that original sin in itself is sufficient to condemn the whole human race or to deserve temporal or eternal punishments."*

These teachers contradict the Apostle, who said: "Through one man sin entered the world, and through sin death, so that death passed to all men, in that all have sinned" (Rom. 5:12). And verse 16: "The guilt of one leads to condemnation." Also, "The wages of sin is death" (Rom. 6:23).

This rejection of error basically reiterates what was said in rejection II.5 and expands on article III–IV.2. While the second head relates its discussion of original sin to the atonement, here original sin is looked at in itself. As we noted before, the canons are written so that each head of doctrine is complete in itself. Here, different biblical texts are cited, but very much to the same point.

Rejection 2: Sin and the Image of God

The Synod rejects the error of those who teach:

> *"Spiritual gifts, or good dispositions, and virtues, such as goodness, holiness, righteousness, could not have had a place in the will of men when they were first created, and so cannot be separated from it in the fall."*

This fights with the description of the image of God that the Apostle teaches in Ephesians 4:24, where it describes the image in terms of righteousness and holiness, which certainly have a place in the will.

The error here claims that the gifts given to man in creation, such as goodness, holiness, and righteousness, were not part of his will and so the will could not lose them in the fall. The implication is that the loss of these gifts in the fall does not prove that the freedom of the will was lost, since these gifts were not a constitutive part of the will.

In rejecting this error, and in reiterating the teaching of article III–IV.1, appeal is made to Ephesians 4, which shows the complete lostness of sinners and the renewal of them in every part in regeneration: ". . . to put off your old self, which belongs to your former manner of life and is corrupt through deceitful desires, and to be renewed in the spirit of your minds, and to put on the new self, created after the likeness of God in true righteousness and holiness" (vv. 22–24, ESV). This teaching of the Apostle Paul makes clear that the regenerating work of the Holy Spirit does indeed give to the Christian and his will that "true" righteousness and holiness that had been lost in the fall. Again, we see that the Arminian teaching rejected here has moved far from the Remonstrance of 1610, point 3, and clearly denies total depravity.

Rejection 3: Sin and the Will

The Synod rejects the error of those who teach:

> *"The spiritual gifts are not separated from the will of man in spiritual death since the will in itself has never been corrupted. It only was impeded through the darkness of the mind and the disordering of the affections. When these impediments are removed, the will makes natural use of its free faculty, that is, it can either will or choose the good put before it, or it can not will or not choose that good."*

> *This is a novelty and an error that leads to elevating the powers of the free will, contrary to what was said by the prophet Jeremiah: "The heart is deceitful above all things and perverse" (Jer. 17:9); and by the Apostle: "Among whom [sinful men] we all also once lived in the desires of our flesh, following the will and understanding of the flesh" (Eph. 2:3).*

This error, expanding on the previous one, teaches that while the human mind and the affections were corrupted by the fall into sin, the human will was not. The will never lost its ability to act and to choose and so was always free to choose the good if the will was led in that way by the mind and affections.

The synod seems a little surprised by this error, labeling it a novelty. Separating the will from the mind and the affections is a new way to try to maintain the freedom of the will in salvation. The synod again rejects this teaching as contrary to the Scriptures, which do see the will as corrupted in the fall. This rejection relates to article III–IV.3.

Rejection 4: Sin and Remaining Good

The Synod rejects the error of those who teach:

> *"Unregenerate man is not properly or totally dead in sin or destitute of all powers for spiritual good. Rather, he can hunger and thirst after righteousness and life, and can offer the sacrifice of a contrite and broken spirit, which is acceptable to God."*

Against this teaching stands the open testimonies of the Scripture: "You were dead in your trespasses and sins" (Eph. 2:1, 5). And "The imagination of the thoughts of the heart of man is only evil all the time" (Gen. 6:5; 8:21).

This error is a denial of the doctrine of total depravity. It teaches that the unregenerate still can have good spiritual desires and actions. The unregenerate can hunger and thirst after righteousness, which is a quotation from Matthew 5:6. They can also offer to God a contrite and broken spirit, which is a quotation from Psalm 51:17. The problem is that the beatitude of Jesus is spoken to His disciples as those regenerate, and the psalm is a psalm of David where he confesses his sin as a regenerate man. The context of these texts shows the error clearly.

The synod refutes this error again by simply quoting the Scriptures, which show the utter lostness of the unregenerate in sin. The dead have no good spiritual abilities or desires. Here again, this rejection is upholding article III–IV.3.

Rejection 5: Regeneration and Common Grace

The Synod rejects the error of those who teach:

> *"Corrupt, natural man could so rightly use common grace— which is to them the light of nature, or gifts remaining after the fall—so that by using this good he could gradually obtain more grace, indeed evangelical and saving grace and salvation itself. And for this reason, God for His part shows Himself ready to reveal Christ to all. God accomplishes for all both sufficiently and efficiently the means necessary for the revelation of Christ, faith, and repentance."*

This is false, according to the experience of all times, about which Scripture also testifies. "He has shown His words to Jacob, His statutes and laws to Israel; He has not done this to any other nation; they do not know His laws" (Ps. 147:19–20). "In the past ages God let all nations walk in their own ways" (Acts 14:16). "They were prevented [Paul and others with him] by the Holy Spirit from speaking the

Word of God in Asia," and "when they had come into Mysia, they tried to go into Bithynia, but the Spirit did not permit them" (Acts 16:6–7).

The "common grace" spoken of in this error is not at all related to Abraham Kuyper's teaching about common grace and the ensuing debate about his teaching. Rather, here "common grace" refers to a grace that is available to and still present in fallen, unregenerate humans. By using that grace, the unregenerate can gain more grace and reach salvation. God is ready to reveal Christ and has made available all the grace needed for salvation. So it is dependent on man to use the grace available and to add grace to grace.

The synod rejects this error as a denial of the biblical doctrine of total depravity. The error is also contrary to all human experience, meaning that experience shows that the knowledge of Christ is not universally available. The synod then cites specific Scriptures that say the same thing. The Scriptures repeatedly teach that God reveals Himself to some and not to others. This rejection looks more closely at the "light of nature" discussed in article III–IV.4.

Rejection 6: Regeneration and New Qualities

The Synod rejects the error of those who teach:

> "In the true conversion of man, new qualities, dispositions, or gifts are not infused into his will by God. The faith by which we are first converted, and from which we are named the faithful, is not a quality or gift infused by God. It is only an act of man that can be said to be a gift in no other way than with respect to the power of attaining it."

These teachers contradict here the Holy Scriptures, which testify that God does infuse in our hearts new qualities of faith, of obedience, and of a sense of His love. "I will put My law in their minds and write it on their hearts" (Jer. 31:33). "I will pour out water upon the thirsty and streams upon the dry land; I will pour out My Spirit upon your seed" (Isa. 44:3). "The love of God is shed abroad in our hearts by the Holy Spirit who has been given to us" (Rom. 5:5). This is also repugnant to the continual practice of the church, which prays with the prophet, "Convert me, Lord, and I will be converted" (Jer. 31:18).

The error here relates to the question about what exactly God gives to sinners in true conversion. The focus of this error is to teach that God does not give or infuse any new qualities to the will of man and does not give the gift of faith. The only gift God has given is the original power of choice to the will of man at creation.

Such a view contradicts the teachings of Scripture that God does give gifts to His own, gifts of knowledge, faith, obedience, and love. It also violates the prayer of the church through the ages that God would act to convert us.

This rejection is particularly important because it clarifies the teaching of article III–IV.11 about these new qualities in the will (cf. article III–IV.16). As we saw, some have asked if these new qualities create an ontological difference between the regenerate and the unregenerate. More pointedly, are the regenerate more human than the unregenerate? Clearly, this is not what the canons are teaching. The new qualities are gifts that liberate from various effects of the fall and renew sinners to life. The regenerate are not different kinds of humans. Their new qualities are faith, obedience, and love.

Rejection 7: Regeneration and Moral Persuasion

The Synod rejects the error of those who teach:

> *"The grace by which we are converted to God is nothing other than a gentle persuasion. Others explain this grace, the noblest manner of working in the conversion of man and the most appropriate to human nature, as working by persuasions. Nothing prevents this moral grace alone from rendering the natural man spiritual. Indeed, God does not produce the consent of the will in any other way than by moral means.*

In this consists the efficacy of divine working, by which the work of Satan is surpassed, namely, that God promises eternal goods while Satan promises only temporal goods."

This is entirely Pelagian and contrary to the whole Scripture. Scripture, against this error, recognizes another much more efficacious and divine manner of working by the Holy Spirit in the conversion of man. "I will give you My heart and I will give you a new spirit in place of the old. I will take away your heart of stone and I will give you a heart of flesh" (Ezek. 36:26).

If the new qualities infused into the will of the regenerate do not represent a basic ontological change, then is conversion simply a matter of moral persuasion? The error here holds that the natural man can be persuaded by moral arguments and can respond to those arguments so that he becomes a spiritual man. The efficacy of divine grace consists in the superiority of its arguments to the arguments of Satan. Satan promises only benefits in this world, while God promises eternal benefits. The natural man has the wisdom and the ability to see that the divine promises are better and to respond to them.

This error is remarkably naive about the nature of the fall and of sin and is rightly labeled "entirely Pelagian." This error is not just semi-Pelagian or tending in the Pelagian direction. This error, like the error of Pelagius, sees no need for grace beyond the "grace" given to man in creation. This error also rejects the teaching of the Bible on the sovereign work of the Holy Spirit in conversion. In conversion, the Holy Spirit not only persuades, He re-creates. This rejection expands on article III–IV.12.

Rejection 8: Regeneration and Human Resistance

The Synod rejects the error of those who teach:

"God in the regeneration of man does not use the powers of His omnipotence, by which He might powerfully and infallibly turn man's will to faith and conversion. God has accomplished all the workings of grace which He uses for converting man. Nevertheless, man can resist and actually

often does resist God when the Spirit intends man's regeneration and wills to regenerate him. Man can certainly impede his regeneration. Indeed, it remains in man's own power whether he will be regenerated or not."

This is nothing other than to remove all efficacy of the grace of God in our conversion. It subjects the action of the omnipotent God to the will of man, contrary to the Apostles, who teach: "We believe because of the efficacy of the strength of His might" (Eph. 1:19). And "God powerfully fulfills in us the gracious benevolence of His kindness and the work of faith" (2 Thess. 1:11). Also, "His divine power has given us all things which pertain to life and piety" (2 Peter 1:3).

This error teaches that God in conversion does not use all His divine power to accomplish His purpose certainly and finally. Rather, even after God has done all His part in preparing for the conversion of man, man still has the power to resist and reject that grace. Man not only has that power but also uses it. Ultimately, it is in the power of man to become regenerated or to refuse regeneration.

The synod rightly sees that this error places the power of man over the power of God as decisive in conversion and removes all effectiveness from divine grace. This error is contrary to the repeated teachings of Scripture on the unfailing effectiveness of divine power in conversion. This rejection relates to part of article III–IV.16.

Rejection 9: Regeneration, Grace, and Free Will

The Synod rejects the error of those who teach:

"Grace and free will are the partial causes concurring together for the beginning of conversion. Grace is not antecedent in the order of causality to the efficacy of the will." That is, "God does not efficaciously help the will of man to conversion before that the will of man moves and determines itself."

This teaching of the Pelagians was condemned long ago by the ancient church, in accordance with the Apostle: "It is not to him who wills or runs but to God who shows mercy" (Rom. 9:16). And "Who makes you different?" and "What do you have that you have not received?" (1 Cor. 4:7). Also "God Himself works in you to will and to do for His good pleasure" (Phil. 2:13).

This error tries to be more subtle than errors 7 and 8 above. It asserts that grace and free will work together to begin conversion. But it then goes on to insist that grace does not act first in conversion or make the will of man able to act. Rather, the will always retains its abilities to act, and free will is as decisive as grace is.

This error is again labeled Pelagian because grace is not decisive but must cooperate on rather equal terms with the free will of man. Again, pointed Scriptures are cited to show that God acts and accomplishes conversion in the sinner. This rejection elaborates on article III–IV.14.

Chapter 12

FIFTH HEAD OF DOCTRINE:

THE PERSEVERANCE

OF THE SAINTS

The doctrine of perseverance embraced by the Reformed was perhaps their most unique doctrine. The uniqueness lay in their teaching that the believer could know that he would persevere by the grace of God. Robert Bellarmine, the great Jesuit theologian of this period, declared that this was the worst heresy of the Reformed. While the Remonstrance of 1610 had claimed uncertainty about this doctrine, it is clear that by the time of the synod, many Arminians had utterly rejected this teaching. They, like Bellarmine, had concluded that this doctrine would lead to moral laxity. The synod carefully and clearly shows what its teaching on this point truly is, and it shows that the charges brought against it are false.

Article 1: Sin Remains in the Regenerate

God, according to His purpose, calls people to communion with His Son our Lord Jesus Christ and regenerates them through His Holy Spirit. He liberates all of these people from the dominion and servitude of sin, but He does not liberate them completely from the flesh and the body of sin in this life.

The fruit of regeneration in the lives of God's people is remarkable indeed. As all Christians confess, the Holy Spirit frees us from the dominion of and slavery to sin. We are no longer entirely controlled and directed by sin in our alienation from God. But we are not completely or fully liberated from sin in this life. Sin continues to be present in and with us. As Christians, we continue to face a lifelong battle against the sin that remains in us. This opening article again begins with a catholic Christian conviction from which the head of doctrine will develop its teaching.

Article 2: The Regenerate Must Constantly Pursue Sanctification

From this continuing sin, the daily sins of weakness arise and blemishes adhere to even the best works of the saints. These sins and blemishes provide a constant cause for the saints to humble themselves before God and to flee for refuge to Christ crucified. The saints seek to mortify the flesh more and more through the Spirit of prayer and through holy exercises of piety. They long for the goal of perfection, until, delivered from this body of death, they reign with the Lamb of God in heaven.

Even the best works that Christ's people perform in this life are marred by sin. This is traditional Christian teaching. The Heidelberg Catechism expresses this powerfully in question and answer 114: "But can those converted to God keep these commandments perfectly? No. In this life even the holiest have only a small beginning of this obedience. Nevertheless, with earnest purpose they do begin to live not only according to some but to all the commandments of God."

How do Christians respond to this problem of continuing sin? This article teaches that the reality of sin in our lives must first humble us. Any temptation to pride in being a Christian or sense of superiority over others must be rejected. *My* sin must humble *me* before *my* God.

This humility must lead us to seek our hope, refuge, and deliverance in Christ alone. His crucifixion is our peace and mercy. In Christ, we will be able more and more to put the flesh to death in us. This mortification is a lifelong process with various ups and downs, for which we gain strength through a life of piety.

Prayer is critical, as we seek the Spirit to help us in our struggle. So are the various exercises of the Christian life from public worship to private devotion. We must also keep before us the goal of perfection, which awaits us in heaven, when we will finally be delivered from all sin. Calvin very much commended to us the discipline of meditating on the future life (see *Institutes of the Christian Religion* 3.9). Such meditation would keep us heavenly minded in the best sense (Col. 3:1)—longing for heaven as fulfilled fellowship with God and final glory beyond all the corruption of sin.

The "body of death" is an allusion to Paul's letter to the Romans and its reflection on the problem of sin in the life of the Christian (Rom. 6:12; 7:24; 8:6, 10–11). In Romans, the contrast is drawn between who we really are in Christ—our inner man—and the remnants of the old man still in us—our outer members. This struggle is the source of great frustration, but also of progress in the Christian life.

Article 3: Perseverance Defined

Because of these remnants of indwelling sin and of the temptations of the world and Satan, the converted could not remain in this grace if they were left to their own powers. But God is faithful. He mercifully confirms them in the grace once given and powerfully preserves them in it even to the end.

The problems that a Christian faces in living the life of faith are real and great. Sin continues to dwell within us and influence us. The world opposes the things of Christ and seeks to tempt Christians away from faithfulness. Satan, who tempted Christ in the wilderness, continues to assail His people. These problems are so great that they would overwhelm and destroy a Christian left to his own powers and resources. We always need the grace and power of God to preserve us in the Christian life. We must indeed pray: "Lead us not into temptation. Deliver us from the evil one."

Here is the canons' simple definition of the Reformed doctrine of perseverance. We persevere in the life of faith only because God is faithful to His plans and promises and merciful despite our sins. He keeps us in the grace that was ours at our regeneration and preserves us in it all through our life to the very end.

Article 4: The Regenerate Can Fall into Serious Sins

That power of God, which truly confirms and preserves the faithful in grace, is greater than that which could be overcome by the flesh. Still, the converted are not always so led and moved by God that they cannot in particular actions fall back from the leading of grace by their own fault. They can be seduced by the desires of the flesh and gratify them. For this reason, they ought always to watch and pray for themselves so that they might not be led into temptations. When they do not do this, they can be carried off by the flesh, the world, and Satan, even into serious and dreadful sins. Indeed, sometimes they actually are carried off by the just permission of God. This is shown by the sad falls into serious sin of David, Peter, and other saints as described in the Holy Scriptures.

Articles 4–8 reflect on various aspects of the continuing problem of sin in the lives of those whom God is preserving. That preservation is not automatic or mechanical. It does not always proceed steadily, nor is it always progressive. The Christian life is always personal. We have personal responsibility to resist sin and seek God through the means He has appointed. God remains always personal in His provisions and helps to us.

Our continuing weakness and sinfulness mean that we can retreat rather than advance at times in the Christian life. Instead of pursuing grace and holiness, we can succumb to the desires of the flesh and sin against God. The only way to prevent this is to watch and pray. That was the admonition that Jesus gave to Peter, James, and John in Gethsemane (Luke 22:39–46). What they failed to heed, we must follow. But we also can fail.

Such failure is not always a matter of minor sins but can involve the Christian in the most serious sins imaginable. The examples of David and Peter are cited here. Adultery, murder, and apostasy—some of the very worst sins—are possible for the Christian. Yet even such sins cannot separate us from the love of God for us in Christ Jesus.

Article 5: Serious Consequences of Serious Sins

By such very great sins, the faithful certainly offend God, incur deadly guilt, grieve the Holy Spirit, interrupt the exercise of faith, and most gravely wound the conscience. Sometimes, for a time, they lose a sense of grace, until through serious repentance they return to life so that the fatherly countenance of God shines again upon them.

Although Christians are elected, regenerate, and promised preservation, the effects of serious sins in their lives are very great indeed. First, such sins offend God. For a Christian, this should be a truly horrible thought. Our love for God should be so great that offending Him and grieving His Spirit should trouble and sadden us profoundly. Today, we often focus on the consequences of sin in our relationships with other people, but our first thought should be of its offense to God.

Second, we must remember that sin remains sin. It is a violation of God's holy law and makes us guilty before the bar of God's justice. For this reason, we must pray throughout our lives, "Forgive us our debts."

Third, such sins interrupt the exercise of faith. The point here is not that the reality of faith disappears but that the blessings of faith in joy and comfort and the uses of faith in prayer and worship may seem not to be operating. The gravely wounded conscience loses something of its sensitivity to sin, and yet at some level the conscience is pained by every consideration of the reality of sin.

At its worst moments, such sin may deprive the Christian of a sense of grace (though not of grace itself). As Peter went out and wept bitterly after denying Jesus three times (Luke 22:62), so a Christian may feel bereft of the love of God for him for a season.

This sad condition ends only when the grace of God leads the sinful Christian to repentance—that is, to a genuine recognition of the offense of the sin and a genuine turning from it. When a Christian repents sincerely, he again experiences the presence and love of God, so beauti-fully expressed in the Aaronic blessing (Num. 6:24–26) as God's face of blessing shining on them.

Article 6: God Preserves His Own

God, who is rich in mercy, because of His immutable purpose of elec-tion, does not utterly take away the Holy Spirit from the converted even in their sad falls. Neither does He let them fall so far that they lose the grace of adoption or the state of justification. He does not let them commit the sin unto death or the sin against the Holy Spirit or be so utterly deserted by the Spirit as to rush into eternal destruction.

While article 5 shows how very serious sin is in the life of the Chris-tian, this article shows that even the most grievous sins do not result in the loss of God's grace and mercy altogether. God always completes the good work He begins (Phil. 1:6). God never lets go of His own. This means that even in the midst of the most calamitous falls into sin, there is hope and comfort when we turn to God. The Holy Spirit remains with us even when grieved or apparently quenched. When we speak of the per-severance of the saints, we recognize the reality of all the struggles in the lives of the saints, but also that they ultimately move toward God. This perseverance occurs because God is always active preserving His own. The perseverance of the saints is the fruit of the preservation of the saints.

Even in grievous sin, we remain the adopted children of God and continue to be justified before Him. These definitive personal and legal connections to God are not severed even by serious sin. (Neither adop-tion nor justification is defined here. Remember, the canons are not a full systematic theology. They assume a knowledge of the meaning of these terms from the Belgic Confession, articles 22–24, and Heidelberg Catechism 32–33, 60–62).

Many Christians worry about committing an unforgivable sin, either the sin against the Holy Spirit (Matt. 12:22–32) or the sin unto death (1 John 5:16). Here the canons assure them that true Christians cannot commit such sins. Such sins are committed only by those who perseveringly oppose and reject the work of Christ and His Spirit in building the kingdom of God. This is never true of real Christians. Here is reassurance indeed. We cannot be lost.

Article 7: God's Restoration of the Fallen

In the first place, God conserves in the elect even in their falls His imperishable seed by which they were regenerated so that it might not be lost or cast away. Next, He renews them to repentance certainly and efficaciously through His Word and Spirit, so that they have heartfelt sorrow to God for their sins. Out of a contrite heart, through faith, they both seek and obtain forgiveness in the blood of the Mediator. They experience again the grace of a reconciled God, adore His mercies through faith, and then eagerly work out their salvation with fear and trembling.

This article summarizes the process by which God works in His elect when they fall into sin. The first point is that the seed of regeneration, planted by the Spirit through the Word, never dies in the elect (see the exposition on article III–IV.17 and 1 Peter 1:23). Next, we are reminded that God will certainly act to bring His regenerated elect back to sincere repentance and sorrow for the sin into which they have fallen. Again, He does this by His Word and Spirit. The Word brings God's holy will to our minds and the Spirit applies it to our hearts to move us. Faith in the elect looks again clearly and powerfully to Christ to find mercy and forgiveness in Him. This faith is aware anew of the blessing of being a child of God and led on to deeper love for God and the eager pursuit of living faithfully for Him. There is nothing mechanical or automatic here, but a beautiful picture of the personal movements of the soul in relationship to the Father, Son, and Holy Spirit.

Article 8: God's Unfailing Preservation

They obtain this not by their merits or powers but from the gracious mercy of God so that they do not fall away totally from faith and grace nor finally remain and be lost in their falls. Such loss not only could happen but certainly would happen if they were left to themselves. But with respect to God, it could not possibly happen, because His plan cannot be changed, His promise cannot fail, nor can the call according to His purpose be recalled. Neither could the merit, intercession, and protection of Christ be rendered void, nor could the sealing of the Holy Spirit be frustrated or destroyed.

This process of reconciliation and restoration after serious falls into sin is entirely from the mercy and grace of God. We cannot earn it and, left to ourselves, have no power to maintain it. In our weakness, we would only produce hopelessness and indifference in ourselves. Despite our weakness, God's grace motivates us to look to God alone for hope and help. God's purpose cannot fail or be thwarted even by us. Again, we see the Trinitarian God at work. The Father's plan, the Son's provision and protection, and the Spirit's preservation cannot and will not fail.

Article 9: The Privilege of Assurance

Concerning this protection of the elect for salvation and the preservation of true believers in faith, the believers themselves can be certain of it. Indeed, they are certain according to the measure of their faith. By that faith they certainly believe that they are and always will remain true and living members of the church and have the remission of sins and eternal life.

Articles 9–13 deal with the issue of assurance in the life of the Christian, specifically whether a Christian can know that he is elect and will persevere in faith. This matter of assurance is a basic element of Reformed theology and receives a great deal of discussion by various theologians. (In these articles, the Latin word *certitudo,* often translated "assurance" in other translations, in this translation is usually rendered "certainty.") This assurance of preservation and protection is a reality in the lives of the elect of which they can be aware and certain.

This article asserts that the process of sanctification and the preserving protection of God is a reality in the lives of the elect of which they can be aware and certain. Our loving heavenly Father does not leave us to doubt and confusion and uncertainty. Scripture nowhere makes a virtue of doubt about our relationship with God. Faith trusts in the promises of God that His love and mercy will never fail. The more that faith grows, the more assured and confident it will be.

Article 10: The Source of Assurance

This certainty is not derived from some particular revelation made beyond or outside the Word. But this certainty comes from faith in the promises of God, which God has revealed most abundantly in His Word for our comfort. It also comes from the testimony "of the Holy Spirit testifying with our spirit that we are the children and heirs of God" (Rom. 8:16). Next, it comes from a serious and holy desire for a good conscience and good works. And if in this life the elect of God were deprived of this solid comfort of obtaining the victory and of the unfailing guarantee of eternal glory, they would be of all men the most miserable.

This article addresses the source of our certainty or assurance. This source is not in some special revelation given to individuals through feelings, or extreme introspections, or trying to climb into heaven to peer into the Book of Life. Rather, we find assurance first by looking with faith to the promises of the Bible that God has made to His children. These promises are applied to our hearts by the Holy Spirit, giving us assurance that the promises are indeed for us.

This assurance is also encouraged by seeing the change made in our lives by the Holy Spirit. Although even our best works are still marred by sin, the regenerating grace of the Holy Spirit truly changes us. We desire holiness and begin to live differently. That change of life, joined to our faith in God's promises, helps us grow in assurance and in the certainty of salvation.

The assurance of salvation—now and forever—is one of the great blessings of the Christian life. We would be miserable and sad indeed if we lived full of doubt and uncertainty about our present relationship with God and even greater uncertainty about what will happen to us in the future. God as our loving Redeemer wants us to know with confidence that we belong to Him—now and forever.

The discussion of assurance in Reformed theology has been long and detailed, with some disagreements. But here we have the foundational, essential elements of this doctrine. The promises of the Word and the reality of a changed life are applied by the Holy Spirit to the faith of the elect to bring comfort, peace, and certainty of salvation.

Article 11: Assurance and Doubt

Further, Scripture testifies that believers in this life may be conflicted with various carnal doubts. They may in grave temptations not always experience the fullness of faith and certainty of perseverance. Truly, God, the Father of all comfort, will not let them be tempted beyond their ability, but with the temptation will provide the way of escape (1 Cor. 10:13). And through the Holy Spirit, He will awaken again in them the certainty of perseverance.

The certainty of salvation is not always a completely stable and steady experience in the life of the believer. Faith trusts God and has a measure of confidence, but it still can be attacked by various doubts and temptations. At times, those doubts and temptations can be so strong that they diminish faith and assurance. Those temptations will never ultimately overwhelm the Christian. God will give a way of escape and will send the Holy Spirit to strengthen us in faith and assurance.

Article 12: Assurance and Piety

This certainty of perseverance is far from making believers proud or carnally secure. On the contrary, it is the true root of humility, filial reverence, true piety, patience in all afflictions, ardent prayers, constancy in cross-bearing and in confessing the truth, and solid joy in God. The consideration of this benefit is a stimulus for serious and continual exercise of gratitude and good works, as is evident from the testimonies of Scripture and the examples of the saints.

This article addresses the effects of assurance on the life and piety of the Christian. The critics of the doctrine of the perseverance of the saints always claim that it will have disastrous effects on the way we live. First, they say, it will make us proud, just as they say that the notion that we are elect will make us proud. Second, they say that it will make us so confident and secure in our status that we will live carelessly or presumptuously, thinking that we can give ourselves over to sin because God is stuck with us.

The real effect of the doctrine of perseverance in the lives of true believers is just the opposite. It encourages us out of thankfulness to be humble, reverent, and pious. It encourages us to be patient in suffering, knowing that God has not and will not abandon us. It leads us to pray, knowing our personal God will hear and help. It strengthens us in truth and joy in all circumstances. The Bible and the experiences of the saints throughout church history show that in fact this doctrine strengthens holy living rather than undermining it.

This point is underscored in the history of Reformed people at the time of the Synod of Dort and afterward. In the Netherlands, the most committed Calvinists were called "precisionists." In England, they were called Puritans. Such people were clearly not secure in their sins or indifferent to holiness.

Article 13: Assurance, Restoration, and Careful Living

A revived confidence of persevering does not produce in those restored from a fall immorality or harm their piety. Rather, with much greater concern, they carefully keep the ways of the Lord which were prepared for them to walk in. In this way, they retain the certainty of perseverance, lest because of the abuse of His fatherly kindness, God would again turn away from them His favorable face and they would fall into more grievous torments of the soul. (The contemplation of His favor is sweeter to the pious than life; the loss of that favor is more bitter then death.)

Even more specifically, this article addresses the situation of those who have been restored from falls into serious sins. Such restoration does not encourage carelessness but rather encourages greater carefulness in the future. Certainly, Peter after his restoration from his sin of apostasy was more faithful and confident in his service to Christ. Diligence like Peter's is necessary, for it is again possible to fall into serious sin and again experience God's severe displeasure.

Article 14: Perseverance and the Means of Grace

It has pleased God to begin His work of grace in us through the preaching of the gospel. So He preserves, continues, and completes this work through the hearing, reading, and meditating on its exhortations, threats, and promises and through the use of the sacraments.

As in the other heads of doctrine, this article states the importance of the means of grace in sustaining the Christian life. As the Spirit works with the Word to begin the life of grace, so He continues to work through it for the well-being of the elect. The Christian is called to hear the Word preached as well as to read and reflect on it privately. All the dimensions of the Word are vital for us: the exhortations that direct us, the threatenings that warn us, and the promises that comfort us. We need all of them always.

Today, some insist that the word *gospel* should only be used strictly to refer to the saving work of Christ and the promise of salvation. But in the Bible and in the history of theology, *gospel* is sometimes used in this strict sense and sometimes in a broader sense, referring to all the teaching of the New Testament. It is used in that broader sense here.

The Word of God and sacraments as the visible Word of promise are also crucial in the life of the Christian and the Christian community. The Spirit works in and through these means to preserve Christians in faith, in hope, and in the pursuit of holiness.

Article 15: Perseverance and Consolation

God has most abundantly revealed in His Word this doctrine concerning the perseverance of true believers and saints and its certainty. He revealed it for the glory of His name and the consolation of pious souls. He impresses it on the hearts of believers. The flesh does not understand this doctrine, Satan hates it, the world derides it, the ignorant and the hypocrites abuse it, and the spirits of error fight against it. But the bride of Christ has always loved it most tenderly as a treasure of incalculable value and she has constantly fought for it. God—against whom no plan can avail and no power can prevail—will take care that she will esteem it always.

This article declares that the doctrines of perseverance and assurance are not peripheral or obscure. This statement is directed against the Arminians who had claimed in their Remonstrance of 1610 that they were uncertain about the doctrine of perseverance and needed to study it more, although they had had years to do so. The canons insist that the doctrines of perseverance and assurance are fully and repeatedly revealed in the Bible. God wanted His people to know these truths because this knowledge glorifies God in His power, mercy, goodness, and love for them. It is also wonderfully comforting to the faithful in the various struggles of their lives. It is so important that God not only reveals it clearly in the Word but also sends His Spirit to plant it deeply in the hearts of His people to encourage them.

While God and His people love the doctrine of perseverance, others do not. People still in the flesh do not understand it and misrepresent it. Satan hates it for the blessing it brings the godly. The world mocks it, thinking in its unbelief that the doctrine must cause carelessness. The ignorant (not knowing any better) and the hypocrites (misusing all God's good gifts) use it improperly. Those trapped in error oppose it viciously. But none of these opponents should discourage us. Indeed, God's people love it as a treasure of immense value and have labored to know it, protect it, and teach it. This conviction God Himself plants in His church and will always preserve it there.

REJECTION OF ERRORS

Rejection 1: Perseverance as Condition

The Synod rejects the error of those who teach:

"The perseverance of the truly faithful is not the effect of election or the gift of God acquired by the death of Christ. Rather, it is a condition of the new covenant, which man must fulfill by his free will before his 'decisive' (as they called it) election or justification."

For the sacred Scripture testifies that perseverance follows from election, and that the power of the death, resurrection, and intercession of Christ is given to the elect. "The elect obtained it, the rest were hardened" (Rom. 11:7). Also, "He who did not spare His own Son, but gave Him up for us all, how will He not with Him give us all things? Who will bring any charge against the elect of God? It is God who justifies. Who is it who condemns? Christ is the One who died, who indeed was also raised, who also sits at the right hand of God, who also intercedes for us: who will separate us from the love of Christ?" (Rom. 8:32).

The error condemned here has several elements. The first is that election does not guarantee perseverance and that the death of Christ did not earn perseverance for the elect. Rather, perseverance is a condition of the new covenant that must be fulfilled by believers. The second is that this condition must be fulfilled by the free will of man. The clear implication is that this free will may or may not fulfill the condition. Third, while a believer may in some sense be elect or justified, he is not ultimately elect or justified until he perseveres to the end.

Any distinction between "initial" and "final" election and justification, however, is contrary to the teaching of the Reformation and of the Bible. The synod cites the Scripture to show that perseverance is indeed the gift of God that flows from election and from the death of Christ. This point follows on article V.8.

Rejection 2: Perseverance and the Will

The Synod rejects the error of those who teach:

"God indeed provides the faithful man with sufficient powers for perseverance, and is prepared to preserve them in him

if he does his duty. God had done for everyone those things that are necessary for persevering in faith and that God wanted to use for preserving faith. But perseverance always depends on the choice of man's will whether he perseveres or does not persevere."

This conviction contains obvious Pelagianism, and while it wants to make men free, it actually makes them sacrilegious. It stands against the perpetual consensus of evangelical doctrine, which takes from man all matter for glorying, and ascribes the praise of this benefit to the grace of God alone. This conviction is contrary to the testimony of the Apostle: "God is the One who will confirm us blameless until the end in the day of our Lord Jesus Christ" (1 Cor. 1:8).

Here the error is that God provides for believers sufficient power and grace so that they can persevere. These powers and graces will succeed if believers do their duty in using those gifts. Still, despite all of God's actions, it remains up to the individual wills of believers whether they will actually persevere to the end.

The error is again labeled Pelagian, as it trades real grace for human freedom. Real grace always leads to humility and praise to God. It also contradicts the Scriptures. This too follows on article V.8.

Rejection 3: Perseverance and Falling from Grace

The Synod rejects the error of those who teach:

"Those truly believing and regenerate can fall away finally and totally from being justified by faith, as well as from grace and salvation. More than that, they frequently actually do fall from them, and perish for eternity."

This opinion renders void the very grace of justification and regeneration and the perpetual care of Christ, against the express words of the Apostle Paul: "If Christ died for us, when we were still sinners, how much more will He through it save from wrath those justified in His blood?" (Rom. 5:8–9). Also against the Apostle John: "He who is born of God does not commit sin because His seed remains in him, and he cannot sin because he is born of God" (1 John 3:9). And also against the words of Jesus Christ: "I give eternal life to My sheep, and they will not perish in eternity, and no one may rip any of them from My hand. My Father who gave them to Me is greater than all, and no one can rip them from the hand of My Father" (John 10:28–29).

This error, which we have seen in other forms in other heads of doctrine, declares that those who have truly been regenerated and have true faith can fall away and be lost. Not only can this happen, but it actually does happen.

The synod rejects this error sharply because it undermines the true biblical doctrine of justification and regeneration. It also destroys our confidence that Christ always watches over and protects His own. Paul, John, and Jesus are quoted to show how great and complete this protection is. This rejection supports article V.6.

Rejection 4: Perseverance and the Sin unto Death

The Synod rejects the error of those who teach:

> *"The truly faithful and regenerate can sin the sin unto death, or the sin against the Holy Spirit."*

After the Apostle John (in 1 John 5:16–17) mentioned those who had committed the sin unto death and had forbidden to pray for them, he immediately joins verse 18 to it: "We know that whoever is born of God does not sin [namely, that kind of sin unto death], but God keeps him who is born of God, and the evil one does not touch him."

The error here touches on a very sensitive pastoral point. Can true believers commit the sin against the Holy Spirit or the sin unto death? The error answers decisively: yes.

The synod not only rejects the error but helpfully explains how the teaching of John on the sin unto death should be understood (1 John

5:16–18). The sin unto death is specifically ruled out as possible for those born of God, as 1 John 5:18 clearly shows. God keeps His own and protects them from the devil and from anything that might threaten the souls of the elect. The synod does not here explain the Bible's teaching on the sin against the Holy Spirit. But implicit here is the whole teaching of the canons, namely, that the same Spirit who regenerates and protects the elect will keep them from this deadly sin against Himself.

Rejection 5: Perseverance and Certainty

The Synod rejects the error of those who teach:

> *"No certainty of future perseverance can be had in this life without special revelation."*

By this doctrine the solid comfort of the truly faithful in this life is taken away and the doubting of the papists is reintroduced to the church. The sacred Scripture throughout requires this certainty, not by special and extraordinary revelation, but from the proper signs of the children of God and the most constant promises of God. Especially the Apostle Paul teaches, "Nothing created can separate us from the love of God which is in Christ Jesus our Lord" (Rom. 8:39). And John, "All who keep His commandments, remain in Him, and He in them; and by this we know that we remain in Him, by the Spirit whom He gave us" (1 John 3:24).

The statement of the error here is very carefully put. All students of the Bible must recognize that individuals in the Bible have certainty of their salvation. Such certainty, this error teaches, is not proper for all believers, but only for a few who receive special revelation about their spiritual state.

The synod rightly responds to this error by pointing out that it is the same teaching as that of the Roman Catholics. The synod rejects this medieval teaching of doubt and fear and upholds the great comfort for Christians found in the biblical doctrine of assurance. This assurance is the right and proper possession of all true believers. See article V.10 for the developed presentation of this teaching.

Rejection 6: Perseverance and Piety

The Synod rejects the error of those who teach:

> *"The doctrine of perseverance and the certainty of salvation, from its nature and inherent quality, is an easy seat for the flesh, and harmful to piety, good morals, prayers, and other holy exercises. On the contrary, to doubt this doctrine is truly praiseworthy."*

These teachers show that they do not know the efficacy of divine grace and the working of the indwelling Holy Spirit. They contradict the Apostle John, who affirms the opposite with these express words: "My beloved, we are now the children of God, but it does not yet appear what we will be. We know that when He shall appear, we will be like Him, for we will see Him as He is. And whoever has this hope in him, purifies himself, as He is pure" (1 John 3:2–3). Furthermore, the examples of the saints of the Old as well as the New Testament refute it, who, notwithstanding their certainty of perseverance and salvation, nevertheless were assiduous in prayers and other exercises of piety.

As we have seen, the impact of theology on piety has been a foundational concern of the canons. The error addressed here brings a very serious charge against the Reformed teaching. The charge is that the doctrine of perseverance necessarily leads the flesh (presumably in believers and nonbelievers alike) to take it easy and to indulge itself. It also necessarily undermines holy living and all efforts to build up faith and holiness. Therefore, it is right to abandon this doctrine.

The synod responds by teaching that this error fails to understand either grace or the work of the Holy Spirit. It quotes the Apostle John in showing that all believers may know themselves to be the children of God and that knowing this leads one to pursue holiness. This synodical teaching does not rest on just one quote from the Bible, however. Throughout the Bible, the examples of those who know that they belong to God show that that knowledge does indeed encourage piety and faithfulness. This teaching depends on what is presented in article V.12.

Rejection 7: Perseverance and Faith

The Synod rejects the error of those who teach:

> *"Temporary faith does not differ at all from justifying and saving faith except in its duration."*

For Christ Himself in Matthew 13:20ff. and Luke 7:13ff. clearly shows the difference between three kinds of those temporarily faithful and those truly faithful. Jesus says that the former receive the seed in rocky ground, while the latter receive it in good ground or good hearts; the former are without root, the latter have a firm root; the former are devoid of fruit, the latter produce their fruit in diverse measure, but constantly and perseveringly.

This error teaches that there is only one kind of faith, and that traditional Reformed distinctions between temporary faith and true saving faith are false. This one faith must persevere to be saving. Where faith fails, it is not because the faith was not true, but because the believer did not properly use the gifts and graces available to him to maintain his faith.

Again, the synod sharply rejects this claim and insists that inherent in the teaching of Jesus about the sower and the seed (Matt. 13) is a distinction between different kinds of faith. True faith is planted by the Word and Spirit in prepared hearts, takes lasting root there, and produces fruit. It is the work of the Holy Spirit that prepares those hearts and produces the roots and fruits there. The faith that is worked in this way by the Spirit is indeed different from brief and fading enthusiasms about Jesus. This rejection expands on the teaching of article V.7.

Rejection 8: Perseverance and Repeated Regeneration

The Synod rejects the error of those who teach:

> *"It is not absurd that a man who has lost his regeneration, may be reborn again, even many times."*

Through this doctrine these teachers deny that the seed of God by which we are reborn is incorruptible, against the testimony of the

*Apostle Peter: "Reborn not of corruptible seed, but incorruptible"
(1 Peter 1:23).*

The error taught here is the logical extension of previous errors. If true conversion and perseverance can be lost, then it can also be regained by the free will of man. If it can be lost and regained once, then it must be that it can be lost and regained more than once.

The synod simply rejects this error by citing Peter's teaching that the seed of the Word by which believers are converted is incorruptible (1 Peter 1:23). Here again, the rejection expands on article V.7.

Rejection 9: Perseverance and the Prayer of Christ

The Synod rejects the error of those who teach:

> *"Christ has nowhere prayed for the unfailing perseverance of believers in faith."*

These teachers contradict Christ Himself, who said, "I have prayed for you, Peter, that your faith fail not" (Luke 22:32). The gospel of John testifies (John 17:20) that Christ prayed not only for the Apostles, but also for all who would believe through their word. Also verse 11, "Holy Father, keep them in Your name," and verse 15, "I do not pray that You would take them out of the world, but that You would keep them from evil."

This final error denies that Christ ever prayed that believers would persevere in faith. Presumably, the point here is that if Christ had prayed such a prayer, it would surely have been answered positively by His Father. But since He never prayed such a prayer, there is no promise of unfailing perseverance.

Again, this error was easy to reject by quoting the Bible, where Christ clearly did pray precisely for such final perseverance. This rejection addresses issues of article V.8.

Chapter 13

_____

CONCLUSION

This is the clear, simple, and candid declaration of the orthodox doctrine on the five articles in the Netherlands, and the rejection of the errors with which the Dutch churches have been troubled for some time. The Synod judges this declaration and rejection to be taken from the Word of God and agreeable to the confessions of the Reformed Churches. So it appears clearly that some most improperly have wanted to inculcate in the people, against all truth, justice, and love, the following false claims:

- *The doctrine of the Reformed Churches on predestination and subjects related to it, by its own proper inclination and tendency, leads the souls of men away from all piety and religion. It is an easy seat for the flesh and the devil and the bow of Satan with which he lies in wait for all, wounds very many, and lethally pierces many with the darts of either despair or false security.*

- *It makes God the author of sin, unjust, a tyrant, and a hypocrite. Nor is this anything other than a new form of Stoicism, Manicheism, Libertinism, and Turkism.*

- *This renders men carnally secure, for indeed by it they are persuaded that the salvation of the elect will not be hurt however they live, and they are so secure that they can perpetrate the most atrocious wickedness. It also teaches that the reprobate will not benefit even if they truly did all the works of the saints.*

- *This teaches that God, by a bare and pure choice of the will, without respect or consideration at all to any sin, created and predestined the greatest part of the world to eternal damnation.*

- *In the same way that election is the foundation and cause of faith and good works, reprobation is the cause of infidelity and impiety.*

- *Many infants of the faithful are ripped innocent from the breasts of their mothers and tyrannically thrown into hell so that neither baptism nor the prayers of the church at their baptism help them.*

And we are accused of teaching many other things of this sort which the Reformed Churches not only do not acknowledge, but also detest with all our heart.

For this reason, the Synod at Dordrecht implores in the name of the Lord all those who piously call on the name of our Savior Jesus Christ not to judge the faith of the Reformed Churches from the calumnies heaped upon it. The Synod also implores them not to judge on the basis of private statements by some teachers, either old or more recent, often also cited in bad faith, or corrupted and distorted into an alien sense. Rather, the Synod implores them to judge the faith of the Reformed Churches from the public confessions of the churches themselves, and from this declaration of the orthodox doctrine unanimously affirmed by all and every member of the Synod. It seriously admonishes those calumniators to recognize how gravely they come under the judgment of God—both as those who present false testimony against so many churches and against so many confessions of churches, and as those who disturb the consciences of the weak, and are busy to render suspect the society of the many who are truly faithful.

Finally, this Synod exhorts all colleagues in the gospel of Christ, that in the handling of this doctrine, both in the schools and in the churches, they consider it piously and religiously. They need to accommodate themselves in speaking and in writing to the glory of the divine name, the holiness of life, and the consolation of troubled souls. They need to think as well as speak with the Scripture according to the analogy of faith. Finally, they need to abstain from all those phrases that exceed the limits prescribed for us in the genuine sense of the Holy Scriptures, and that could furnish a right occasion for the shameless sophists to insult or even falsely accuse the doctrine of the Reformed Churches.

May the Son of God Jesus Christ, who is seated at the right hand of the Father to give gifts to men, sanctify us in the truth, lead those who are erring to the truth, close the mouths of those who falsely calumniate sound doctrine, and provide the faithful ministers of His Word with the Spirit of wisdom and discretion so that all their communications may result in the glory of God and the edification of their hearers.

The conclusion is an integral part of the canons. It makes several important points in summary form that are helpful for understanding the issues before the synod. It begins by asserting forcefully that the canons present in an honest and straightforward manner the doctrine that the churches confess and teach. This doctrine is derived from the Scriptures and conforms to the doctrinal standards of the Reformed churches. Here again we see theology, piety, and strategy combined. The theology is the doctrinal teaching of the synod. The piety is the honesty and simplicity with which the synod speaks. The strategy is to contrast the honesty of the synod with the "false claims" of its critics.

Specifically, the conclusion wants to deny again several specific accusations that the Arminians have unfairly and inaccurately brought against the teaching of the Reformed churches. It lists six lies that have been told about Reformed teaching, lies that the synod wants clearly to repudiate.

The first false claim is that the doctrine of predestination necessarily tempts believers to compromise a life of piety, moving them to descend with greater or less seriousness into either despair of salvation or a false security of election.

The second false claim relates to the doctrine of God. The Reformed are charged with turning God into a tyrant or the cause of sin and adopting a form of determinism. (Interestingly, this determinism is linked in part to Islamic teaching—"Turkism"—showing an awareness of this religion.)

The third false claim expands on the dangers of carnal security mentioned in the first point that can encourage the elect to think that they can live in any wicked way and still be spiritually safe. It also repeats the false charge that the reprobate can earnestly desire heaven, live for it, and still be lost.

The fourth false claim is that the Reformed teach that the reprobate—"the greatest part of the world"—are predestined and eternally condemned without any regard for sin.

The fifth false claim expands on the fourth. It claims that the Reformed teach that as God gives faith and good works to the elect, in just the same way He gives unbelief and wickedness to the reprobate.

The sixth false claim is that "many" infants are tyrannically thrown into hell, and neither baptism nor the prayers of the church can help.

The synod declares that it not only rejects the teaching of these false claims but actually detests it. Interestingly, these false claims are expressed in strong, sometimes emotional, terms with apparently the language the Arminians actually used. Strikingly, the synod does not analyze or respond to these accusations. In one sense, it just lets them stand. For the synod, its canons have already clearly and passionately answered these false claims, and so their unfairness and inaccuracy are obviously wrong.

We can see those answers and refutations to these claims in many places in canons. For example: claim 1 is refuted in rejection V.6; claims 2, 3, 4, and 5 are refuted in articles I.5, 7, 15; and claim 6 is refuted in article I.17.

These claims do not need further comment here except on claim 5. This claim begins with the Latin words *eodem modo* (in the same way) and has elicited a significant amount of discussion among theologians in recent times. What is crucial here is that the synod rejects a symmetry or exact parallel between God's election to life and God's reprobation to damnation. The Arminians had suggested that just as God gives the gift of faith and repentance to the elect to lead them to eternal life, so

He gives the gift of sin to the reprobate to lead them to condemnation. The synod rejects any such symmetry. The canons clearly teach that God is not the author of sin and that the reprobate alone are responsible of their sin, guilt, and condemnation. Here again we see that the Reformed are not pursuing a logically consistent theology but are being faithfully biblical. By contrast, the Arminians are actually the ones whose theology is driven by logic.

The synod begs all Christians to study and evaluate the teaching of the Reformed churches only on the basis of the confessions they had adopted and now from the canons of the synod. Specifically, it asks that Christians not be guided in such understanding by those who are not Reformed and heap false charges on the church—such as the six points listed above. Also, the Reformed churches ask not to be evaluated by the private writings of Reformed individuals, often quoted out of context and misrepresented. (This statement implicitly concedes that Reformed individuals may have written some things of which the synod would not approve.) It solemnly warns critics of the spiritual dangers to themselves and to others of misrepresenting the teaching of the churches.

The synod then addresses ministers and teachers in the Reformed churches to deal with these matters carefully and piously. These doctrines are taught by God in the Scriptures for "the glory of the divine name, the holiness of life, and the consolation of troubled souls." The church must be faithful in teaching them just as God has. Teachers and preachers must speak as the Scriptures do and must avoid phrases (sometimes called "harsh phrases") or expressions that can be misunderstood or abused either by the faithful or by those who reject Reformed teaching.

The conclusion ends with a prayer: first to preserve the faithful in the truth, second to lead those in error to the truth, third to shut the mouths of false teachers, and fourth to bless faithful ministers to teach the truth wisely and helpfully.

The conclusion effectively summarizes both the truth and the piety to which the canons as a whole aspire. Its appeal for fairness and its prayer for those in error show the synod as sincerely trying to be pastoral, removed from the anger and bitterness that sometimes characterized theological debate in the decade before the synod. The Calvinists were of course victorious, and it is easier to be gracious as the winner. Still, this conclusion does capture the spirit of Reformed Christianity at its best.

Chapter 14

———

CLOSING REFLECTIONS

The Synod of Dort accomplished what it set out to do. It articulated and protected the Reformed understanding of the Bible recovered in the Reformation. It rejected the Arminian challenge to Calvinism. For a time, it united most of the Reformed churches of Europe in a synod that reached a unanimous decision on key doctrinal points. It made important decisions for the life and future of the Dutch Reformed Church: a Bible translation, catechism teaching, baptism in a missionary context, the Sabbath, and a church order. It promoted theological fidelity and piety. It saved the Reformation by clarifying and buttressing key elements of *sola fide, sola gratia, solus Christus,* and *sola Scriptura,* all under the rubric *soli Deo gloria.* Many have confused the Reformation with its effects. The effects of the Reformation were immense over a long time in politics, education, economics, science—indeed, in every area of human endeavor. But the essence of the Reformation was the recovery of biblical religion. And that is what the Synod of Dort helped to save.

The synod did not accomplish all that it might have wanted to do. It did not give the Reformed churches a new confession to unite them all as the Lutherans were united by the Augsburg Confession. It did, however, provisionally affirm the Belgic Confession as acceptable to all (the British reserving only the right to dissent from its teaching on church government). It did not provide a definitive statement on the Reformed understanding of the Sabbath, but it did provide a helpful basic, if provisional, approach to the Sabbath. And this statement has continued to guide the Dutch Reformed churches through their history. It did not free the church from the Erastian control of the civil government. That government would not allow the meeting of another national synod for almost two hundred years, and when that synod met, it was much more a department of state than the Synod of Dort had been. It did not convince the Lutherans that Reformed theology was the best expression of the Reformation. It did not succeed in protecting European culture or even the churches against the rise of secularism, optimism, individualism, and a revolutionary spirit. But it did provide the Reformed churches with a great resource, one that summarizes the Bible's teaching at key points on God, man, Christ, the Holy Spirit, salvation, grace, and the church.

In our day, we are seeing something of a renewed interest in the Reformed theology of salvation. That is encouraging. The Synod of Dort reminds us, however, that Reformed Christianity (and biblical Christianity!) is much more than theology. Christian piety and the life of the church are central to it. May reflecting on the work of the synod stimulate a renewed interest in the fullness of Reformed Christianity.

The Synod of Dort was an important event in the history of the church, well worth remembering and celebrating after four hundred years. It has drawn the affirmation of millions of Christians for centuries, not as a matter of tradition but as a matter of biblical fidelity. The Synod of Dort worthily taught and preserved for the churches a God-glorifying religion, a God-centered life, and a God-given comfort.

On May 29, 1619, the last activity of the synod was to gather in the Great Church of Dordrecht for a worship service. The pastor there, Balthasar Lydius, who was also a delegate to the synod, preached the final sermon. His text was a most fitting conclusion to the work of the synod. It was not a text that focused on the any of the five Calvinistic answers to Arminianism. Rather, it was a text that celebrated the gracious character of salvation:

You will say in that day:
"I will give thanks to you, O LORD,
　　for though you were angry with me,
your anger turned away,
　　that you might comfort me.
"Behold, God is my salvation;
　　I will trust, and will not be afraid;
for the LORD GOD is my strength and my song,
　　and he has become my salvation."
With joy you will draw water from the wells of salvation.
(Isa. 12:1–3, ESV)

—

APPENDICES

—

Appendix 1

ARMINIUS: A NEW LOOK

After Jacobus Arminius died on October 19, 1609, Petrus Bertius, his close friend since their student days at university in Leiden, presented a funeral oration reflecting on his life and work. Near the end of his address, Bertius reported that when the physicians informed Arminius that he was fatally ill, he received the news with a "noble display of moderation and heroic firmness."[1] Those characteristics—nobility, moderation, heroism—have continued to dominate the biographical reflections of Arminians on Arminius, from the time of Bertius to our time.

The Remonstrant histories of Gerard Brandt and Caspar Brandt in the seventeenth and eighteenth centuries take a similarly positive view of Arminius' moderation in the face of Calvinist intransigence. G.J. Hoenderdaal continued that outlook, writing of Arminius' controversy in 1982, "He did not seek the dispute; he would rather have avoided it."[2] This interpretation of Arminius has resonated with many readers who are inclined in any case to see Calvinism as a particularly joyless, heartless, domineering form of Christianity.

The fullest statement of this positive view in English is the generally fine biography of Arminius by Carl Bangs in 1971.[3] More recently, there has been something of a renaissance of the study of Arminius in English. Richard Muller, Keith Stanglin, and Thomas McCall have contributed important studies, particularly on the theology of Arminius.

These scholars (with the exception of Muller) are Arminians. They have greatly deepened our knowledge of Arminius while continuing the basically positive understanding of Arminius presented by Bangs.[4] Ironically perhaps, the careful work done by Arminian scholars provides us with new information that allows for a reconsideration of the standard positive interpretation of the life of Arminius.

Thomas Kuhn, in his influential work *The Structure of Scientific Revolutions* (1962), argued convincingly that fundamental changes in basic scientific hypotheses usually occur when so much evidence accumulates that is contrary to the old theory that the old theory suddenly collapses and is replaced by a new one. Perhaps the time has come for the weight of the evidence gathered by recent scholars to be used for a very different interpretation of the life of Arminius than the one long followed, especially since the reinterpretation of Arminius' life presented by Bangs.

To reexamine the positive interpretation of Arminius that has dominated scholarship, we will take a close look at four key arguments of Carl Bangs that are foundational to his interpretation. First, Bangs argues that the Dutch Reformed Church in Arminius' day had two currents within it: the older, broader native Erasmian stream and the newer, narrower foreign stream of strict Calvinism. Arminius, a product and champion of the older stream, got caught up in the efforts of the strict Calvinists to eliminate that older stream. Second, Bangs argues that Arminius was surrounded by and reacted negatively to a triumphant and pervasive supralapsarianism among the strict Calvinists. Third, Bangs concludes that Arminius was committed to the older, Erasmian theological stream in the Netherlands for all of his life. He did not change, but the world around him was changing. Fourth, Bangs insists that Arminius was attacked for his theology repeatedly and unfairly by strict Calvinists throughout his life. Each of these four foundational interpretive elements in Bangs' understanding of Arminius needs to be reexamined, because each of them is seriously wrong.

Before we look at each of these four arguments, we must remember two difficulties in reconstructing the life and thought of Arminius: (1) We have no extant writings from Arminius from before 1590, so we have no hard evidence from him of his theology in the first thirty years of his life. (2) Arminius published nothing in his lifetime (except a small number of printed copies of his public disputations circulated locally in Leiden), so his contemporaries had little on which to base an evaluation of his theology except oral reports about his preaching and teaching.

While recognizing these difficulties, the basic biography of Arminius is simple:

- 1559–75: Youth and early education
- 1575–81: Student at Leiden University
- 1582–87: Student in Geneva and Basel
- 1588–1603: Pastor in the Reformed Church of Amsterdam
- 1603–9: Professor of theology at Leiden University

Two Currents in the Dutch Reformed Church?

First, we need to reflect on the character of the Dutch Reformed Church in the days of Arminius. This is, of course, a very big question, but Bangs' claims are too broad and not ultimately convincing. For example, he writes: "The plot thickens when Calvinist clergy, and their people, fled north from the southern provinces, driven out by Spain and the Catholics. They brought with them their energy, their money, their talents, their trade connections, and a new brand of Calvinism, precise and intolerant. Then, as the Remonstrant historian Gerard Brandt put it, the term 'Reformed' came to have two meanings, one for the old Hollanders, another for the new preachers."[5] Later in the book, Bangs comments: "What was happening in the 1590s is that the Calvinists, seeking to impose their theology on the Dutch churches, ran into constant resistance from the older Reformers and their sympathizers. Snecanus and Arminius were not alone in their refusal to capitulate to the pressures of Beza and his sympathizers in Holland. The controversy which was beginning to flare in many quarters now caused some consternation among the more 'orthodox' Calvinists themselves, who found their colleagues taking positions which seemed to them to be too extreme to be defended."[6] Is Bangs' picture of two kinds of Reformed churches accurate?

One of the newer standard histories of this period, Jonathan Israel's *The Dutch Republic*, presents a different picture. Israel sees the central contrast not between two Reformed churches but between the Reformed ministers on the one hand and the powerful merchant regents on the other: "As Grotius put it, where the preachers followed Calvin, the regents preferred the Reformation of Erasmus. . . . By the 1590s, hardly any regents were still openly Catholic. But only a small minority were zealous Calvinists who supported the aspirations of the Reformed preachers. . . . This clash of principles expressed itself also in a clash of interpretations of the Revolt. For the Calvinists it was above all a struggle about religion, for the 'true faith.' For the regents it was a struggle for freedom from oppression and tyranny."[7]

Israel notes a distinctive vitality to Calvinism in Holland that was not imposed on the people: "The Holland regents, in 1587, worked on the assumption that about one-tenth of the province's population belonged to the Reformed Church. By German, or English, standards, this might seem sparse. But when it is considered that this had been achieved without coercion, that there were numerous non-Calvinist Protestants, and that the prevailing political and military insecurity was bound to discourage many from joining the public Church, the figure of 10 per cent is really rather impressive."[8] In particular, he notes that Amsterdam was a strong center of Calvinism at the very time in which Arminius began his pastoral work there. The Alteration, as it was known, took place in Amsterdam in 1578, turning the city from an officially Roman Catholic city to a Reformed one. The Calvinism there was strong: "Leicester convened a new National Synod, at The Hague, at which a strictly Calvinist 'Church order' was drawn up, designed to strip the town councils of power in Church affairs, while simultaneously strengthening state backing of the public Church. Several pro-Leicester, Calvinist towns in Holland—notably Amsterdam, Dordrecht, and Enkhuizen—accepted the 1586 'Church order,' but most Holland towns rejected it."[9]

Israel recognizes that there was a small minority of clergy in the Netherlands who dissented from the clear Calvinism of the Reformed

Church, but a steady pattern of disciplining such clergy was established before the ordination of Arminius. Most notably, Caspar Coolhaes was a minister who was disciplined in Leiden and ultimately deposed and excommunicated in 1582 in the very years when Arminius was a student there. Arminius knew about several disciplinary actions that the Reformed Church took against this small number of ministers, as he would refer to them in his 1608 *Declaration of Sentiments*.

In addition, Israel is much more nuanced than Bangs in evaluating the impact of Calvinist refugees from the south:

> As confessionalization proceeded, and more of the ordinary populace came under the influence of the preachers, Calvinists had more scope for mobilizing popular opinion against the regents. Of the particular significance, in this context, was the influx of Protestant refugees from South Netherlands, after 1585. The immigrants were not the cause of the tension between consistories and regents or between Calvinist orthodoxy and less dogmatic Protestant attitudes. But they certainly aggravated matters, by strengthening Calvinist orthodoxy and adding a social dimension to a tension basically political and theological in character. In this way, Calvinist orthodoxy became the ideology of those—often guild-members, militiamen, and semi-literate artisans—who opposed the regents.[10]

Israel makes clear that Calvinists immigrants from the south did not create Calvinist orthodoxy in the north but rather strengthened it.

Stanglin and McCall summarize the views of Richard Muller, the leading expert on Reformed orthodoxy in this period: "Richard Muller . . . argues that the definition of Reformed theology codified at Dordt was already the standard interpretation of the confession and catechism in Arminius's lifetime, an interpretation that was reinforced in previous synods that disciplined alternative viewpoints. Thus there is no anachronism involved in contrasting Arminius with the Reformed. Arminius's attempt to exploit the ambiguity of the confessional documents was unconvincing to his peers and out of step with their authorial intent."[11] There were not two Reformed churches as Bangs claimed, but rather a small of group of dissenters, with which Arminius ultimately identified, from the dominant Reformed consensus.

Dominant Supralapsarianism?

Second, Bangs suggests that Arminius reacted to the growing dominance of Bezan supralapsarianism. For example, he writes, "It was Beza's form of Calvinism which was promoted in Geneva when Arminius went there to study."[12] Is Bangs correct in this contention?

Stanglin and McCall implicitly reinforce Bangs' perspective by focusing two-thirds of their discussion of Arminius and predestination on supralapsarianism (pp. 106–29), even though the reason for their focus is theological, rather than historical: "Arminius expends great energy opposing supralapsarianism. He sees it as a species of a more common genus of predestination (rather than something *sui generis*), and he says that, among the different options, its advocates 'climb the highest.'"[13] In another place, Stanglin reinforces the notion of rather pervasive supralapsarianism: "It is not that his Leiden colleagues were forcing supralapsarianism on Arminius; but, since it was the norm in that environment, he found it to be especially worthy of refutation. If Arminius seems to devote an inordinate amount of time and energy against supralapsarianism, then one should remember the people whom he faced on a daily basis."[14] Supralapsarianism, however, was not as pervasive as Bangs claimed, and predestination had become a significant concern for Arminius long before he went to Leiden.[15]

Muller, by contrast, has argued, "Geneva was not at all dominated by supralapsarianism."[16] He records that Lambert Daneau, an infralapsarian who taught Arminius at Leiden in 1581, had been a pastor in Geneva from 1574 to 1581 and worked closely and cooperatively with Beza.[17] In another place, Muller writes: "In Geneva, Arminius must also have encountered the recently published *Harmonia* of the Reformed confessions (1581) prepared by Beza, Daneau and Salvart as a Reformed response to the Lutheran *Concordia*. This work also is infralapsarian and is founded not on the confession of Beza but on Bullinger's *Confessio Helvetica posterior.* Cleary, there was no supralapsarian monolith for Arminius to encounter."[18] Certainly, supralapsarianism was not dominant in Basel when Arminius studied there with Johann Jacobus Grynaeus (1540–1617). Grynaeus was an infralapsarian who had taught in Heidelberg and urged Basel to adopt the Second Helvetic Confession.

While Arminius was genuinely concerned about supralapsarianism, his first extensive writing on predestination was his critical correspondence with Franciscus Junius, a well-known infralapsarian.[19] Arminius at times seemed to attack supralapsarian in part as a strategy to try to divide infralapsarian Calvinists from supralapsarian Calvinists. It never worked as a strategy. Surely, Muller's summary conclusion is exactly right: "The usual interpretation of Arminius' thought as generated entirely in reaction to the supralapsarianism of a 'Bezan orthodoxy' is untenable. Not only is this thesis incapable of explaining Arminius' departures from the paradigm of Reformed orthodoxy on topics other than predestination, such as the highly important topic of Christology, it is also based on a misunderstanding of Arminius' education in theology in Leiden and Geneva and cannot explain even the predestination side of Arminius' thought."[20] Arminius came to reject all Calvinist forms of unconditional predestination, not just supralapsarianism.

Unchanging Theology?

Third, we must examine Bangs' claim that the character of Arminius' theology remained fundamentally unchanged throughout his life. Until the work of Bangs, scholars had accepted the statement of Bertius that Arminius had followed the theology of Beza until around 1590, when he changed his mind. In his funeral oration for Arminius, Bertius described the process of that change beginning with the request of Martin Lydius, who had been a minister in Amsterdam, that Arminius respond to a pamphlet written in Delft titled *An Answer to Some of the Arguments Adduced by Beza and Calvin; From a Treatise concerning Predestination, on the Ninth Chapter of the Epistle to the Romans.* Bertius maintains:

Arminius himself also was not averse to this proposal; for, having recently left the University of Geneva, his ears seemed to retain the sound of Beza's lectures and arguments on this subject. He made the requisite preparations, therefore, and betook himself to the work. But while he was contriving a proper refutation, and had begun accurately to weigh the arguments on both sides, and to compare different passages of scripture together—while he was thus harassing and fatiguing himself, he was conquered by the force of truth, and, at first, became a convert to the very opinions which he had been requested to combat and refute. But he afterwards disapproved of them, as promulgated by the brethren of Delft, because he did not think the doctrine contained in them to be correct according to the scriptures. . . . But the deep and interesting inquiries into which his mind was led on this occasion, were, by the Divine rod of correction and the guidance of the Holy Spirit, turned towards those opinions which he finally embraced, and which to the close of his life he constantly maintained.[21]

Bangs commented on this statement of Bertius: "No dates are given, but Bertius leaves the impression that this took place around 1591. Caspar Brandt in retelling the same story places its beginning back to 1589."[22] Bangs, however, rejected this claim of Bertius, insisting that the evidence shows that Arminius did not change his mind, especially on predestination, in any fundamental way. This claim by Bangs has been accepted generally, including by such careful scholars as Richard Muller and Keith Stanglin.[23] But was Bangs correct in his claim? What is the evidence?

Bangs presents his case in his biography of Arminius.[24] His first line of argument is a letter written by Arminius on March 18, 1591, to his former professor in Basel, Grynaeus. Bangs quotes from the letter: "There is a lot of controversy among us about predestination, original sin, and free will."[25] Arminius does seem perplexed, but he does not clearly state where he stands in these controversies. This letter provides no specific information on the theological position of Arminius on predestination at this time and none at all on whether he had changed his mind. This letter is completely irrelevant to the question at hand. Moreover, the statement of Bertius about Arminius' change of mind is generally seen as referring to 1589 or 1590, well before the letter to Grynaeus. So the letter to Grynaeus provides no evidence that would refute the statement of Bertius.

In his second line of argument, Bangs makes two points: "Finally, there is some negative evidence, or significant arguments from silence. . . . First, there is no clear evidence that Arminius ever accepted Beza's doctrine of predestination and its concomitants. Second, he makes no point of having undergone a theological transition. He constantly portrays himself as teaching an ancient position in the church and one widely held among the Reformed pastors in the Low Countries. He sees his opponents as innovators, not himself."[26]

On the first point, as to whether he ever believed in unconditional predestination, we have no evidence at all from Arminius as to what he thought about predestination before 1590. He has left us no writings from before this time. We do know, however, that he received letters of recommendation from Grynaeus and Beza as to his Reformed orthodoxy. This does not prove he was supralapsarian, but it also does not suggest that he openly espoused conditional predestination. We also know that he sustained his ordination examinations in Amsterdam, which, as we have seen, had a strongly Calvinist church and clergy.

On the second point, whether Arminius even admits to changing his theology, Bangs himself acknowledged that Arminius writes very little about himself in his letters: "The greater part of the extant letters consists of theological treatises, with maybe a word of personal greetings at the end. One seizes on every personal word."[27] Later in his life, Arminius does claim to stand with the ancient church on predestination in several of his writings, but that offers no evidence as to how long he had held those views.

Much later in the biography, Bangs cites a letter by Arminius dated April 6, 1608, in which he wrote: "Neither am I ashamed to have occasionally forsaken some sentiments which had been instilled by my own masters, since it appears to me that I can prove by the most forcible arguments that such a change has been made for the better."[28] Bangs immediately adds, "The last sentence, by the way, is the sole occurrence known to me of any report by Arminius that he had once adhered to views he now rejected." But since Arminius wrote so little about himself, this statement must be taken very seriously. He certainly does not indicate which views he changed, but in his writings his "most forcible arguments" were about the doctrine of predestination and his formative "masters" had been strong teachers of predestination.

If the contention of Bangs that Arminius never changed his views on predestination seems to lack any substantive support, how reliable is the claim of Bertius that he did change? Bertius was a friend of Arminius from their days together as students at the University of Leiden, and they remained friends throughout their lives. He tells this story not years after Arminius' death but immediately after it. He does not make his statement in passing, but with significant details. No one at the time who knew Arminius challenged it. There does not seem to be any clear rhetorical reason for Bertius to have made it up for the funeral oration.

By contrast, Bangs does have a reason to reject the story. His claim of an unchanging Arminius uncontroversially embracing conditional predestination at the beginning of his career supports Bangs' picture of two streams in the Dutch Reformed Church. In fact, however, it was not the nature of the Dutch Reformed Church that was in flux but the theology of Arminius. Bangs' contention contributes to his picture of Arminius as one valiantly unchanging in the face of growing opposition. Certainly, Bangs was sincere in believing that the story of Bertius was not credible, but the evidence in fact supports Bertius rather than Bangs.

One additional fact is perhaps relevant here. Muller as well as Stanglin and McCall has shown that Arminius used the concept of middle knowledge in the development of his doctrine of conditional predestination. (Bangs shows no awareness of this doctrine in the thought of Arminius.) Middle knowledge was taught by Luis de Molina (1535–1600), a Spanish Jesuit, in his work *Concordia liberi arbitrii cum gratiae donis* (1588).

We do not know when Arminius read this work, but we do know that he had the second edition (1595) in his personal library.[29] Since this work of Molina appeared just before the time Arminius changed his views on predestination according to Bertius, it is possible that Molina's book had a key role in that change, and that the doctrine of middle knowledge gave him a way to affirm conditional predestination in apparent harmony with divine sovereignty. Stanglin and McCall note: "Arminius never refers to them [Molina and his Spanish Jesuit colleague Francisco Suarez (1548–1617)] positively by name, but some of the differences between Arminius and his Reformed contemporaries can be traced to the tacit influence of these writers."[30] Of course, Arminius never refers to the influence of Suarez or Molina on him, since that would have given his Calvinist opponents the evidence they needed to depose him.

One specific issue that Molina did raise, and which was very important to Arminius in his later writings, was related to the goodness of God, election, and the origin of sin in humans. For example, in responding to what he regarded as hyper-Augustinian theology, Molina wrote, "Again, what grievance will God have on Judgment Day against the wicked, since they were unable not to sin as long as God did not efficaciously incline and determine them to the good, but rather solely by His own free will decided from eternity not so to determine them?"[31] Molina may have raised, or more likely, helped resolve this issue for Arminius.

Unfair Attacks?

On the fourth point of Bangs, was Arminius pursued and persecuted by strict Calvinists? To answer this question, it is necessary to look at the three periods of his life about which we have the most information: as a student in Switzerland (1582–87), as a pastor in Amsterdam (1588–1603), and as a professor in Leiden (1603–9).

Switzerland (1582–87)

The first episode in Arminius' life that needs reevaluation is his time in Switzerland. The chronology of his studies there is not entirely clear. He finished his studies at Leiden in 1581 and registered in Geneva on

January 1, 1582. The traditional dating of his life holds that he left Geneva in the middle of 1582 to study in Basel, returning to Geneva in the middle of 1583. Bangs presents a different dating, arguing that he left Geneva for Basel in the middle of 1583 and returned a year later. A history of the University of Basel records that he led a disputation there in September 1582, but Bangs argues that that date must be wrong and must mean September 1583. Bangs adduces Arminius' close friend Jan Uytenbogaert who wrote that Arminius particularly left Geneva because of trouble with an Aristotelian professor, Petrus Galesius, who did not arrive in Geneva until 1583.[32] Uytenbogaert is likely to be a reliable witness generally, but he did not write up these memories until 1647. Bertius seems to support his going in 1582, stating that Arminius left Geneva "after a short time."[33] Again Bangs' reconstruction is at best problematic.

Whether Arminius was in Geneva initially for six months or eighteen months, Bertius does comment on the zeal with which he defended his philosophical Ramism against the Aristotelians and how he offended some of them. Bertius wrote that Arminius "could not secure the favour and regard of some of the principal men in Geneva" because of "his invincible attachment to the philosophy of Peter Ramus, which he publicly defended in the warmest manner."[34] It was not the Calvinists who caused Arminius trouble during his first period in Geneva for theological reasons, but Arminius who confronted Aristotelians (who were also Calvinists) over philosophical issues.

Whatever problems Arminius had in Geneva, he seemed to do well in Basel. Bertius as well as Uytenbogaert records that Arminius was so highly regarded in Basel that the faculty wanted to award him a doctoral degree. He certainly received a fine letter of recommendation from Johannes Jacobus Grynaeus, the leading professor of theology in Basel.

Grynaeus' letter, dated September 3, 1583, is quite revealing:

Since we ought to refuse, to no learned and pious man, such testimonials as are worthy of obtaining credit for learning and piety in behalf of those to whom they are granted, such testimonials are on no account to be denied to James Arminius, of Amsterdam. For he lived in the University of Basel a life of piety, temperance and study; and in our Theological disputations he very often proved to all of us that he possessed the gift of the spirit of discernment, in such a measure as to elicit from us our sincere congratulations. Lectures were likewise lately delivered out of the ordinary course, at the request and by the command of the Faculty of Theology; on which occasion he publicly expounded some chapters of the Epistle to the Romans, and excited within us the greatest hopes of his soon becoming qualified to undertake and sustain the province lawfully assigned to him of communicating instruction, with great profit to the Church, provided he continues to stir up the gift of God which is in him. I commend him therefore to all pious persons, and especially to the church of God which is collected together in the famous city of Amsterdam; and I reverently ask it as a favour, that some regard may be paid to this learned and pious youth, and that he may never be compelled to experience any interruption in his Theological studies which have been happily commenced and continued to the present time.[35]

This letter shows that Grynaeus is very positive about Arminius. Since Grynaeus was a champion of unconditional predestination who urged the church in Basel in these years to adopt the Second Helvetic Confession, it would appear that he did not hear anything from Arminius that was clearly opposed to that doctrine. The letter also shows that Arminius' interest in the epistle to the Romans, on which he would preach for years in Amsterdam, goes back at least to his student days in Basel. We do not know precisely which chapters Arminius covered in Basel, but the lectures do not seem to have been at all controversial theologically.

After Arminius returned to Geneva, Bertius tells us, "he judged it proper to curb his former impetuosity."[36] Similarly, Uytenbogaert wrote of Arminius' second period in Geneva that Arminius "did not dispute so much, conducted himself in a milder manner, and was not so enamored with the Ramist philosophy as formerly."[37] His friends show that he was better behaved during his second stay in Geneva.

Theodore Beza, the leading theologian in Geneva, wrote another positive letter of recommendation for Arminius to Amsterdam.[38] Beza wrote to the Rev. Martin Lydius, a minister of the church of Amsterdam, these words of recommendation for Arminius:

> To describe in a few words, be pleased to take notice, that from the period when Arminius returned from Basle to us at Geneva, both his acquirements in learning and his manner of life have been so approved by us, that we form the highest hopes respecting him, if he proceed in the same course as that which he is now pursuing, and in which, we think, by the favour of God, he will continue. For the Lord has conferred on him, among other endowments, a happy genius for clearly perceiving the nature of things and forming a correct judgment upon them, which, if it be hereafter brought under the governance of piety, of which he shews himself most studious, will undoubtedly cause his powerful genius, after it has been matured by years and confirmed by his acquaintance with things, to produce a rich and most abundant harvest. These are our sentiments concerning Arminius, a young man, as far as we have been able to form a judgment of him, in no respect unworthy of your benevolence and liberality.[39]

Beza does indeed recommend Arminius "from the time Arminius returned to us from Basel," perhaps an implicit criticism of him during his first stay in Geneva.

On August 19, 1585, city leaders in Amsterdam wrote to Beza, presumably pondering further financial support for Arminius, with several questions that Bangs summarizes: "They wanted to know about his personal development. Is he stubborn and arrogant? Does he obstinately defend his own personal opinions? Is he making proper use of his education? The burgomasters were evidently nervous about the earlier episode of Arminius' defense of Ramus."[40] Apparently, word had gotten back to Amsterdam about the problematic behavior of Arminius in Geneva, which is not surprising, since between 1559 and 1586 some 190 Dutch students studied in Geneva.[41]

The letters of recommendation from Grynaeus and Beza were clearly intended to elicit continued financial support from the church of Amsterdam for Arminius' theological studies. They present strong testimonies to Arminius' brilliance, piety, and learning in 1583 and, perhaps, 1585. Grynaeus' letter reflects much more personal familiarity with Arminius than does Beza's. Financial aid for Arminius from Amsterdam continued for the whole time of his study in Switzerland. No clear evidence survives as to why Amsterdam provided financial support for Arminius,[42] but it must surely have reflected earlier recommendations from Calvinists, perhaps from Danaeus, who had taught him in Leiden.

Certainly, Arminius' time in Geneva was significant. According to Bertius, while in Geneva, Arminius heard Beza preaching on Paul's letter to the Romans "to the great and deserved admiration of the multitudes who heard him."[43] It may have been Beza, ironically, who further encouraged Arminius' interest in Romans, on which he began to lecture in Basel. (Perhaps this testimony of Bertius is further evidence of theological harmony between Arminius and Beza before 1590.)

Near the end of his time in Geneva, with the church in Amsterdam urging him to return, Arminius decided to travel to Italy. Such a decision is certainly understandable from the perspective of an eager student, but his seven months in Italy and then a few more months in Geneva before returning to the Netherlands certainly justify James Nichols' comment that his decision represented "a degree of youthful rashness."[44] Arminius finally arrived back in Amsterdam no later than September 1587.

The reports of his friends indicate that while he was in Switzerland, Arminius was impetuous at times and had both caused trouble and been appreciated. Here is the pattern that we will see repeated in his life. The pattern is not an unobtrusive man who is attacked by mean Calvinists. Rather, we see a very bright and talented person who was willing to initiate confrontation with those with whom he disagreed and could be quite adamant in advancing his views. Rather than a moderate Arminius mistreated by mean Calvinists, we see an Arminius who could be impetuous and stubborn but who was treated with a great deal of kindness by Calvinists.

Pastor in Amsterdam (1588-1603)

In Amsterdam, he reported to the classis in October 1587 and to the consistory in November. Bangs cites the consistory minutes: "Jacobus Arminius, an alumnus of this city, having come from Geneva, appeared in the consistory and delivered his testimonial from the school in Geneva, which was signed by Beza."[45] This testimony, which we do not possess, was apparently another one from Beza on behalf of the whole faculty. In February 1588, Arminius was examined by classis, and he was ordained on August 27, 1588. It is not clear why there was a delay of almost seven months.[46]

While no specific record survives of Arminius' subscribing the confessional standards of the church (the Belgic Confession and the Heidelberg Catechism), in the strongly Calvinist church of Amsterdam, he must have subscribed. Bangs wrote: "The candidates were also to be required to sign the Belgic Confession according to the actions taken by the National Synod of Dordrecht (1578) and the National Synod of Middelburg (1581). This, as will be seen, was not uniformly observed."[47] H.H. Kuyper wrote in 1899, "Already from the first General Synod the decision was made in the Church Order that all preachers must subscribe the confession as the expression of unity."[48] The synods of Dort (1574), Dort (1578), Middleburg (1581), and The Hague (1586) all required subscription to the Belgic Confession, but none adopted a specific form of subscription.

In terms of Arminius' later career, the crucial section of the Belgic Confession was article 16 on predestination: "God showed himself to be as he is: merciful and just. He is merciful in withdrawing and saving from this perdition those whom he, in his eternal and unchangeable counsel, has elected and chosen in Jesus Christ our Lord by his pure goodness, without any consideration of their works. He is just in leaving the others in their ruin and fall into which they plunged themselves." Here is a clear, brief statement of unconditional predestination that is not supralapsarian and with which Arminius apparently agreed in 1588.

When Arminius was ordained in August 1588, Arminius must have known, in light of his studies in Geneva, the character of confessional Calvinism. He received two letters of recommendation from Beza and sustained a thorough examination by the Amsterdam classis. It is extremely unlikely that Beza and the classis would have failed to discover if Arminius believed in the conditional predestination that he later taught. It is much more likely that Bertius was correct and that Arminius held to some form of unconditional predestination at the time of his ordination. This is not to say that he was an enthusiastic supralapsarian. That would not have been required in Geneva or in Amsterdam.

Marriage. On September 16, 1590, a little more than two years after his ordination, Arminius married Lijsbet Reael. This event was, of course, very important personally for Arminius, but may also have been important for his theological development. Arminius had lost his own family, and his new family connections by marriage brought him into a prominent, prosperous merchant family in Amsterdam. "By his call to the Amsterdam ministry and by his marriage to Lijsbet, he was caught up in an extended network of professional, political, economic, and family relationships which extended into every corner of the leading families of Amsterdam."[49] Lijsbet's father, Laurens Reael, probably shared the views of most of his associates in Amsterdam. He held to the Reformed faith but wanted the church and ministers to be under the supervision of the civil government.

By 1591, Arminius had clearly come to share the Erastian views of his father-in-law rather than the view of most of the Dutch Reformed clergy, which was Calvin's view of the relative independence of the church. Arminius may have adopted Erastian views already in Basel, but the influence of his new family at the very least reinforced such views. His new connections might have been a factor in encouraging him to reconsider the theology with which he returned from Geneva, for according to Bertius, the period 1589–91 is the time in which he changed. It may also be that his new connections gave him the courage to become independent of and think differently from his ministerial colleagues. Certainly, in 1591, he served on the committee appointed by Jan van Oldenbarnevelt, the leading government official in the United Provinces, which drew up an Erastian church order for the church. (None of these church polity issues is really discussed in Bangs.) This church order was sharply Erastian and was so controversial with the majority of the church that it could not be implemented.

Preaching. Early in his ministerial work in Amsterdam, Arminius decided to preach on Romans and Malachi, pursuing interests he had had at least since his time in Basel. His preaching was a very detailed study of the text. He found himself in trouble for his preaching on Romans 7 in 1591 and on Romans 9 in 1593. In his sermons on Romans 7, he rejected the standard Reformed interpretation that originated with Calvin and argued instead that Paul's presentation of internal struggles reflects the problems of an unregenerate person rather than a regenerate Christian. In his sermons on Romans 9, he rejected the standard Reformed uses of this text to support unconditional election.

On Romans 9, according to Bangs,[50] Arminius acknowledged that he had taken a different interpretation from the standard Reformed one, but he insisted that he agreed with the Belgic Confession and Heidelberg Catechism.

> He reiterated his assent to the Confession and Catechism, offering only one scruple—over the interpretation but not the words of the sixteenth article of the Belgic Confession. It is the article on "eternal election," which affirms that God delivers and preserves "all whom he, in his eternal and unchangeable council, of mere goodness hath elected in Jesus Christ our Lord." His scruple was this: Does the "all" refer to believers, or is it an arbitrary decree to bestow faith? He accepted the first interpretation and rejected the latter. The terms of the article, however, he accepted. The consistory found Arminius' statement acceptable and declared the matter closed, urging fraternal fellowship until such a time as a general synod should determine the proper interpretation of the article.[51]

Bangs is dependent for this account on Caspar Brandt, an early eighteenth-century Remonstrant historian. There is no independent sixteenth-century record of such a consistorial decision. However exactly the trouble was cleared up, several points are clear: the controversy was sparked by Arminius, who knew that he was challenging the received Calvinist point of view and that the Calvinist majority of the consistory was willing to find a way to keep the peace with Arminius. Is this a case of a moderate Arminius being unfairly attacked by Calvinists or a case of a provocative, even troublemaking Arminius with whom Calvinists found a way of working?

Writing. Although Arminius did not publish any of what he wrote during his years as a pastor in Amsterdam, he did write several works of importance. First, we have his study of Romans 9. In 1596, Gellius Snecanus, a minister in Friesland, published a study on Romans 9. His position was very similar to what Arminius says he preached in Amsterdam in 1593, and apparently Arminius composed his own treatise on Romans 9 in 1596 as a response to Snecanus.[52]

Near the beginning of his treatise, titled "A Brief Analysis of the Ninth Chapter of St. Paul's Epistle to the Romans," Arminius writes:

> For, when I saw that you had remarked, in the Apostle's scope and treatment of the principal arguments, just what, not so very long before, I had set forth publicly to the people committed to my care, in explaining the same chapter, I was greatly strengthened in that view. . . . I freely confess that that part [of Scripture] always seemed to be enveloped in the deepest shade, and most difficult of explanation, until the light shed upon it in this way dispersed the darkness, and gave my understanding a clear view of the place lit up by its brilliance.[53]

This interesting bit of autobiography seems to imply that Arminius for some time before he preached in 1593 had not accepted the standard Reformed interpretations of Romans 9 and had been in a quandary as to its meaning. This comment is consistent with the idea that sometime between 1589 and 1591 Arminius began to change his views on predestination, since Romans 9 is one of the central texts on that doctrine.

In most of his writings on predestination, his central objection to any doctrine of unconditional predestination is that for him it makes God the author of sin. Significantly, here in this first treatise, he does not explicitly raise this issue. Still, he does raise related issues: he says that one cannot be a sinner if one has not sinned freely.[54] He also criticized Beza:

> If any one simply says that God has the power of making man a vessel to dishonour and wrath, he will do the greatest injustice to God, and will contradict clear Scripture. Wherefore Beza himself does not dare to say that *simply*, but that those things are to be understood of the decree, which He does not execute till after man, having become a sinner, has made himself deserving of wrath. But he so subjoins the execution to the decree as to suspend the proximate cause of the execution on the decree itself; which comes to just the same thing as if he had said simply, that God determined to make some men vessels [to dishonour, others vessels] to honour; some vessels of wrath, others vessels of mercy; and, that He might do this, to make all men sinners primarily, that He might afterwards actually make some, by justice, vessels of wrath and dishonour, others, by mercy vessels of mercy and honour.[55]

In this criticism of Beza he certainly implies that Beza makes God the author of sin.

Here Arminius' approach is not explicitly to attack or reject Calvin's doctrine of unconditional predestination. Rather, he simply argues that Romans 9 does not support that doctrine, as Arminius says at the end of the analysis, "And thus I think I have shown *that this passage of the Apostle does not serve to confirm that opinion which many suppose to rest on the foundation of this Chapter*."[56] This approach, often taken in his writings, is aptly captured by Stanglin and McCall: "Arminius's major treatises that deal with predestination give much more attention to what he opposes than to what he proposes."[57] Not positive Arminius, but Arminius the critic.

His second major work while a pastor was probably written in 1597,[58] namely, his collected correspondence with Franciscus Junius (1545–1602) titled in the English translation *Friendly Conference of James Arminius, the Illustrious Doctor of Sacred Theology, with Mr. Francis Junius, about Predestination, Carried on by Means of Letters* (the title given to this work by the Arminians is strange, indeed, in that Junius was much better known and much more illustrious in the sixteenth and seventeenth centuries than Arminius). In this work, Arminius repeatedly raises the question of whether the doctrine of unconditional election made God the author of sin. Interestingly, he comments, "I should like, however, to be taught how the necessity of sin being done can depend on the ordination and decree of God otherwise than by the mode of cause whether efficient or deficient: which latter is reduced to an efficient, when the efficiency of the deficient is necessary to avoid sin. Beza himself confesses it to be incomprehensible how God can be free from blame, and man exposed to blame, if man has fallen by the ordination of God and necessarily."[59] Ironically, one might argue that Arminius seems to want a more rational or perhaps rationalistic theology than Beza did. Arminius certainly is adamant for a relatively unimportant minister in correspondence with a very distinguished professor:[60] "For my assertion remains unshaken, that 'God is made to be the author of sin, if He be said to have ordained that man should fall and become wicked, in order to open for Himself a way to declare His glory in that manner which He had already by an eternal decree appointed.'"[61] This writing of Arminius is the first in which he explicitly raises the issue of God as the author of sin, which would remain his most serious objection to the doctrine of unconditional election. Junius, after quite a lengthy correspondence, put an end to it, while Bangs writes that Arminius eagerly wanted to continue it, for he was a "dogged controversialist."[62] No moderate Arminius here.

A third major writing of Arminius in his years as a pastor in Amsterdam was his *An Examination of the Treatise of William Perkins concerning the Order and Mode of Predestination.* Perkins, the great English Puritan, published his study of predestination in 1598. Arminius wrote his examination in 1602, the year in which Perkins died, and did not publish it.

Near the beginning of his examination, Arminius writes: "I must diligently read [your work, Perkins,] . . . and see whether you . . . could remove, in that work, the difficulties which have long disquieted my mind."[63] This statement suggests that Arminius has not always clearly embraced conditional predestination and was at least formally uncertain. It surely shows that he is clearly aware of his problems with received Calvinism.

Arminius again shows that his great concern is with the issue of God as the author of sin. "If anyone . . . says that God has arranged this, as an occasion for Himself, by decreeing that man should fall, and by carrying forward that decree to its end or limit, we ask the proof of that assertion, which, in my judgment, he will be unable to give. For that sentiment is at variance with the justice of God, as it makes God the author of sin, and introduces an inevitable necessity for sin."[64] As usual, his response to Perkins is mostly a matter of rejecting Perkins' arguments as unconvincing.

He does at one point offer his own positive definition of election in these terms:

"Election is the decree of God, by which, of Himself from eternity, He decreed to justify in (or through) Christ, believers, and to accept them unto eternal life to the praise of His glorious grace." But you will say, "The faith is made dependent on the human will, and is not a gift of divine grace." I deny that sequence, for there was no such statement in the definition. I acknowledge that the cause of faith was not expressed, but that was unnecessary. If any one denies it, there may be added after "believers" the phrase "to whom he determined to give faith." But we should observe whether, in our method of consideration, the decree, by which God determined to justify believers and adopt them as sons, is the same with that by which He determined to bestow faith on some, but to deny the same to others. This seems to me not very probable.[65]

Later in the treatise, he writes: "In the second place, you assert, that 'divine Election is the rule of giving or withholding faith. Therefore Election does not pertain to believers, but faith rather pertains to the elect, or is the gift of Election.' You will allow me to deny this, and to ask for the proof, while I plead the cause of those whose sentiment you here oppose. Election is made in Christ. But no one is elected in Christ, unless he is a believer."[66] For Arminius, election is not the unconditional predestination of individuals but the selection of a class of people conditioned on belief.

Arminius equivocates on the question of the origin of faith in believers: "Whether the grace, which is offered to man, may be also received by him by the aid of grace, which is common to him with others who reject the same, or by grace peculiar to him, is perhaps in controversy."[67] Surely, it is more than a little curious that a Reformed theologian at the beginning of the seventeenth century is uncertain about the origin of faith.

Professor in Leiden (1603–9)

In 1603, two of the three chairs in theology at Leiden University were open. Franciscus Junius and Lucas Trelcatius the Elder had died of the plague. The trustees of the university appointed Lucas Trelcatius the Younger to replace his father and Arminius to replace Junius. Some of the Calvinist clergy objected strongly to the appointment of Arminius. The issue was resolved when all sides agreed to have Gomarus, the surviving professor of theology at Leiden, interview Arminius and make a recommendation. Gomarus conducted the interview and declared himself satisfied with the orthodoxy of Arminius and supported granting him a doctoral degree. Gomarus was key to maintaining peace between Arminius and some of his critics.

Why would Gomarus conclude that Arminius was an orthodox Reformed theologian? There are only a limited number of answers to that question: (1) Gomarus did not ask adequate questions of Arminius, (2) Arminius did not give honest or complete answers to the questions, (3) Arminius changed his mind on some issues after the interview, or (4) some combination of the three preceding answers. In light of what we have seen in Arminius' earlier writings, some combination of numbers one and two is most likely. Here again we do not have a case of noble Arminius, but a case where at least some Calvinists treated him well.

Notorious disputations in 1604–5. A particularly notable and often quoted episode at Leiden in an eighteen-month period from February 1604 to August 1605 reveals serious misunderstandings promoted by many historians about the relationships between Arminius and Gomarus. The three members of the theological faculty at the University of Leiden—Franciscus Gomarus, Lucas Trelcatius the Younger, and Jacobus Arminius—regularly wrote theses on key theological topics and then supervised, as a central part of the students' theological education, public debates or disputations on those theses. The topics followed a regular systematic theological order, with each professor taking turns in order. The theses usually ran to about five to seven printed pages. On February 7, 1604, in the regular order of topics, Arminius presided over a disputation on predestination. On October 31, 1604, Gomarus departed from the regular order of topics to lead his own disputation on predestination. Arminius' public disputation "On Divine Predestination" is relatively brief and straightforward, fifteen theses in just over four printed pages.[68] Gomarus' thirty-two theses on predestination later in the year run to about twelve pages, longer than usual.

In his "Chronology" near the beginning of his biography, Bangs wrote of 1604: "Arminius presents theses on predestination. Gomarus counter-attacks."[69] In the text, Bangs elaborates on Gomarus' action: "It was not until October 31, 1604, that the theological battle in Leiden began in earnest. Gomarus touched it off by holding a public disputation on predestination, out of turn and not part of the established schedule. He began with an 'acrimonious preface,' according to Brandt, excusing his speaking out of turn on the grounds that error was abroad—no direct mention of Arminius, but the message was plain."[70] Bangs is clearly depending on the Remonstrant historian Gerard Brandt, who had written, about seventy years after the event, that Gomarus had acted "out of his turn, and contrary to the method that had been before agreed upon."[71] Brandt, in turn, seems dependent on Stephen de Courcelles, a

Remonstrant theologian who edited and published Arminius' *Examination of the Theses of Dr. F. Gomarus Respecting Predestination* for the first time in 1645. In his preface, de Courcelles wrote of Arminius:

> Let not any one think, then, that he entered upon that contest of his own free choice; but he was drawn into it, contrary to his intention, by the necessity of defending himself. For he perceived that the Theses which he here refutes were not composed by Gomarus, according to the safe usage of the University, in order to exercise the Candidates of Theology, but were written out of order, to provoke him, whom he knew to be of the opposite opinion. Wherefore Arminius thought it a matter of duty not to leave Divine truth undefended, of which he was a Doctor and Minister.[72]

No evidence exists for Brandt's claim that Gomarus wrote an "acrimonious preface" to his theses, not even in de Courcelles' preface.

The claim of Brandt is still repeated by Keith Stanglin and Thomas McCall: "One of the renowned treatises of Arminius actually arose from the public disputation of his colleague, Gomarus, who composed his theses on predestination in opposition to Arminius on 31 October 1604."[73] Elsewhere, Stanglin wrote:

> Disputation number 30 in the cycle, which happened to be on predestination, fell to Arminius on 7 February 1604. Gomarus did not approve of what was said in the disputation, for he responded on 31 October 1604 with his own public disputation on predestination. Gomarus's move to publish theses on a topic that had just been covered eight months earlier in the curriculum was viewed as insulting, for he did it "out of turn, and contrary to the method that had been before agreed upon." [Again citing G. Brandt.] The very next day, Arminius wrote a letter to Jan Uytenbogaert, his close friend and ministerial colleague, calling Gomarus *offensissimus*. That Arminius took Gomarus's disputation as a polemical refutation of his own is demonstrated by the

fact that Arminius responded directly to Gomarus's disputation point by point in writing.[74]

At first glance, all of this evidence seems very straightforward, but it begins to unravel because of Stanglin's own thorough work on the public disputations. Stanglin shows that the claim of Brandt that Gomarus had acted contrary to the method agreed upon was not true:

> The other type of public practice disputation was outside of the planned order (*extra ordinem*) of the *repetitio*. In contrast to the *repetitio* disputations, which moved in order through the series of connected theological topics (*ex ordine*), these disputations dealt with so-called *quaelibet* material, that is, a randomly chosen subject that held no connection with the material being handled at the time. These random disputations—which have medieval antecedents in the quodlibetal questions handled by Aquinas, Scotus, and Ockham, among others—were held at Leiden University about twice a month at an ad hoc assembly. . . . Since working through the complete *repetitio* would take at least one year or as many as three years, and a professor or student might not otherwise have the opportunity to handle a certain topic in this public setting, the professors, perhaps in collaboration with students, often took advantage of this ability to propose topics out of the usual *repetitio* order. . . . Moreover, these randomly proposed disputations gave professors an opportunity to deal with any topic that arose in their own reading or interaction with one another. Gomarus's 1604 disputation on predestination, as a response to Arminius's disputation on the same topic, is a clear example of this type. These disputations generally were known by titles other than *disputatio*. Rather, their most common designation was *theses theologicae*.[75]

According to Stanglin's own analysis, Gomarus had not done anything unusual in 1604 by proposing his own theses on predestination.

More than that, the action itself does not show that he was reacting to or criticizing Arminius. Indeed, according to Stanglin, Gomarus apparently later stated that he had not disagreed with Arminius' theses on predestination: "In Gomarus's Bedencken, published late in 1609 in response to Petrus Bertius's funeral oration, Gomarus again points to the late 1603 disputation on justification, claiming that Arminius had then taught purely (*suyverlick*) on this doctrine. He goes on to claim that he had suspended his judgment of Arminius until his 1605 disputation on free choice (Disp. Pub. XI)."[76] Even as disagreements became public later, Gomarus insisted that his great concern with Arminius was not on predestination (and not in 1604), but the ways in which his teaching would undermine the Protestant doctrine of justification.[77]

What are we to make, then, of Arminius' reaction to Gomarus' theses that Gomarus was most offensive? Apparently, at the time Arminius expressed his offense, he only knew what Uytenbogaert had told him. The fact that Arminius took offense does not prove that Gomarus meant to offend or even that he had actually done anything offensive. In all likelihood, Arminius took offense not to the action of Gomarus in presenting theses but to the content of those theses. Of course, Arminius may have mistakenly thought that Gomarus was attacking him when that was not Gomarus' intention.

What we know with certainty is that Arminius immediately set to work on a detailed, lengthy analysis and refutation of Gomarus' theses.[78] Apparently, Arminius completed this work late in 1604 or early in 1605. Arminius' preface to this work seems to imply that he intends this work to be published: "You will not take it amiss, most illustrious Gomarus, if I weigh, according to the Scriptures, those Theses which you composed not so long ago, and propounded for public disputation, and if I state candidly and modestly what I find wanting in them. Solemnly and in God's presence I protest that I take up this task, not from a desire of contention, but from an earnest wish to inquire into and search out the truth."[79] The conclusions he reached on the teaching of Gomarus, however, are virulent indeed and are perhaps the reason he decided not to publish them. Of Gomarus' teaching on predestination, Arminius wrote:

I, however, freely and openly affirm, that it seems to me to follow certainly from those Theses, that God is the author of sin; nor this alone, but also that God really sins, nay, that God alone sins: whence it necessarily follows that sin is not sin, because God cannot sin. . . . But I, forsooth, am certain in my own conscience, from the word of God and of His Christ, that this doctrine is false and profane, in no manner contrary to the kingdom of Satan, but very well adapted for establishing and confirming it. For which reason also, since all that is false traces its prime origin from that kingdom, I should not hesitate to affirm that this doctrine has crept into the hearts of good men by the subtilty and craft of Satan; and that they, on their side (though unaware of it, and with other intentions), have accomplished for the kingdom of darkness a work not sufficiently to be repented of. Yet I trust that the good God has pardoned them this very thing, as having done it in ignorance, and as being prepared to submit to those who may teach them better things.[80]

The charges here are extremely serious, but the quotation seems to have two disingenuous elements. First, at the very end of the treatise, the suggestion of some mitigation of Gomarus' responsibility because he wrote in ignorance does not seem sincere. Gomarus was a professor of theology, and his conclusions on predestination surely cannot be attributed to ignorance. Second, Arminius writes that he is making his conclusion about Gomarus "openly," but there was nothing open about it. (Stanglin, in the quotation above, similarly writes that Arminius "responded directly" to Gomarus.) Arminius did not publish this work in his own lifetime and made no public statement about these convictions until 1608 in his *Declaration of Sentiments.*

The extreme nature of Arminius' reaction to Gomarus leads to another question about his integrity. Within a few months of completing his *Examination,* in response to an inquiry from the Classis of Dordrecht about controversies at Leiden, on August 10, 1605, Arminius signed a public statement along with this fellow theology professors, Franciscus

Gomarus and Lucas Trelcatius, which declared "that among themselves, that is, among the Professors of the Faculty of Theology, no difference existed that could be considered as in the least affecting the fundamentals of doctrine."[81] Was Arminius being honest? It is hard to see how Arminius could have written what he did in his *Examination* and then could claim that he agreed with Gomarus on the fundamentals of doctrine. Surely, teaching that makes God the author of sin is a fundamental doctrine.

On the other hand, we must ask if Gomarus was honest in suggesting that he had no trouble with Arminius or his teaching in 1604. While Gomarus wanted to teach somewhat differently on predestination in 1604, had Arminius in his 1604 disputation on predestination said anything that would have seriously offended Gomarus? Arminius wrote in thesis 2, "Predestination therefore, as it regards the thing itself, is the Decree of the good pleasure of God in Christ, by which He resolved within himself from all eternity, to justify, adopt, and endow with everlasting life, to the praise of his own glorious grace, believers on whom He had decreed to bestow faith (Eph. i; Rom. ix.)."[82] Further, he wrote in thesis 7, "But we give the name of 'Believers,' not to those who would be such by their own merits or strength, but to those who by the gratuitous and peculiar kindness of God [*erant credituri*] would believe in Christ."[83] These statements of Arminius as far as they go represent views completely compatible with Calvin's teaching on predestination and would not have offended Gomarus. He does not raise in these theses his concerns about the origin of sin or the source of faith.

The evidence shows that Gomarus did nothing unusual or offensive in presenting theses on predestination in 1604. His supralapsarian views did greatly offend Arminius, who responded with vicious criticism of Gomarus' teaching, which he kept private while publicly claiming agreement with Gomarus on basic doctrines. It is Arminius who seems bitter and rather dishonest in this period, not Gomarus. If the positive Arminius narrative falls apart on close examination of this one key piece of evidence, the whole narrative begins to unravel.

Free will. In July 1605, Arminius conducted a public disputation titled "On the Free Will of Man and Its Powers." While the theses of the disputation themselves were not controversial, controversy soon swirled around him. Bangs explains this:

> Two days later, in a letter to Adrian Borrius, he reveals his thinking on these questions. "I transmit you my theses on free will, which I have composed in this [guarded] manner, because I thought that they would thus conduce to peace. I have advanced nothing which I consider at all allied to a falsity. But I have been silent upon some truths which I might have published, for I know that it is one thing to be silent respecting a truth and another to utter a false-hood, the latter of which is never lawful to do, while the former is occasionally, nay very often, expedient." Those hostile and those sympathetic to Arminius have divided on the ethical question.[84]

Stanglin addresses the ethics of this situation: "What Arminius wrote to his friend about the caution he took in the public disputation on free choice was apparently said publicly at the disputation itself, for Gomarus was aware of the statement. Whatever Arminius meant by withholding some opinion at the disputation on free choice, his decision not to declare every-thing was no secret, but acknowledged openly."[85] If Stanglin was right, then Arminius was not duplicitous, as many have thought, but was provocative. Surely, Gomarus would have wondered and worried about what his other unspoken opinions were. Gomarus' doubts about Arminius were growing.

Rectoral address. Early in 1605, Arminius was elected by his col-leagues to serve a one-year term as Rector Magnificus of the university.[86] As was the custom at the end of his term, on February 8, 1606, he delivered a rectoral address. His was titled "On Reconciling Religious Dissensions among Christians." This oration is very illuminating and seems to be intentionally controversial.

The address begins with a very strong statement about the value of religious union, using some curious examples:

> But, to close this part of my discourse, the very summit and con-clusion of all the evils which arise from religious discord, is, the

destruction of the very religion about which all the controversy has been raised. . . . Of this a very mournful example is exhibited to us in certain extensive dominions and large kingdoms, the inhabitants of which were formerly among the most flourishing professors of the Christian Religion: but the present inhabitants of those countries have unchristianized themselves by embracing Mahomedanism, a system which derived its origin, and had its chief means of increase, from the dissensions which arose between the Jews and the Christians, and from the disputes into which the Orthodox entered with the Sabellians, the Arians, the Nestorians, the Eutychians, and the Monothelites.[87]

Is he just saying that these controversies weakened Christianity, or in light of his strong statements against dissension, is he suggesting that these controversies should not have taken place? Surely, he must mean the former, but he is strangely unclear.

In speaking of the harmful effects of controversy on the confidence of common people in Christian religion, he declared:

When the people perceive that there is scarcely any article of Christian doctrine concerning which there are not different and even contradictory opinions; that one party calls that 'horrid blasphemy' which another party has laid down as "a complete summary of the truth"; that those points which some professors consider the perfection of piety, receive from others the contumelious appellation of "cursed idolatry"; and that controversies of this description are objects of warm discussion between men of learning, respectability, experience and great renown . . . , they begin then to indulge in the imagination, that they may esteem the principles of religion alike obscure and uncertain.[88]

The words "cursed idolatry" are cited from Heidelberg Catechism 80 and there refer to the character of the Roman Catholic Mass. Again, is Arminius just showing the danger of disagreements, or is he equating the fault of the Roman Catholic and Reformed parties in the religious divisions?

While Arminius does not take sides in any of the dissensions that he uses as examples or ever say that some disagreements are necessary and cannot be negotiated away, he does at last turn to the situation in the Netherlands: "It is my special wish, that there may now be among us a similar cessation from the asperities of religious warfare, and that both parties would abstain from writings full of bitterness, from sermons remarkable only for the invectives which they contain, and from the unchristian practice of mutual anathematizing and execration."[89] Again, he does not specify the nature of the theological issues between the parties. It is striking that he refers to two parties, apparently seeing the division in terms of what would later be known as the Remonstrants and Contra-Remonstrants, or Arminians and Calvinists. Later, however, he refers to "all the parties that disagree."[90]

The great suggestion of Arminius to create unity is the meeting of a synod: "That remedy is, an orderly and free convention of the parties that differ from each other. . . . Let the members deliberate, consult, and determine what the word of God declares concerning the matters in controversy, and afterwards let them by common consent promulge and declare the result to the Churches."[91] Remarkably, this synod does not seem to be part of the regular order of the particular, provincial, or national synods of the Dutch Reformed Church. Indeed, the institutional church does not seem to figure in Arminius' efforts to heal disagreements, no doubt because he knew how little influence he had in the church.

Arminius proposes a strongly Erastian solution: "The Chief Magistrates, who profess the Christian religion, will summon and convene this Synod, in virtue of the Supreme official authority with which they are divinely invested, and according to the practice that formerly prevailed in the Jewish Church, and that was afterwards adopted by the Christian Church and continued nearly to the nine hundredth year after the birth of Christ, until the Roman Pontiff began through tyranny to arrogate the authority to himself."[92] (Is Arminius here implicitly equating the Calvinist opposition to Erastianism with the Roman tyranny?) He even suggests that the magistrates preside over the synod: "For the sake of order, moderation, and good government, and to avoid confusion, it will be necessary to have presidents subordinate to Christ Jesus. It is my sincere wish that the magistrates would themselves undertake that office in the Council; and this might be obtained from them as a favour."[93] He may be thinking of Constantine at the Council of Nicaea or of Luther's great reforming treatise *To the Christian Nobility of the German Nation*, but he must have known that his suggestion would anger most of his fellow Reformed ministers.

His most astounding recommendation for the synod was that it should function with only the Bible as its authority and that all delegates "be absolved from all other oaths directly or indirectly contrary to this [supreme allegiance to the divine word] by which they have been bound either to churches or their confessions, schools and their masters, or even to princes themselves (except in matters of their proper jurisdiction)."[94] The synod would not be bound, as the church was, by the confession and catechism. While Arminius always insisted that he did not teach anything contrary to the confessional standards of the church,[95] he must have known how inflammatory his recommendation would be.

Only five weeks after Arminius' address, the States General of the United Provinces granted permission for the meeting of a national synod, but its only mandate was to revise the confession and catechism.[96] The large Calvinist majority in the church was unwilling to meet in a synod with such a mandate, and this synod never met.

An intriguing question seems not to have been posed by the Arminian scholars: Since Arminius had so many connections through his wife's family to regents in Holland, had one of them encouraged Arminius to make this suggestion? This call for a synod that was not bound to the church's confession and catechism seems much more confrontational than anything else that Arminius had done publicly as a professor at Leiden. Had he been assured of support and help from the Erastian regents in bringing about this result? Regardless of whether there is any extant evidence to answer this question, we must recognize the sharply confrontational nature of his action.

Other issues. Arminius often claimed to agree with the confessional standards, and perhaps he never publicly taught contrary to them. His call for a synod, however, reinforced the suspicions of many ministers that he was trying to change the established theological commitments of the church. It is useful here to show that he clearly disagreed with the teaching of the confession and catechism, not only on predestination, but on a number of other issues. On original sin, Stanglin and McCall summarize Arminius' views: "To put the matter briefly, for Arminius, the claim that original sin is primarily a deprivation of original righteousness is accompanied by the claim that original sin does not make one liable to further punishment."[97] This position stands in contrast to Belgic Confession article 15: "We believe that through the disobedience of Adam original sin is extended to all mankind; which is a corruption of the whole nature and a hereditary disease, wherewith even infants in their mother's womb are infected, and which produces in man all sorts of sin, being in him as a root thereof, and therefore is so vile and abominable in the sight of God that it is sufficient to condemn all mankind."

On faith as trust, again Stanglin and McCall summarize: "For Arminius, the problem lies first with the Reformed conviction that saving faith includes not only knowledge and assent, but also *fiducia*, or confident assurance. In other words, assurance is, by definition, thought to be a necessary component of saving faith. . . . Arminius contested this assertion that led Christians to despair. Instead, he distinguished assurance (*fiducia*) from faith (*fides*), declaring that assurance follows as the ordinary result of saving faith, but is not necessarily simultaneous with faith."[98] But the Heidelberg Catechism teaches: "What is true faith? True faith is not only a sure knowledge, whereby I hold for truth all that God has revealed to us in His Word, but also a firm confidence which the Holy Spirit works in my heart by the gospel, that not only to others, but to me also, remission of sins, everlasting righteousness and salvation are freely given by God, merely of grace, only for the sake of Christ's merits" (Q&A 21).

On faith and justification, John Valero Fesko has done a careful study showing that Arminius taught that faith itself is imputed for righteousness, which is seriously at odds with the standard Reformed understanding that faith is the instrument by which the righteousness of Christ is received. Fesko quotes Arminius: "If I understand at all, I think this is the meaning of the phrase, God accounts faith for righteousness: And thus justification is ascribed to faith, not because it accepts, but because it is accepted."[99] As Fesko notes, Arminius' understanding of faith stands against the teaching of Heidelberg Catechism 61: "Why do you say that you are righteous by faith alone? Not because I please God by virtue of the worthiness of my faith, but because the satisfaction, righteousness, and holiness of Christ alone are my righteousness before God, and because I can accept it and make it mine in no other way then by faith alone."[100]

On the possibility of Christian moral perfection, Stanglin and McCall write: "Although he admits that it is strictly possible for the regenerate to fulfill the moral law perfectly in this life, Arminius does not leave the impression that such perfection actually happens often, if at all."[101] But the Heidelberg Catechism teaches: "But can those who are converted to God keep these commandments perfectly? No; but even the holiest men, while in this life, have only a small beginning of this obedience" (Q&A 114). It is surely not surprising that Arminius might have wanted changes to the confession and catechism.

Trelcatius and the divinity of Christ. In 1606, a theology student challenged Arminius about his teaching on an aspect of the divinity of Christ, specifically on whether Christ was *autotheos* (God from Himself). The student accused Arminius of disagreeing with Trelcatius on this point. Muller commented on this dispute: "In the ensuing debate, Arminius' interpretation of the doctrine of the Trinity differed pointedly from that of his Reformed colleagues in the university. Arminius held that the Son's begottenness pertained not only to his person but also to his divinity. Thus, while Trelcatius and the Reformed viewed only the Trinitarian relation, begottenness, as generated, so that the second person of the Trinity could be said to have his sonship by generation but to have his essence of himself, Arminius argued that Christ had both his sonship and his divinity or essence by generation."[102] The views of Arminius, rather than those of Trelcatius, seem to be the innovative ones. Again, as Muller argues: "Arminius' grounding of the economic subordination of the Son to the antecedent will of the Father in the concept of a generated *deitas* or divine *essential* is foreign not only to the Reformed and Lutheran views of Trinity but also to the views of all the great medieval doctors."[103]

Muller seems to understand the concerns of Arminius' Calvinist critics: "Arminius' patristic scholarship left something to be desired—and the resemblance of his polemical statements to those of [Valentin] Gentile eventually convinced his Reformed opponents that he tended toward an anti-trinitarian, subordinationistic, and even Arian view of God."[104] Stanglin and McCall defend Arminius' Trinitarian orthodoxy but acknowledge Trinitarian problems in the later history of the movement: "It is clear that Arminius intends nothing short of a defense of the full divinity of the Son, but it is just as clear (from the resultant history) that the theology of many later Arminians tended toward subordinationism."[105]

Arminius was apparently annoyed with Trelcatius on this matter but did not speak directly to him about it, perhaps because he did not respect the intellect of Trelcatius.[106] Once again, we see Arminius adopting controversial views and confronting his colleagues and students with them. Here he is the innovator and troublemaker.

Rumors. One of the very real problems Arminius faced in the last years of his life was the circulation of rumors about his beliefs and teaching. Many false charges flew in many directions, and Arminius was not the only one misrepresented. Nevertheless, Arminius was often at the center of various charges, and the fact that he had not published anything no doubt fueled them.

One recurring charge is summarized by Gerard Brandt in this way: "Among the things reported of him at that time [1608], and which have been since often repeated, was, that he advised his Pupils or Scholars to read the books of the Jesuits and of Koornhert, and spoke contemptibly of those of Calvin."[107] In September 1608, Arminius wrote to a burgomaster in Amsterdam, Sebastian Egberts, to deny these charges vigorously. He declared that he commended the works of Calvin to his students and then stated: "That this has been my advice, I can prove by numberless witnesses; whereas they cannot produce one whom I have counseled to read the Jesuits or Koornhert's books: let them show but one only, and the falsity will appear. Thus stories, or rather fables, arise from a single nothing."[108]

Today, we are perhaps surprised that the reading of theological opponents would be controversial. No doubt, some Calvinists were unfairly trying to build a case against Arminius that he was serving the interests of the Roman Catholic Church. The long war with Spain might have made the books of Spanish Jesuits such as Suarez and Molina particularly controversial. We can see that Arminius regarded the charges as sufficiently serious that he denied them absolutely.

One student, however, did testify very clearly against Arminius on this point. Caspar Sibelius, a student at Leiden from 1608 to 1609, declared: "I observed, among a number of fellow students enrolled in the private theological class of doctor Arminius, many things that, had I been ignorant, might easily have led me into dark and abominable errors. For in that class we were utterly drawn away from reading the works and treatises of Calvin, Beza, Zanchi, Martyr, Ursinus, Piscator, Perkins, and other learned and valuable theologians of the church of Christ, we were commanded to examine only holy scripture, but equally so the writings of Socinus, Acontius, Castellio, Thomas Aquinas, Molina, Suarez and other enemies of grace were commended to us."[109] Whether the rumors or charges were true, the situation in the university and in the broader church and society had become so serious that the civil government concluded that it must take action.

The Declaration of Sentiments. In the midst of growing controversy, Arminius was asked to present his views in person to the rather sympathetic states of Holland in The Hague on October 30, 1608. Arminius read this statement, known as *The Declaration of Sentiments*, in Dutch to the assembly. After his death, it was translated into Latin and published.

The first part of the *Declaration* is historical, explaining why Arminius had often been unwilling to enter into discussions with various groups of ministers to state and defend his views. The second part is theological, analyzing and rejecting various Calvinist views of predestination and then presenting on his own views on predestination and a number of related issues.

In the course of his *Declaration of Sentiments*, Arminius refers twice to several controversial ministers in the Reformed Church in the United Provinces: Caspar Coolhaes, Herman Herberts, Cornelius Wiggerts, and Tako Sybrants. As we have already seen, Coolhaes was deposed and excommunicated in 1582, and Wiggerts was suspended in 1593 and deposed in 1596. Herberts was suspended by the church in 1591 but was kept in office by the magistrates. Sybrants, while long opposed by the Calvinist clergy, survived in his post through the protection of the magistrates.

Arminius' first appeal to these ministers in the historical section of the *Declaration* was in Erastian terms, as he explained why he had not cooperated in a conference in 1605 with ministers from Holland: "I wish the brethren would remember this fact, that although every one of our ministers is subject as a member to the jurisdiction of the particular Synod to which he belongs, yet not one of them has hitherto dared to engage in a conference without the advice and permission of the magistrates under whom he is placed."[110] He then appeals to the four ministers as examples of this requirement of the involvement of the magistrates.

His second appeal is under his theological arguments, specifically: "XX. Lastly. *This doctrine of Predestination* has been rejected *both in former times and in our own days,* by the greater part of the professors of Christianity."[111] He develops this statement: "1. But, omitting all mention of the periods that occurred in former ages, facts themselves declare, that the Lutherans and Anabaptist churches, as well as that of Rome, account this to be an erroneous doctrine. 2. However highly Luther and Melanchthon might at the very commencement of the Reformation have approved of this doctrine, they afterwards deserted it."[112] In these comments, Arminius shows that he is not a very good historian of doctrine with regard either to the Roman church or to Luther.

He continues with the situation in the Netherlands:

4. Besides, by many of the inhabitants of these our own provinces this doctrine is accounted a grievance of such a nature, as to cause several of them to affirm, that on account of it they neither can nor will have any communion with our Church: Others of them have united themselves with our Churches, but not without entering a protest, "that they cannot possibly give their consent to this doctrine." But, on account of this kind of Predestination, our Churches have been deserted by not a few individuals, who formerly held the same opinions as ourselves: Others also have threatened to depart from us, unless they be fully assured that the Church holds no opinion of this description. . . . 6. *Lastly.* Of all the difficulties and controversies which have arisen in these our Churches since the time of the Reformation, there is none that has not had its origin in this doctrine, or that has not at least been mixed with it. What I have here said will be found true, if we bring to our recollection the controversies that existed at Leyden in the affair of Koolhaes, at Gouda in that of Herman Herberts, at Horn with respect to Cornelius Wiggertson, and at Mendenblick in the affair of Tako Sybrants. This consideration was not among the last of those motives which induced me to give my more diligent attention to this head of doctrine, and endeavour to prevent our Churches from suffering any detriment from it; because, from it, the Papists have derived much of their increase.[113]

Such a doctrine of predestination, he argues, has caused trouble wherever it has gone.

These arguments would not have impressed the Calvinists, who would have responded that the character of the church is defined by its doctrinal standards, not by its critics, and that the church sought to discipline the four men.

Arminius' concluding rejection of supralapsarianism is very sharp. As Bangs noted, "Arminius now comes out fighting. No longer is he content to say merely that many views should be tolerated in the church; he finds this position intolerable."[114] Arminius writes: "*This doctrine completely subverts* THE FOUNDATION OF RELIGION IN GENERAL, *and of the Christian Religion in particular.*"[115] These words echo his evaluation of the teaching of Gomarus on predestination in his "Examination" in 1605. They again raise the question of Arminius' honesty when he argued that he had no fundamental disagreements with Gomarus in 1605.

After the lengthy rejection of Calvinist views of predestination, Arminius presents the clearest and fullest statement of his own views on predestination that we have from his own pen. Still, this statement in four propositions is not long or detailed. As Bangs wrote: "It is surprisingly brief."[116]

The first proposition refers to Christ: "I. The FIRST absolute decree of God concerning the salvation of sinful man, is that by which he decreed to appoint his Son Jesus Christ for a Mediator, Redeemer, Saviour, Priest and King, who might destroy sin by his own death, might by his obedience obtain the salvation which had been lost, and might communicate it by his own virtue."[117] Here Arminius articulates his insistence that Christ is the foundation of election against the standard Reformed teaching that Christ is the executor of election and the foundation of salvation. (The Reformed, of course, always said that the eternal Son in the councils of eternity with the Father and the Spirit was the foundation of election.)

The second proposition makes clear his conviction that God does not unconditionally elect individuals, but elects those who meet the condition of faith: "II. The SECOND precise and absolute decree of God, is that in which he decreed to receive into favour *those who repent and believe,* and, in Christ, for HIS sake and through HIM, to effect the salvation of such penitents and believers as persevered to the end; but to leave in sin and under wrath *all impenitent persons and unbelievers,* and to damn them as aliens from Christ."[118]

In the third proposition, Arminius writes of the means by which God makes faith available to sinners. Then, in the fourth proposition, he presents his views on how a sinner actually comes to faith: "IV. To these succeeds the FOURTH decree, by which God decreed to save and damn certain particular persons. This decree has its foundation in the foreknowledge of God, by which he knew from all eternity those individuals who *would,* through his preventing [i.e., prevenient] grace, *believe,* and through his subsequent grace *would persevere,* according to the before-described administration of those means which are suitable and proper for conversion and faith; and by which foreknowledge, he likewise knew those who *would not believe and persevere.*"[119] Here Arminius is using middle knowledge and presenting his views honestly and straightforwardly. But his candor here highlights the limits, and perhaps even deceit, of his 1604 theses on predestination.

In twenty brief points, Arminius defends his propositions. He concludes his twentieth point with these words about his teaching on predestination: "It cannot afford any person just cause for expressing his aversion to it; nor can it give any pretext for contention in the Christian Church."[120] Such a statement in the midst of all the controversy in the church is at very best disingenuous. Is he appealing to the desire of the magistrates for order? As some of his arguments show a serious misreading of history, here he seems seriously to misread the contemporary situation in the church. He has attacked various Reformed doctrines, and he claims not to understand the reaction he is facing. Here again, we do not see the moderate Arminius but rather Arminius the "dogged controversialist."

Conclusion

The evidence we have examined shows conclusively that the four key contentions of Bangs that undergird his positive picture of Arminius are wrong. Arminius was not part of an older, Erasmian Reformed current in the church. Such a current did not exist. Arminius was not surrounded by a pervasive supralapsarianism among the orthodox Calvinists. Arminius did most likely change his theology of predestination from Calvinist to non-Calvinist around 1590. And Arminius, far from being unfairly attacked again and again by Calvinists, was usually the initiator of controversy.

Arminius experienced controversy in Geneva, Amsterdam, and Leiden with a variety of people over philosophy, ecclesiology, exegesis, and theology. Is it credible that it was always someone else who caused the trouble? Or is it more likely that Arminius was something of a troublemaker? Surely, he knew that Beza and others were Aristotelians before he went to Geneva. Surely, he knew the contents of the Belgic Confession and Heidelberg Catechism to which the church subscribed in Amsterdam. Surely, he knew that the majority of ministers in the Netherlands opposed the Erastianism that he embraced in 1591. Surely, he knew Calvin's exegesis of Romans 7 and 9, followed by most all the Reformed, before he preached a very different understanding of those texts. He certainly knew the theological commitments of Gomarus and Trelcatius at Leiden on free will and predestination before he went there. Yet, somehow a number of historians have accepted that whenever Calvinists objected to Arminius' challenge to the established positions of the Reformed churches, they were the ones causing trouble. No one forced him to subscribe or to become a pastor or professor.

He was likely more than a controversialist, however. He was likely a dissembler who abused the good will and efforts of the Calvinists to maintain peace with him in the church. If he never changed his theology, then was he honest with Beza, who gave him a letter of recommendation? Was he honest with the classis in 1588 when he was examined for ordination? Was he honest with Gomarus in their conversation in 1603, which led to Gomarus' recommending him for the appointment to teach at Leiden? Was he honest with Gomarus, Trelcatius, and the churches in 1605 when together the three of them assured the churches that they were united theologically? If he did change his theology in a way that contradicted the Belgic Confession, was he under no moral obligation to report this to the church?

Arminius knew that he was part of a small minority of ministers in the church who wanted to change its doctrines by allying themselves with the power of the magistrates. He was not more confrontational than some others in the church. He was a bright and creative theologian. But he had no right to reject theological views that he had pledged to uphold. He had a right to promote his views. Neither he nor his supporters can contend that those who disagreed with him—the majority of the ministers—were wrong to promote their views. Arminius should be evaluated in the same way as all his contemporaries, not as an obviously morally superior figure. Perhaps, after all, Abraham Kuyper best epitomized Arminius when he called him a "crafty fox."[121]

Appendix 2

───

GENERAL PATTERN IN EACH
HEAD OF DOCTRINE

The Synod of Dort in writing the canons followed a general pattern in each head of doctrine. To understand the canons, it is very helpful to see that structure and the ways in which each head of doctrine follows it. The following fourteen points summarize that pattern:

1. Each is written in a popular rather than a scholastic style.
2. Each head of doctrine is complete in itself.
3. Each head of doctrine begins with positive articles presenting the Reformed theology and concludes with rejections of errors refuting specific Arminian teaching.
4. Each begins with a commonly accepted Christian, catholic doctrine.
5. Each develops the head of doctrine from the common Christian conviction to the distinctively Reformed position: I.1–6; II.1–7; III–IV.1–2, 4–5; V.1–2.
6. Each has one article that summarizes the distinctive Reformed doctrine on this point: I.7, 15; II.8; III–IV.3, 11; V.3.
7. Each gives some specific elaborations and applications of the doctrine: I.8–14, 16–18; II.9; III–IV.4–5, 7–17; V.4–15.
8. Each addresses the justice of God and the fault of man: I.1,

5, 18; II.1–2, 6; III–IV.4, 9, 15; V.8.

9. Each examines the effects of the doctrine on Christian living: I.6, 12–13, 17; II.8–9; III–IV.7, 9, 10, 12, 15; V.1–2, 4, 7, 10–15.

10. Each (except one) examines Christian assurance in relation to the doctrine: I.2, 16; III–IV.13, 15; V.9–13.

11. Each shows the importance of the means of life: I.3, 7, 14; II.5; III–IV.6, 8, 11–12, 17; V.14.

12. Each is shaped against specific Arminian teachings and formulations both in some of the articles and many of the rejection of errors.

13. Each has more quotations from the Scriptures in the rejection of errors than in the articles.

14. Each head of doctrine, to preserve its completeness, has some repetition in the subjects covered in its rejection of errors; for example, original sin is considered in rejection I.8; rejection II.5; and rejection III–IV.1.

——

AN OUTLINE OF
THE CANONS OF DORT

The brief but detailed outline of the canons in this appendix will help the reader and student see the ways in which canons develop their theological points.

I. Redemption planned
    A. Common Christian convictions
        1. Man is lost in sin; article 1 (Eph. 2:1–3)
        2. God redeems through His Son, sending preachers and giving faith; articles 2–5 (John 3:16; Rom. 10:14–15; Eph. 2:8)
        3. Faith is given according to God's plan; article 6 (Rom. 9:10–15)
    B. Reformed doctrine of unconditional election defined; article 7 (Eph. 1:3–12)
    C. Elaborations of the doctrine of election
        1. One kind of election, not many; article 8 (Rom. 8:28–30)
        2. Election not based on foreseen qualifications; article 9 (Eph. 2:8–10)
        3. Election is of persons, not of conditions; article 10 (Eph. 1:4)

4. Election is unchangeable; article 11 (Rom. 8:31–32; 9:6)
D. Answers to alleged problems caused by the doctrine
   1. Election and assurance; articles 12–13 (Rom. 4:18–5:11; 8:16; 1 John 3:7–10)
   2. Election and preaching; article 14 (Eph. 1:1–11)
E. Reformed doctrine of reprobation defined; article 15 (Rom. 9:6, 10–23)
F. Answers to alleged problems caused by reprobation
   1. Reprobation and assurance; article 16 (Isa. 42:1–3; Matt. 12:18–20)
   2. Reprobation and covenant; article 17 (1 Cor. 7:14)
G. Election, reprobation, and God-centered religion; article 18 (Rom. 11:33–36)
H. Rejections of errors
   1. Election and one decree
   2. Election and many decrees
   3. Election and faith
   4. Election and preparation
   5. Election and foreseen qualities
   6. Election and perseverance
   7. Election and assurance
   8. Election and passing over
   9. Election and worthiness

II. Redemption accomplished
A. Common Christian convictions
   1. God's justice requires satisfaction for sin; article 1 (Ex. 34:6–7; Gal. 6:7–8)
   2. God gives His Son, who alone can satisfy; articles 2–3 (2 Cor. 5:18–21; 1 John 2:2; John 4:42)
   3. Christ satisfies as God and man; article 4 (Matt. 1:20–23)
   4. Call to believe is to be preached to everyone; article 5 (Matt. 28:18–20; Acts 2:37–39)

    5. Cause of unbelief is in the unbeliever, not in Christ; article 6 (Matt. 23:27)

    6. Christ is the cause of faith; article 7 (Col. 2:13–14)

B. Reformed doctrine of definite atonement defined; article 8 (Matt. 20:28; John 10:15; 11:51–52)

C. Elaboration of doctrine of definite atonement: Christ will always have a church; article 9 (Matt. 16:18)

D. Rejections of errors

    1. Atonement and effectiveness

    2. Atonement and covenant

    3. Atonement and free will

    4. Atonement and faith

    5. Atonement and original sin

    6. Atonement accomplished and applied

    7. Atonement and the love of God

III–IV. Redemption applied

A. Common Christian convictions on depravity

    1. Man was created good, but has become wicked in mind, will, and affections; article 1 (Rom. 3:9–18)

    2. Original sin from Adam; article 2 (Rom. 5:17–19)

B. Reformed doctrine of total depravity defined; article 3 (Gen. 6:5)

C. Common Christian convictions on regeneration

    1. Nature cannot regenerate sinners; article 4 (Rom. 1:18–25)

    2. The law cannot regenerate sinners; article 5 (Rom. 8:3)

D. How God works regeneration

    1. By the Spirit through preaching; article 6 (John 3:1–6)

    2. Sovereignly to whom He will; article 7 (Jer. 9:23–24)

    3. Through a sincere call to believe; articles 8–9 (Matt. 11:28–30; 13:1–23)

4. As a gift to the elect; article 10 (Eph. 2:8, 9)

E. The Reformed doctrine of regeneration defined; article 11 (Gal. 5:22–25)

F. Implications of the Reformed doctrine of regeneration

    1. A completely efficacious act of God alone; article 12 (John 6:63–65; 2 Cor. 5:17)

    2. Ineffably; article 13 (John 3:8)

    3. Actually creating faith; article 14 (Phil. 2:12–13)

    4. Believers and unbelievers respond differently to the work of regeneration; article 15 (Luke 17:12–19)

    5. God works faith as a response in a personal, not mechanical way; article 16 (Acts 2:46–47)

G. Regeneration and the means of grace; article 17 (2 Cor. 5:11, 18–19; 6:1)

H. Rejections of errors

    1. Sin and original sin

    2. Sin and the image of God

    3. Sin and the will

    4. Sin and remaining good

    5. Regeneration and common grace

    6. Regeneration and new qualities

    7. Regeneration and moral persuasion

    8. Regeneration and human resistance

    9. Regeneration, grace, and free will

V. Redemption preserved

A. Common Christian convictions

    1. Regeneration does not mean the end of sin or suffering; article 1 (Rom. 8:17–25)

    2. The regenerate must strive for holiness; article 2 (Phil. 3:12–16)

B. Reformed doctrine of perseverance defined; article 3 (Phil. 1:6)

C. Perseverance and the continuing problem of sin

1. Weakness of the flesh can result in serious sins; article 4 (2 Sam. 11)
2. Such sins seriously disturb one's relationship with God; article 5 (Ps. 32:3–4)
3. God does not permit the destruction of that relationship; article 6 (1 Peter 1:1–5)
4. God renews a disturbed relationship; article 7 (Ps. 51:1–11)
5. Man is weak, but God is steadfast; article 8 (Ps. 32:6–7, 10)

D. Perseverance and assurance
   1. Assurance of perseverance is possible for believers; article 9 (Heb. 10:19–23)
   2. Assurance is found in the promises of the Word and in holy living; article 10 (Rom. 4:18–5:11; 8:16; 1 John 3:7–10)
   3. Assurance is attacked, but overcomes; article 11 (Rom. 7–8)
   4. Assurance produces humility and piety; article 12 (Eph. 5:8–18)
   5. Assurance after serious sin produces more care in the future; article 13 (Ps. 51:12–19)

E. Perseverance and the means of grace; article 14 (Heb. 10:25)
F. Perseverance and consolation; article 15 (John 10:28)
G. Rejections of errors
   1. Perseverance as condition
   2. Perseverance and the will
   3. Perseverance and falling from grace
   4. Perseverance and the sin unto death
   5. Perseverance and certainty
   6. Perseverance and piety
   7. Perseverance and faith
   8. Perseverance and repeated regeneration
   9. Perseverance and the prayer of Christ

RELATION OF THE POSITIVE ARTICLES OF THE CANONS TO THE REJECTION OF ERRORS

First Head of Doctrine

Art. 3: R of E 9
Art. 6: R of E 8
Art. 7: R of E 1, 9
Art. 8: R of E 2
Art. 9: R of E 4, 5
Art. 10: R of E 3
Art. 11: R of E 6
Art. 12: R of E 7
Art. 15: R of E 8
R of E 1: Art. 7
R of E 2: Art. 8
R of E 3: Art. 10
R of E 4: Art. 9
R of E 5: Art. 9
R of E 6: Art. 11
R of E 7: Art. 12
R of E 8: Art. 6, 15
R of E 9: Art. 3, 7

Second Head of Doctrine

Art. 8: R of E 1–7
Art. 9: R of E 6
R of E 1–5, 7: Art. 8
R of E 6: Art. 8–9

Third and Fourth Heads of Doctrine

Art. 1: R of E 2
Art. 2: R of E 1
Art. 3: R of E 3–4
Art. 4: R of E 5
Art. 11: R of E 6
Art. 12: R of E 7
Art. 14: R of E 9
Art. 16: R of E 8
R of E 1: Art. 2
R of E 2: Art. 1
R of E 3: Art. 3

R of E 4: Art. 3

R of E 5: Art. 4

R of E 6: Art. 11

R of E 7: Art. 12

R of E 8: Art.16

R of E 9: Art. 14

Fifth Head of Doctrine

Art. 4: R of E 7

Art. 6: R of E 3 and 4

Art. 7: R of E 8

Art. 8: R of E 1, 2, and 9

Art. 10: R of E 5

Art. 12: R of E 6

R of E 1: Art. 8

R of E 2: Art. 8

R of E 3: Art. 6

R of E 4: Art. 6

R of E 5: Art. 10

R of E 6: Art. 12

R of E 7: Art. 4

R of E 8: Art. 7

R of E 9: Art. 8

A NEW TRANSLATION OF THE DOCTRINAL STATEMENT BY THE SYNOD OF DORT ON THE SABBATH [1]

On the Sabbath

1. In the fourth commandment of the divine law, part is ceremonial and part is moral.
2. The ceremonial was the rest of the seventh day after creation, and the rigid observance of that day prescribed particularly for the Jewish people.
3. The moral truly is that a certain and appointed day is fixed for the worship of God and so much rest as is necessary for the worship of God and for holy meditation on Him.
4. Since the abrogation of the Sabbath of the Jews, the day of the Lord must be solemnly sanctified by Christians.
5. This day has always been observed since the time of the Apostles by the ancient catholic church.
6. This day must be so consecrated to divine worship that on it one ceases from all servile works, except those of love and

present necessity; and also from all such refreshing activities[*] as impede the worship of God.

---

* The Latin word translated "refreshing activities" is *recreationibus*, which has traditionally been translated "recreations." That traditional translation has connotations in English that the Latin word would not have had in the seventeenth century. The word stands in contrast to "servile works" and means "restorations," "recoveries," or "refreshings."

ACKNOWLEDGMENTS

With thanks to many who helped with this project: from early professors, Roger Nicole, Lewis Spitz, Wilhelm Pauck, and Heiko Oberman; to all my colleagues at Westminster Seminary California, especially Scott Clark; to the encouragers at Ligonier Ministries, R.C. and Vesta Sproul, Chris Larson, and Kevin Gardner; to Barb Van Solkema; and to my dear friend Andrew Cammenga.

NOTES

Foreword

1   Joel R. Beeke, *Reformed Preaching: Proclaiming God's Word from the Heart of the Preacher to the Heart of His People* (Wheaton, Ill.: Crossway, 2018), 256–64.

Introduction

1   Walter Rex, *Essays on Pierre Bayle and Religious Controversy* (The Hague, Netherlands: Martinus Nijhoff, 1965), 80.

Chapter 1

1   For a more detailed look at subscription to the doctrinal standards in the life of the Dutch Reformed churches, see W. Robert Godfrey, "Subscription in the Dutch Reformed Tradition," in *The Practice of Confessional Subscription*, ed. David W. Hall (Oak Ridge, Tenn.: The Covenant Foundation, 2001), 67–75.

2   These two synods were attended by delegates from the Reformed churches in the provinces of Holland and Zeeland. "The synods held in Dordrecht in 1574 and 1578 were mainly of a provincial character" (*Handbook of Dutch Church History*, ed. Herman J. Selderhuis [Goettingen, Germany: Vandenhoeck and Ruprecht: 2015], 239). Yet their work was recognized by and in harmony with the national synods.

3   With the establishment of a Dutch monarchy after the Napoleonic era, new regulations were given to the Dutch Reformed Church by the king in 1816 establishing a national synod, but on very different terms than those of the earlier national synods. Many Calvinists in 1816 believed that those terms were not at all Reformed. As the *Handbook of Dutch Church History* states: "The general Synod only looked after administrative matters, not doctrinal ones. The king appointed the members of the higher authorities, that is, the Synod and the regional administrations" (446).

4   Within orthodox Calvinism, a difference had developed on the question of the order of the decrees of election in the mind of God in eternity. Here the minds of the finite must tread very carefully in trying to understand the mind of the infinite. The two interpretations came to be known as infralapsarianism and supralapsarianism. The key Latin word embedded in these terms is the word *lapsus*, meaning the fall of humans into sin. The disagreement was over the place of God's eternal decree of the fall in relation to His other decrees about election. The infralapsarians taught

that the decree distinguishing the elect from the reprobate occurs on the basis of the decree of the fall. They saw this order as crucial for upholding the goodness and justice of God. The supralapsarians taught that the decree distinguishing the elect from the reprobate preceded the decree of the fall. They saw this order as crucial for upholding the sovereignty of God. While this disagreement was significant, each side recognized the other as within the bounds of Calvinist orthodoxy.

5   *The Works of James Arminius*, trans. and eds. James Nichols and William Nichols (Grand Rapids, Mich.: Baker, 1986), 1:634.

6   Arminius, *Works*, 1:653–54.

7   For a helpful study of the varieties of later Arminianism, see J.I. Packer, "Arminianisms," in *Through Christ's Word*, eds. W.R. Godfrey and J.L. Boyd III (Phillipsburg, N.J.: P&R, 1985), 121–48.

8   *Acta et Documenta Synodi Nationalis Dordrechtanae* (1618–1619), eds. Donald Sinnema, Christian Moser, and Herman J. Selderhuis (Goettingen, Germany: Vandenhoeck and Ruprecht, 2015), 1:167.

9   This translation is from the Latin text in Philip Schaff, *The Creeds of Christendom*, vol. 3 (Grand Rapids, Mich.: Baker, 1935).

Chapter 2

1   For details, see W. Robert Godfrey, "John Hales' Good-Night to John Calvin," in *Protestant Scholasticism*, eds. Carl Trueman and R.S. Clark (Carlisle, England: Paternoster, 1999), 165–80.

2   See appendix 5 for a new translation of that statement on the Sabbath.

3   See W. Robert Godfrey, "Tensions within International Calvinism: The Debate on the Atonement at the Synod of Dort, 1618–1619" (Ph.D. diss., Stanford University, 1974), 251–52.

4   The Latin text translated here is from *Acta Synodi Nationalis* (Dordrecht, Netherlands: I.J. Caninius, 1620), 287–89.

Chapter 3

1   This translation of the canons is based on the Latin text in Schaff, *The Creeds of Christendom*, vol. 3.

Chapter 8

1   The Latin word *caput* literally means "head" and comes also to mean a chapter or section.

2   *Canon* here is derived from a Greek word for "rule" or "standard."

3   For more details, see W. Robert Godfrey, "Popular and Catholic: The Modus Docendi of the Synod of Dordt," in *Revisiting the Synod of Dordt*, eds. Aza Goudriaan and F.A. van Lieburg (Leiden, Netherlands: Brill, 2011), 243–60.

4   Out of fifty-nine positive articles, only eleven contain biblical quotations or references (nine in the first head of doctrine, and one each in the third and fourth heads and the fifth head. In the thirty-four rejections of errors, only two (rejections II.3, 6) have no such quotations or references.

Chapter 9

1 For a fuller discussion, see W. Robert Godfrey, "A Promise for Parents: Dordt's Perspective on Covenant and Election," in *Church and School in Early Modern Protestantism*, eds. Jordan Ballor, et al. (Leiden, Netherlands: Brill, 2013), 373–86.

2 Francis Turretin, *Institutes of Elenctic Theology*, ed. J. Dennison (Phillipsburg, N.J.: P&R, 1992), 12.4.7 (2:190–91).

Appendix 1

1 Bertius' funeral oration is printed in Arminius, *Works*, vol. 1. The citation is from p. 45.

2 G.J. Hoenderdaal, "Jacob Arminius," in *Orthodoxie und Pietismus*, ed. Martin Geschat (Stuttgart, Germany: Mohr Siebeck, 1982), 62, cited in Keith Stanglin and Thomas McCall, *Jacob Arminius* (Oxford, England: Oxford University Press, 2012), 205f.

3 Carl Bangs, *Arminius: A Study in the Dutch Reformation* (Nashville, Tenn.: Abingdon, 1971).

4 See Richard Muller, *God, Creation, and Providence in the Thought of Jacob Arminius* (Grand Rapids, Mich., 1991), 10, and Stanglin and McCall, 21f.

5 Bangs, 22.

6 Bangs, 198.

7 Jonathan Israel, *The Dutch Republic: Its Rise, Greatness, and Fall 1477–1806* (Oxford, England: Oxford University Press, 1995), 369.

8 Israel, *The Dutch Republic*, 365.

9 Israel, *The Dutch Republic*, 370.

10 Israel, *The Dutch Republic*, 371f.

11 Stanglin and McCall, 202.

12 Bangs, 71.

13 Stanglin and McCall, 108.

14 Keith D. Stanglin, *Arminius on the Assurance of Salvation* (Leiden, Netherlands: Brill, 2007), 34.

15 While a pastor in Amsterdam, Arminius wrote in 1602 a long analysis of William Perkins' defense of a supralapsarian approach to predestination.

16 Muller, *God, Creation, and Providence*, 19

17 Muller, *God, Creation, and Providence*, 17.

18 Richard A. Muller, "The Christological Problem in the Thought of Jacobus Arminius," *Nederlands Archief voor Kerkgeschiedenis* 68-2 (1988), 148.

19 Muller, *God, Creation, and Providence*, 26.

20 Muller, "Christological Problem," 146.

21 Arminius, *Works*, 1:29f.

22 Bangs, 138.

23 Muller, *God, Creation, and Providence*, 9f, and Stanglin, *Assurance*, 32.

24 Bangs, 138–41.
25 Bangs, 139.
26 Bangs, 141.
27 Bangs, 19.
28 Bangs, 296. Nichols and Nichols give the date of this letter in Arminius, *Works*, 1:168.
29 Stanglin and McCall, 68.
30 Stanglin and McCall, 45; see also 68, 102.
31 Luis de Molina, *On Divine Foreknowledge* (part IV of the *Concordia*), trans. A. Freddoso (Ithaca, N.Y.: Cornell University Press, 1988), 139.
32 Bangs, 71.
33 Arminius, *Works*, 1:23.
34 Arminius, *Works*, 1:23.
35 Arminius, *Works*, 1:25.
36 Arminius, *Works*, 1:24f.
37 Cited by Bangs, 73.
38 Bangs, 73, insists that the letter must be dated June 3, 1585, although it is dated 1583 in both the *Epistolae* and the *Works*. Bangs offers no evidence for his claim. Is it likely that if Beza wrote in June 1585, that the city of Amsterdam would ask for a letter of recommendation in August 1585?
39 Arminius, *Works*, 1:24–25n.
40 Bangs, 73.
41 Bangs, 66.
42 Bangs, 64f.
43 Arminius, *Works*, 1:22.
44 Arminius, *Works*, 1:27.
45 Bangs, 111.
46 Bangs, 112f., records and rejects the claim of the seventeenth-century Calvinist minister and historian Jacobus Triglandius that Arminius' examination revealed theological problems that had to be resolved before his ordination.
47 Bangs, 110.
48 Cited in W. Robert Godfrey, "Subscription in the Dutch Reformed Tradition," in *The Practice of Confessional Subscription*, ed. David W. Hall (New York: University Press of America, 1995), 68.
49 Bangs, 132.
50 Bangs, 142–50.
51 Bangs, 149.
52 Bangs, 194.
53 Arminius, *Works*, 3:485.
54 Arminius, *Works*, 3:504.

55 Arminius, *Works*, 3:514.

56 Arminius, *Works*, 3:519; see also 496, 497, 505, 509, 510.

57 Stanglin and McCall, 134.

58 Bangs, 203.

59 Arminius, *Works*, 3:76.

60 Junius was professor in Heidelberg from 1584 to 1592, when he went to Leiden to teach until his death, although he was invited to teach in Geneva.

61 Arminius, *Works*, 3:87.

62 Bangs, 203.

63 James Arminius, *Writings*, trans. and ed. W.R. Bagnall (Grand Rapids, Mich.: Baker, 1977), 3:281.

64 Arminius, *Writings*, 3:297f.

65 Arminius, *Writings*, 3:311.

66 Arminius, *Writings*, 3:489.

67 Arminius, *Writings*, 3:481; also, "But, is there, then, a two-fold Election on the part of God? Certainly, if that is Election, by which God chooses to righteousness and life, that must be different, by which He chooses some to faith, if indeed he does choose some to faith: which, indeed, I will not now discuss, because it is my purpose only to answer your arguments. . . . That true and saving faith may be totally and finally lost, I should not at once dare to say: though many of the fathers frequently seem to affirm this" (3:490f.).

68 "On Divine Predestination," is just over four pages in Arminius, *Works*, 2:226–30.

69 Bangs, 15.

70 Bangs, 263.

71 Gerard Brandt, *The History of the Reformation and Other Ecclesiastical Transactions in and about the Low-Countries* (London: T. Wood, 1720–23), 2:31, cited in Stanglin, *Assurance*, 31. Brandt was originally published in Dutch in four volumes, 1671–1704.

72 Arminius, *Works*, 3:523.

73 Stanglin and McCall, 38.

74 Stanglin, *Assurance*, 26.

75 Stanglin, *Disputations*, 17–18.

76 Stanglin, *Disputations*, 66.

77 G.P. van Itterzon, *Franciscus Gomarus* ('s-Gravenhage: Netherlands: Martinus Nijhoff, 1930), 123, 178; P.J. Wijminga, *Festus Hommius* (Leiden, Netherlands: D. Donner, 1899), 68.

78 Arminius, "Examination of the Theses of Dr. F. Gomarus Respecting Predestination," in *Works*, 3:526–658.

79 Arminius, *Works*, 3:526.

80 Arminius, *Works*, 3:657–58.

81 Arminius, *Works*, 1:39.

82 Arminius, "Disputation XV, On Divine Predestination," thesis 2, in *Works*, 2:226.

83 Arminius, "Disputation XV," thesis 7, in *Works*, 2:228.

84 Bangs, 269.

85 Stanglin, *Disputations*, 92.

86 Stanglin and McCall commented, "Arminius' election to this position reflects the broad and deep respect he so quickly commanded among the faculty outside of his college" (32f.). They do not discuss, however, how many on a relatively small faculty served a one-year term.

87 Arminius, *Works*, 1:452f.

88 Arminius, *Works*, 1:441f.

89 Arminius, *Works*, 1:472f.

90 Arminius, *Works*, 1:486.

91 Arminius, *Works*, 1:473.

92 Arminius, *Works*, 1:473ff.

93 Arminius, *Works*, 1:506.

94 Cited in Bangs, 278.

95 E.g., Bangs, 268; Stanglin and McCall, 137.

96 Bangs, 280.

97 Stanglin and McCall, 149.

98 Stanglin and McCall, 177f.

99 John Valero Fesko, "Arminius on Justification, Reformed or Protestant," in *Church History and Religious Culture* 94 (2014), 7.

100 Fesko, 11.

101 Stanglin and McCall, 172.

102 Muller, "Christological Problem," 152.

103 Muller, "Christological Problem," 160.

104 Muller, "Christological Problem," 153f.

105 Stanglin and McCall, 90.

106 Stanglin, *Assurance*, 30f.

107 Brandt, 2:51.

108 Brandt, 2:52.

109 Cited in Muller, *God, Creation, and Providence*, 27f.

110 Arminius, *Works*, 1:601.

111 Arminius, *Works*, 1:639, emphasis original.

112 Arminius, *Works*, 1:640–42.

113 Arminius, *Works*, 1:643f, emphasis original.

114 Bangs, 309.

115 Arminius, *Works*, 1:634, emphasis original.

116 Bangs, 312.

117 Arminius, *Works*, 1:653, emphasis original.

118 Arminius, *Works*, 1:653, emphasis original.

119 Arminius, *Works*, 1:653–54, emphasis original.

120 Arminius, *Works*, 1:656.

121 Cited by Stanglin and McCall, 8.

Appendix 5

1   For the Latin text, see *Acta et Documenta Synodi Nationalis Dordrechtanae (1618–1619)*, vol. 1, eds. Donald Sinnema, et al. (Goettingen, Germany: Vandenhoeck and Ruprecht, 2015), 167. For the issues of concern to the delegates from Zeeland, see H.H. Kuyper, *De Post-Acta of Nahandelingen van de Nationale Synode van Dordrecht* (Amsterdam: Hoeveker and Wormser, 1899), 180–83, 190–93.

SCRIPTURE INDEX

SUBJECT INDEX

Cover Image

Jacob Adriaensz. Backer, *Johannes Wttenbogaert (1557–1644). Remonstrant Minister in The Hague*, 1638. Public domain.

Interior Images

Claes Jansz. Visscher, *Johannes Bogerman (1576–1637)*, 1619. Public domain.

Anonymous, Portrait of Franciscus Gomarus, *Hoogleeraar te Leiden 1594–1611 Leider der Contra-Remonstrantie Geb. 1563*, Gest. 1647. Public domain.

ABOUT THE AUTHOR

Dr. W. Robert Godfrey is a Ligonier Ministries teaching fellow and chairman of Ligonier Ministries. He is president emeritus and professor emeritus of church history at Westminster Seminary California and an ordained minister in the United Reformed Churches in North America. He is a graduate of Stanford University (A.B., M.A., and Ph.D.) and Gordon-Conwell Theological Seminary (M.Div.).

He is the featured teacher for the six-part Ligonier teaching series *A Survey of Church History*. He is author of several books, including *God's Pattern for Creation, An Unexpected Journey: Discovering Reformed Christianity, Reformation Sketches: Insights into Luther, Calvin, and the Confessions, John Calvin: Pilgrim and Pastor,* and *Learning to Love the Psalms*.